THE CATHOLIC UNIVERSITY OF AMERICA
CANON LAW STUDIES
No. 118

CANONICAL ELECTIONS

AN HISTORICAL SYNOPSIS AND COMMENTARY

A DISSERTATION

Submitted to the Faculty of Canon Law of the Catholic University of America in Partial Fulfillment of the Requirements for the Degree of

DOCTOR OF CANON LAW

BY THE

REV. ANSCAR PARSONS, O. M. CAP., J. C. L.

1939

THE CATHOLIC UNIVERSITY OF AMERICA PRESS
WASHINGTON, D. C.
1939

Imprimi Potest:

THEODOSIUS FOLEY, O. M. CAP.,
Minister Provincialis.

Detroitensis, Mich., die XI Junii, 1939.

Nihil Obstat:

VALENTINUS T. SCHAAF, O. F. M., J. C. D.,
Censor Deputatus.

Washingtonii, D. C., die XII Junii, 1939.

Imprimatur:

✠ MICHAEL J. CURLEY, D. D.
Archiepiscopus Baltimorensis.

Baltimorae, Md., die XII Junii, 1939.

Printed by
WORMAN PRINTERY INCORPORATED
Teutopolis, Illinois

TO

MY FATHER AND MOTHER

TABLE OF CONTENTS

CHAPTER EIGHT

CHAPTER NINE

CHAPTER TEN

CHAPTER ELEVEN

CHAPTER TWELVE

INTRODUCTION

The purpose of the present work is to outline the history of canonical election and to present a commentary on canons 160-178 of the Code which treat of elections in general. The papal election and the process of postulation are beyond the proper scope of this dissertation. Some attention has been given to the elections of religious, because these are the most frequent canonical elections today; but, since the work is concerned with elections in general, references to specific elections are introduced merely by way of illustration and no pretense is made of offering an exhaustive discussion.

The subject of canonical elections is one of the most thoroughly digested sections of the law. A rich literature of pre-Code works exists. Since the law of the Code leaves the former law substantially unchanged, much of this literature is of value today. However, one important observation must be made. Before the Code a canonical election was, primarily, the election of a bishop by a cathedral chapter. The principal change made by the Code had the effect of detaching the law of elections from the milieu of the cathedral chapter where it developed and of creating a general law which is applicable alike to religious, laymen in their confraternities, diocesan consultors, cathedral canons. The commentator of our own day must, therefore, endeavor to find the most general applications of the law which governs all types of elections; and, since in many instances the Code safeguards the special regulations of particular groups, it will also be necessary to balance the prescriptions of the general law with those of particular enactment.

A study of the past history and present workings of canonical election shows that the Church has faith in true democracy. Truth does not necessarily lie with the majority (therefore the stress which the old canonists laid on the *sanior pars),* but the majority of men when actuated by the proper motives and when acting in the concord of the Holy Spirit can and usually do arrive at the truth.

The writer is happy to take this occasion to express his gratitude to the Very Reverend Theodosius Foley, O. M. Cap., Minister Provincial, for the opportunity of pursuing the study of Canon Law at the Catholic University of America; to his confreres of the Capuchin Province of St. Joseph for many past favors; to the Very Reverend Claude Vogel, O. M. Cap., Ph. D., and the Capuchin Friars of the Province of St. Augustine for their kindness and Franciscan hospitality during his residence at Capuchin College, Brookland, D. C.; to the Dean and Faculty of the School of Canon Law for their helpful criticism and painstaking revision of this dissertation; and to the Librarians and other members of the Catholic University staff for services extended during three years of graduate study.

CHAPTER ONE

Canonical Elections in General

ARTICLE I. *Election a Method of Ecclesiastical Appointment.*

Canonical election is one of the methods employed by the Church for providing worthy incumbents for ecclesiastical offices. The Code sets forth the principle of public law that no office can be validly obtained in the Church unless it is duly granted by competent ecclesiastical authority.[1] This principle is a clear deduction from the teachings of Fundamental Theology. The Church is a perfect society, hierarchically constituted, and therefore its posts of jurisdiction and power cannot be seized by force nor obtained by usurpation. Even though a candidate for ecclesiastical office be elected by a group of voters, presented by a noble family, or nominated by a king, these actions are devoid of effect unless they are followed by a formal act of the ecclesiastical authority.

Therefore, a complete canonical appointment involves two juridical acts: 1) designation of the person who is to receive office; 2) actual bestowal of the office. The first act may be termed the material element and may take place by direct appointment, by nomination, by presentation, by postulation or by election. The other act is the formal element which is always performed by competent ecclesiastical authority. In direct appointment the two elements are joined in one act, since the superior designates the person

[1] Can. 147.

and gives him the office at one and the same time (*libera collatio*). But in the other methods of appointment the two elements are kept distinct. An election must be completed by confirmation; nomination and presentation must be followed by ecclesiastical institution; a postulation must be admitted or granted by the lawful superior. Finally, certain elections which require no confirmation are completed by the mere consent of the one chosen, because the law has attached ratification to the act of acceptance.[2]

Thus, in an election the assembly of voters can do no more than designate the person for the office. Full title and ecclesiastical jurisdiction are acquired by a subsequent act, namely, by the confirmation of a competent superior or (when the law so ordains) by the candidate's simple acceptance of the election.

ARTICLE II. *Definition of Canonical Election.*

Nominally, election means a choice among many persons, things, or courses of action. In its stricter legal sense it means the choice of a person for public office. The Code offers no formal definition of a canonical election in the strict sense. Indeed, the words *electio* and *eligere* are used rather loosely in the Code.[3] Canonists also use the term to designate any sort of appointment or approbation including presentation, nomination, postulation, and direct appointment.[4] In canons 160-178, however, the term "election" is used in the strict sense. The process described in these canons is the canonical calling of a qualified person to a vacant ecclesiastical office or benefice by an assembly of law-

---

[2]Cf. Can. 148 § 1.

[3]Cf. canons 232, § 1; 399, § 1; 446, § 1; 516, § 1; 560; 1359, § 1; 1360; 1393, § 3; 1520, § 1; 1573, § 1; 1580, § 2; 1589, § 1; 1598, § 3; 1607, § 1.

[4]Cf. Schmalzgrueber, Lib. I, tit. 6, n. 1.

ful voters.[5] This strict meaning is the sense applied to the term "election" throughout this study.

An election is a truly *canonical* act. The call is given by following the careful procedure of canons 160-178. The result of the electoral process gives to the one elected a true right before the law. However, the assembled voters do not confer the office, but merely give a *call* to the office. In other words, as a result of the election the one chosen has a strict claim (*ius ad rem*) to confirmation by the competent superior who thereby completes the canonical appointment. The person chosen must be *qualified*, that is, free from impediments and worthy of the charge. The office for which an election is held must be *vacant*. Those who participate must be *lawful voters*, that is, they must enjoy the right of suffrage and they must exercise true freedom of choice. They must, moreover, vote as a duly *assembled* collegiate body.

ARTICLE III. *Distinction of Election from Other Methods of Appointment.*

The definition of election in the strict sense is clarified by contrasting it with other methods of appointment to which the term is sometimes loosely applied. Election differs from *free appointment* (*libera collatio*),[6] because such a free and direct appointment is always the act of a superior, whereas election is usually the act of subjects choosing their superior. In free appointment the person is named and the title is conferred by one and the same act of the superior, but this is not true of election.

---

[5]Cf. Passerini, *De Electione Canonica*, I, 35; Wernz, *Ius Decretalium*, II, n. 352; Ferraris, *Bibliotheca*, v. "Electio", I, 3; Reiffenstuel, Lib. I, tit. 6, n. 4; Bernardus Papiensis, *Summa Decretalium*, p. 307; Maroto, *Institutiones Iuris Canonici*, I, 721-722.

[6]Cans. 152-159.

Postulation, as described in canons 179-182, is similar to an election; but in postulation the candidate is not altogether qualified for the office, in as much as he lacks some specific requirement, for instance, the necessary age. The voters do not really *elect* the candidate; rather, by electoral petition they *ask* the superior to effect the appointment. Postulation rests on the good will of the superior, who is free to admit or to reject the one chosen, whereas the election of a duly qualified person must in justice be confirmed.

In the act of *presentation* those who present a candidate exercise the right not of suffrage but of patronage.[7] Election is the act of an assembly; presentation is usually the act of one individual. Even when the right to present a candidate belongs to a group, the members of this group are not bound by the formalities inherent in a canonical election, but merely follow the law prescribed for the performance of a collegiate act.[8] They need not be convoked and they may indicate their choice by letter or by proxy.[9] The right of presentation allows the patron to name more than one person and to submit additional names;[10] election is concerned with one final choice, which gives the one so named an exclusive right.

The term *nomination* is applied to several things in canon law. Most normally it signifies the act of naming or designating a person to whom institution in office is later to be conferred by the proper superior. In this sense nomination is intimately allied to, or even, practically synonymous with, presentation.[11] The distinction between the two results rather from the circumstantial difference that *nomination* is the designative act of a religious superior or of a person of clerical status, whilst *presentation* is the designative act of a lay patron.

---

[7]Can. 1448-1471.

[8]Can. 101 § 1, n. 1; cf. can. 1460 § 1.

[9]Cf. Maroto, *Institutiones*, I, 725.

[10]Can. 1460 § 4.

[11]Cf. Bastnagel, *The Appointment of Parochial Adjutants and Assistants*, p. 164, not. 103.

Nomination may also refer to a particular phase of the procedure at a canonical election, namely, the preliminary discussion of possible candidates. Again, it can point to the case in which an electoral college has used its right or privilege to resort to *solemn nomination.*[11a] In this case the electoral body surrenders its right to employ a formal election and instead determines upon submitting two or three names from which a choice is to be made by the superior who enjoys the right of confirming the person in office. Finally, *commendation,* like presentation, is closely akin to nomination. The method followed by the hierarchy of the United States in listing the names of men qualified for the office of bishop is a method of commendation.[12]

All of the foregoing methods differ substantially from an election in the strict sense of the word.

ARTICLE IV. *Kinds of Elections.*

Elections may be distinguished by reason of the *mode of procedure* followed by the voters. Two forms are mentioned by the Code: scrutiny[13] and compromise.[14]

A third form, that of acclamation, was mentioned in the decretal *"Quia propter"*[15] and was discussed by all authors before the Code. It may be used in the election of the Roman Pontiff according to the Constitution *"Vacante Sede Apostolica"*.[16] Whether it may still be used in other elections will be discussed in the paragraph which treats of the form of election.

[11a] Coronata *(Institutiones,* I, 247, not. 2) holds that this form is admitted by c. 28, X, *de electione et electi potestate,* I, 6, and may be followed also after the Code.

[12] S. C. Consist., July 26, 1916—*AAS,* VIII (1916), 400.

[13] Can. 171.

[14] Can. 172

[15] C. 42, X, *de electione et electi potestate,* I, 6.

[16] Pius X, Dec. 25, 1904, n. 55—*Codex I. C.,* Documentum I.

Again, elections are divided *by reason of their effect.* Some elections require for their complete effect the mere acceptance of the one elected; as soon as he consents to the election he acquires full right to the office.[17] Others require the confirmation of a competent superior before the person elected acquires full title.[18]

Elections may also be distinguished *by reason of the office* for which the one elected is chosen. Ecclesiastical offices are divided into: 1) Offices in the strict sense, namely, offices permanently established, conferred according to canonical norms, and involving some share in ecclesiastical orders or jurisdiction; 2) offices in the broad sense, namely, offices which promote some spiritual purpose, but do not enjoy a share in ecclesiastical orders or jurisdiction.[19] The article in the Code on elections (canons 160-178) refers directly to offices in the strict sense.[20] The choice of a person for an office in the broad sense, for instance, for a religious office in a lay institute, is specifically distinct from the first type of election. It would not be governed by canons 160-178, if canon 507, § 1, had not so directed.[21]

A final distinction must be made between elections properly so-called and "elections" that are not strictly canonical. The former are those which conform to the strict definition already given and which proceed according to the rules listed in canons 160-178. The latter includes various cases[22] in which a group selects a person in accord with the rules for collegiate action as contained in canon 101, § 1, n. 1, but does not observe all the formalities of canonical election. A particular instance would be the choice of synodal examiners, synodal judges, and parochial consultors as mentioned in canons 385, § 1, and 1574. These canons do not

---

[17]Can. 176, § 2.

[18]Can. 176, § § 2-3.

[19]Can. 145, § 1.

[20]Cf. can. 145, § 2. See also Vermeersch-Creusen, *Epitome,* I, 188.

[21]Cf. Larraona, "De Electionibus Religiosorum", *CpR,* VIII (1927), 290.

[22]See, e. g., cans. 1452; 1460, § 1, etc.

require a canonical election. The bishop of course could grant the synod the right to choose these officials by way of canonical election. But, if he presents exclusive lists of names from which a choice must be made, or if he in any way restrains the liberty or constrains the option of the electors, then the notion of a strictly so-called canonical election is lost.

ARTICLE V. *Provisional Definition for Historical Inquiry.*

A canonical election today is a clearly defined legal procedure distinct from all similar canonical actions. Prior to a consideration of the present law an effort will be made to trace the history of this ecclesiastical institution. Naturally, the clean-cut definition of modern law cannot be realized in the electoral procedure of the early Church. Often an action of the early Church may have been called "election" when the modern canonist would label it "petition", or "commendation", or "nomination".

Investigation cannot be begun with the exact definition which is the net result of centuries of development. But neither can it be commenced with a definition too general or vague, such as "appointment" would be. This search begins with the provisional definition of election as "the designation of a church officer by a group". The group may not be organized as strictly as a modern electoral college. The designation may not confer upon the person a *ius ad rem,* but if there is some active designation of a person by a group, then there exists an historical antecedent of a present-day canonical election.

PART ONE

HISTORICAL SYNOPSIS

CHAPTER TWO

THE PRIMITIVE ELECTION "PER CLERUM ET POPULUM"

ARTICLE I. *Elections in the First and Second Centuries (c. 30-150 A. D.)*

1. *Acts of the Apostles*

In apostolic times election appears for the first time in the Church at Jerusalem, when the Twelve said to the multitude of the disciples: "Brethren, look ye out among you seven men of good reputation . . . whom we may appoint over this business . . . And they elected Stephen [and six others.] . . . These they set before the apostles; and they praying, imposed hands upon them."[1] In this text which is (with the possible exception of the choice of Matthias)[2] the earliest text on ecclesiastical elections, the "multitude of the disciples" are described as taking part in the election. All must have had some voice in the proceedings, because the text implies that one purpose of this election was to mollify the dissatisfaction of the Greeks and their widows. This end would be attained if the aggrieved parties were able to pick those who would take care of the alms in the future. The apostles in this instance thought it well to give heed to the voice of the community. However, this is merely an isolated fact and from it one cannot conclude to a permanent law of elections in apostolic times.

[1]Acts, VI, 3-6.

[2]The choice of Matthias does not seem to have been an election in the proper sense, since the assembly of the faithful expressly refrained from a deliberate choice. However, the preliminary decision to make Joseph Barsabas and Matthias the two candidates was probably the result of some form of election. Cf. Acts, I, 15-26.

2. *The Didache*

The first trace of anything like a permanent ordinance or law is contained in the *Didache.* This purports to be the teaching of the Twelve and directs: "Elect for yourselves bishops and deacons."[3] One can conclude from this that sections of the Church in Syria maintained a right of election and that they traced this right to an ordinance of the apostles themselves.

3. *The Letter of St. Clement*

About the time of the appearance of the *Didache* St. Clement tells the Church at Corinth that the apostles laid down rules for the appointment of bishops and deacons. He notes that a form of *general consent* was a part of these apostolic ordinances: "Our apostles also knew, through our Lord Jesus Christ, that there would be strife on account of the office of the episcopate. For this reason, therefore, inasmuch as they had obtained a perfect foreknowledge of this, they appointed those ministers already mentioned, and afterwards gave instructions, that when these should fall asleep, other approved men should succeed them in the ministry. We are of opinion, therefore, that those appointed by them, or afterwards by other eminent men, with the *consent of the whole church* . . . cannot be justly dismissed from the ministry."[4]

The word "consent" used by St. Clement in describing the action of the community signifies subsequent ratification rather than positive choice. Consent of itself tends to be automatic and implies nothing more than general approval.

Therefore, of itself the text of Clement says nothing about election as the term is understood in this study. The

---

[3] XV, 1-2—Franz Xaver Funk, *Patres Apostolici* (Tübingen, 1901), I, 32.

[4] *Epistola Clementis, I,* XLIV, 1-3—Funk, *op. cit.*, I, 154.

eminent men of the Church named the new member of the episcopate. The whole community was given the opportunity of testifying concerning the merits of the chosen man and, if no serious defects were discovered, the entire Church acclaimed the choice and signified their consent to the appointment.

4. *Details of Procedure*

The documents at hand tell nothing concerning the details of an ecclesiastical election during the first decades of the Church. One might suppose that in this, as in so many other affairs of the infant Church, the Synagogue served as a model. Schürer, however, finds that in the synagogues at the time of Christ and the early Christians "there is at least no trace of any direct deliberation and determination of the whole congregation in individual cases of discipline and government of the kind which we meet with in the Christian Church at Corinth."[5] Gerdes supposes that the popular assemblies of the Roman Republic were imitated by the Christians.[6] The etymology of the word which is used by St. Luke in the *Acts* and by the *Didache*,[7] would indicate that the choice was made by show of hands as in the popular assemblies of ancient Athens. It seems certain that during the first and second centuries the whole Church, both clergy and people, had some voice in the nomination of Church officers, but nothing definite is known concerning details of procedure.

The principal part in the choice of the clergy was exercised by the eminent men of the community. The majority of the faithful could give testimony as to the fitness of the candidates. They could approve the choice of the

---

[5]Emil Schürer, *A History of the Jewish People* (Edinburgh, 1885), II (div. 2), 59.

[6]*Die Bischofswahlen in Deutschland unter Otto d. Grossen 953-973* (Hamburg, 1878), p. 2.

[7]Acts, XIV, 23; *Didache*, XV, 1-2—Funk, *Patres Apostolici*, I, 32.

"eminent men", but it is doubtful whether they had a right of election in the sense of being able by positive act to designate a person.

ARTICLE II. *Third Century Elections. (c. 200-314)*

After the age of the Apostles and of the Apostolic Fathers (c. 30-155 A. D.), no further information[8] on the question of ecclesiastical appointments is available until the time of St. Cyprian (248-258).[9] However, the harmony between Cyprian's description of ecclesiastical government and the reports of Clement and Ignatius serves to support Cyprian's own assertion that the appointments of bishops at his time were carried on "de traditione divina et apostolica observatione."[10]

Cyprian's description of the appointment of a bishop is important, not only because he declares that the practice of his time was ancient and traditional, but also because he says that the method described is followed in almost all provinces. Epistle LXVII, which contains the fullest description, was written from Africa to a church in Spain. Cyprian alludes to the fact that the Spanish practice is in accord with the African custom. In several other letters, to which reference will duly be made, he describes the election of Pope Cornelius and shows that it was carried out in the customary manner. Thus, the letters of St. Cyprian

---

[8]Authorities sometimes cite a passage from Tertullian's *Apologeticum* (written about 197 A. D.), in which he says (XXXIX, 6) that the "seniores" (presbyteri ?) who preside at the assemblies of the Christians attain office "non pretio sed testimonio"—*MPL*, I, 469; Eusebius *(Historia Ecclesiastica*, VI, 10-11—*MPG*, XX, 542-543) records two elections which took place at Jerusalem about 200, but he may be interpreting events of the third century in the light of a practice which was in vogue in the fourth.

[9]The dates refer to the years of Cyprian's episcopate.

[10]*Epistola* LXVII, 5—Guglielmus Hartel, *S. Thasci Caecilii Cypriani Opera Omnia*, II, 739, in *Corpus Scriptorum Ecclesiasticorum Latinorum* (Vindobonae, 1866-), III b.

contain information on the question of episcopal elections in three great provinces of the western Church, Africa, Italy, and Spain.

In order to hold ordinations in the proper manner, St. Cyprian writes, "the neighboring bishops of the same province come together to those people for whom a prelate is to be ordained, and the bishop is appointed in the presence of the people who know most fully the lives of each and everyone. This was done in the ordination of our colleague, Sabinus. He was given the bishopric and hands were imposed upon him, in virtue of the suffrage of the whole fraternity and the judgment of the bishops who had come together or who had written letters to you concerning him."[11]

From this and other texts[12] it is clear that the neighboring bishops as well as the local clergy and people had part in the appointment of a new bishop. But, what was the respective rôle of each?

Juridical Evaluation of a Third Century Election.

1. *The Role of Clergy and People*

It is difficult to determine definitely the juridical value of the part played by the local clergy and the people. Funk[13] and Gerdes[14] would conclude that the local community had a strict right of election. Phillips[15] reduces the part of the

[11] *Ibid.*

[12] E. g., *Ep.* LV, 8; LXVIII; XLIV—Hartel, II, 629, 599, 745.

[13] "Die Stellen [in Cyprian's letters] lassen in ihrer Gesamtheit keinen Zweifel uebrig dass der Gemeinde nicht bloss ein Vorschlagsrecht, sondern ein Wahlrecht im vollen Sinne des Wortes zukam."—*Abhandlungen und Untersuchungen* (Paderborn, 1897), I, 28.

[14] "Über den Candidaten wurde in der Weise der alten Volksversammlungen, vermuthlich durch Scherben abgestimmt ('universae fraternitatis suffragium', Ep. LXVII)"—*Die Bischofswahlen*, p. 2.

[15] The election of clergy and people of which Cyprian speaks "erscheint. . . keineswegs als eine eigentliche förmliche Wahl."—Georg Phillips und Friedrich H. Vering, *Kirchenrecht* (Regensburg, 1889), VIII, 10.

people to loud acclamations, assuring the bishops, the real electors, that their choice was welcome to the community. Van Espen[16] regards the choice of the people as a simple "postulation", which the bishops were free to admit or to reject.

Funk and Gerdes attach much importance to the word *suffragium,* which St. Cyprian employs quite frequently to designate the action of the people.[17] Certainly, if Cyprian uses the word in the classical Roman sense, then the bishops in the third century were elected with all the accessories of republican rule, with written ballots and by numerical majority. If this is so, then the practice died without leaving a trace, for when full accounts appear in the next century the proceedings are entirely oral.[18]

There are texts which seem to show that the action of the people tended to become chiefly negative. About a decade before St. Cyprian's time Alexander Severus (222-235) inaugurated the practice of submitting to the people the names of those whom he proposed to appoint as governors and procurators. The people were urged to manifest and prove any crimes of which the candidate might be guilty. The Emperor declared that he was moved to adopt this method because the Christians follow the same system in appointing their priests.[19] Cyprian, too, does not seem to demand anything very positive from the people, if his appeal to Numbers XX, 25-28, has any significance, for in that text the people merely witness (and apparently approve) the consecration of Eleazar as high priest.

---

[16]Zegerus Bernardus Van Espen, *Jus Ecclesiasticum Universum* (Lovanii, 1753), I, tit. 13, cap. 1, nn. 8-11.

[17]*Ep.* LV, LIX, LXVII—Hartel, II, 629, 672, 673, 738, 739.

[18]Compare the election of St. Ambrose (Socrates, *H. E.*, IV, 30—*MPG*, LXVII, 543); and that of St. John Chrysostom *(op. cit.*, VI, 2—*MPG*, LXVII, 662).

[19]*Monumenta Ecclesiae Liturgica,* ed. Ferdinand Cabrol and Henri Leclercq (Parisiis, 1900-1902), n. 4881; Francois J. M. Raynouard, *Histoire du Droit Municipal en France* (Paris, 1829), I, 137.

On the other hand, the action of the people counted for so much that Cyprian can say of Cornelius: "populi universi suffragio deligitur"[20] and he can place upon the people the responsibility for a bad choice.[21] From the midst of his torments the layman Flavianus suggested to the Christians among the on-lookers that they choose Lucianus to replace the martyred Cyprian, apparently believing that his suggestion would have effect.[22] In later times there were instances of a child[23] or of a woman[24] calling out a name in the electoral assembly. These and other descriptions indicate that the people and the local clergy had an influence which fluctuated in accord with the flexible character of the whole procedure at the time.

2. *The Part Taken by the Bishops*

It would be easy to accumulate authorities who so interpret Cyprian's words as to make the college of bishops the determining element in the entire procedure. "The election of the bishop does not take place without the suffrage of the faithful of the church that is to be provided for, and without the votes of the clergy. The bishops take part in the election, on them it depends, and from them it receives its validity."[25] The right of election truly pertained to the bishops.[26] The bishops elected effectively.[27]

---

[20]*Ep.* LIX—Hartel, II, 673.

[21]*Ep.* LXVII—Hartel, II, 737.

[22]*ASs, Februarii,* III, 464.

[23]Rufinus, *Historia Ecclesiastica,* II, 11—*MPL,* XXI, 521-522.

[24]Gregory of Tours, *Historia Francorum,* II, 13—*MPL,* LXXI, 210-212.

[25]Pierre Battifol, *Primitive Catholicism* (transl. Henri L. Brianceau, New York: Longmans, 1911), p. 334.

[26]William Beveridge, *Synodicon sive Pandectae Canonum et Conciliorum* (Oxonii, 1672), II, append., p. 47.

[27]A. Boucharlat, *Les Elections Episcopales sous les Merovingiens* (Paris, 1904), p. 16.

Though there was great flexibility about the procedure where clergy and people were concerned, one thing was fixed with juridical definiteness, namely, the action of the bishops. This was the core of the process. Nothing was final until the bishops consented to confer upon the candidate episcopal consecration. This consent on the part of the bishops had the juridic force which was later to attach to *confirmation* of the election. From this point of view one may certainly assert that the bishops played the most important part in the entire election. That the bishops also had an important share in actively designating the person of the candidate is probable.

If at times the bishops were content merely to guide and moderate a discussion of nominations and postulations, clergy and people knew that the presiding bishops were the final judges who gave validity to the appointment. Such decisive power rested with the bishops that their action was the first to be regulated by conciliar law. Though the flexible rôles of clergy and people were left to traditional practice for determination, the council of Arles in 314 made a clean-cut regulation for the bishops. It was declared a usurpation for any single individual to take upon himself the ordaining[28] of a bishop. A college of at least seven bishops should confer about an affair of such importance. If seven cannot be had, then three should act.[29]

---

[28]Cf. *infra,* note 30. The arguments used to show that can. 4 of the Council of Nice is concerned with appointment to office as well as with ordination to the episcopate apply with equal force to can. 20 of the Council of Arles.

[29]Can. 20—Harduin, I, 266. The first of the *Canons of the Apostles* (Harduin, I, 10) contains a similar prescription: "Episcopus a duobus aut tribus ordinetur." If the *Canons of the Apostles* were drawn up about 300, then the canon cited is quite in line with the legislation of Arles (314), Nice (325), Antioch (341) etc. Most modern authorities, however, attribute them to the fifth century.—Bernardus Lijdsman, *Introductio in Jus Canonicum* (Hilversum in Hollandia, 1924-1929), 2 vols., I, 99.

ARTICLE III. *The Council of Nice and Fourth Century Elections.*

The consent of the provincial bishops to confer episcopal consecration was the true confirmation of whatever part clergy and people had taken in the designation of the bishop-elect. The tendency to regulate this action of the bishops which had been manifested at the council of Arles (314) was apparent also at Nice (325). Canon 4 directed that a bishop be appointed[30] by all the bishops of the province. If this becomes difficult either on account of urgent necessity or because of distance, three bishops at least should meet together and, the suffrages of the absent also being communicated in writing, the ordination should then take place. But in every province the ratification of what is done is left to the metropolitan.[31]

The foregoing ordinance was supplemented by canon 6 which declared that, if anyone be made a bishop without the metropolitan, such a one is not to be regarded as a bishop; but, if two or three bishops from a natural love of contradiction oppose the common vote of the rest, then the choice of the majority should prevail.[32]

These canons are a confirmation of the ancient custom which Meletius had broken by appointing and consecrating bishops with the approbation of the metropolitan of Alexandria and without the consent of the comprovincials.[33] No single bishop could take it upon himself to consecrate anoth-

[30]Canon 4 regulates the election as well as the ordination of bishops. This is the sense from the wording of the original Greek as well as from the circumstance that at that time election and ordination were joined. Cf. Phillips-Vering, *Kirchenrecht,* VIII, 14, n. 4; Funk, *Abhandlungen,* I, 28; Beveridge, *Synodicon,* II, append., p. 48, where it is pointed out that if the canon refers merely to ordination there would be no reason for getting the votes of the absent; therefore, he concludes: "Canon . . . non de ordinatione tantum aut consecrationis actu, sed de ipsa etiam electione intelligendus."

[31]Harduin, I, 323.

[32]*Ibid.*

[33]Beveridge, *Synodicon,* II, append., p. 48.

er bishop. In the time of St. Cyprian the bishops presided as moderators and final judges of the election. The local clergy and people had the right of participation, certainly by giving testimony and consent, probably to the extent of positive suffrage. What effect had the Nicean canons on this procedure?

1. *"The Neighboring Bishops"—the Synod and Metropolitan.*

Where St. Cyprian desired the presence of several neighboring bishops, Nice required all those of the province under the presidency of the metropolitan. In the mid-third century the bishops went to the church which had been deprived of its bishop, but after the first quarter of the fourth century the practice was rather to bring the question of a new appointment before the bishops assembled in synod. Canons 16, 19, and 23 of the Council of Antioch (341) indicate this practice.[34] Canon 16, for instance, says that it is an act of usurpation for a bishop to intrude himself into a see without a full synod's concurrence. The canon then defines a complete synod as one at which the metropolitan is present.

Subsequent councils continued to restate the canons of the I Council of Nice with regard to episcopal elections. Canon 6 of the Council of Sardica is a very obscure text, but if one should adopt the interpretation of the Council of Constantinople (382) it directs that if in a certain province there is only one bishop left besides the metropolitan, he should be summoned to elect with the metropolitan, and if he does not come, then the metropolitan should proceed to an election together with bishops of the neighboring province. The text seems to insist more on the presence of a college of bishops, than on the fact of their being from the same province.[35]

---

[34]Harduin, I, 600, 603.

[35]Harduin, I, 640. The Council of Sardica was held probably about 343.

Canon 12 of the Council of Laodicea, held between the years 370 and 380[36], canon 2 of the Roman synod of 386[37], and canon 39 of the council of Carthage in 397[38] show by their enactments that the law of the Council of Nice continued in force. "Nec unus episcopus episcopum ordinare praesumat . . . Hoc enim in synodo Nicaena constat esse definitum", Pope Siricius writes in an encyclical letter which was directed to Italy, Africa, and other sections of the West.[39] The Council of Carthage in 397 was so concerned with having a college of bishops present for the election that at first they proposed that 12 be required. Ultimately, however, the minimum of three, as prescribed by the Council of Nice, was maintained.[40] The direction of Pope Innocent I (402-417) to maintain in all elections that which "synodus Nicaena constituit atque definivit"[41] and the letter of Pope Hilary (461-468) to the bishops of Spain (465) declaring that with regard to ordinations the prescriptions of the divine law and the decisions of the Council of Nice are to be carefully carried out[42] show that the force of this law persevered through the fourth and into the fifth century. The part of the bishops in an episcopal election was clearly defined in law. But what of the local clergy and people?

2. *The Part of the People in Episcopal Elections after 325.*

Canon 4 of the I Council of Nice discussed the election of bishops without the least reference to the participation of the people and canon 13 of the Council of Laodicea (370-380) declared: "Quod non sit permittendum turbis electiones eorum facere qui sunt ad sacerdotium provehendi."[43]

[36]*Idem*, I, 784.
[37]*Idem*, I, 857.
[38]*Idem*, I, 965.
[39]*Idem*, I, 857.
[40]Canon 12—Harduin, I, 951.
[41]*Ep.* to Victricius of Rouen (404)—Kirch, *Enchiridion*, n. 720.
[42]Harduin, II, 788.
[43]Harduin, I, 784.

The silence of the Council of Nice and the express declaration of the Council of Laodicea would seem to exclude the people. However, there are evidences to show that they continued to share in elections throughout the fourth century. These reports derive from Antioch,[44] Constantinople,[45] Alexandria,[46] and Milan.[47]

These facts would indicate that another interpretation must be sought for the decree of the Council of Laodicea and the silence of the Council of Nice. Beveridge says that the Council of Nice did not legislate regarding the part of the people because there was no need. Canon 4, as was said above, was directed against Meletius. He broke the ancient custom when he dared to appoint on his own initiative without consulting other bishops, but the other part of the "ancient custom", namely the consultation of the people, he seems not to have violated.[48] Beveridge adds that the silence of the Council of Nice, far from introducing a change, is to be interpreted in the light of the phrase "confirmentur antiquae consuetudines", which runs like a theme through all the acts of the Council. A confirmation of this view is found in the Arabian versions, two of which add to canon 4 " . . . fiatque cum consensu populi"[49] and " . . . populo consensum praebente".[50]

Canon 13 of the Council of Laodicea is interpreted as excluding the ὄχλοι, the noisy and tumultous crowd, which Dionysius Exigus rendered as *turbae*.[51] Had they wished to exclude the laity they would have said λάοι or λαίκοι. Far

---

[44]Eusebius, *Vita Constantini*, III, 60-62—*MPG*, XX, 1127.

[45]Socrates, *H. E.*, V, 8—*MPG*, LXVII, 578.

[46]*Op. cit.*, VII, 7—*MPG*, LXVII, 750.

[47]*Op. cit.*, IV, 30—*MPG*, LXVII, 543.

[48]Beveridge, *Synodicon*, II, append. p. 48.

[49]Harduin, I, 463.

[50]*Idem*, I, 479. The "Paraphrasis Arabica" is of great importance, Harduin observes.

[51]*Codex Canonum Ecclesiae*—*MPL*, LXVII, 166.

from changing the current discipline this canon confirmed it from abuse.

Canon 16 of the Council of Antioch (341) seems to show that both synod and people shared in the normal electoral procedure. It says that if a bishop without a see intrudes himself into a vacant see without the synod's concurrence, the appointment is invalid *even if* the whole people elect him.[52] The implication seems to be that the part of the people is important, but not as weighty as the judgment of the synod.

3. *The Part of the Local Clergy in Elections after 325.*

Specific references to the local clergy are wanting in the legislation of the Council of Nice and of subsequent councils of the fourth century. However, the facts adduced to show that the people continued to have part in the elections apply with equal or greater force to the clergy. Whenever the *populus* is directly set in contrast to the *episcopi*, it is clear that both clergy and people are included in this generic term, with the clergy playing the chief rôle.[53] Furthermore, besides their position in the local church, it is probable that the clergy had a consultative voice in the synod. The Council of Antioch directed the priests and deacons to go to the synod if they wished to secure their rights. There is reason to think that even apart from cases of litigation the inferior clergy attended the synods without, however, enjoying a decisive voice.[54]

---

[52]Harduin, I, 600.

[53]In canon 16 of the Council of Antioch the concurrence of the synod is opposed to the election "by the whole people."—Harduin, I, 600; the Council of Hippo (392) in canon 20 calls for the witness of the people.—Mansi, III, 922. Compare this canon of the Council of Hippo with canon 1 of a collection attributed by Harduin to the IV Council of Carthage (398): "Qui episcopus ordinandus est, antea examinetur . . . tunc cum consensu *clericorum* et laicorum . . . ordinetur episcopus." —Harduin, I, 978.

[54]Canon 20—Harduin, I, 602; cf. Hinschius, *System*, III, 474.

ADDENDUM TO ARTICLE III

Note on Elections in the East after the Fourth Century

It is of some importance to follow out the development of the Eastern electoral law, especially because the third canon of the VII General Council (787) and the twenty-second canon of the VIII (869) were taken up into the *Corpus Iuris Canonici,* and these canons reflect Eastern rather than Western practice.

Elections in the East tended to develop along different lines than in the West. In the East the people were entirely excluded at a much earlier date. The noisy and tumultuous crowd is not to dominate elections, canon 13 of the Council of Laodicea had said and, even if this did not exclude all share of the laity, the movement towards restriction had begun and the East tended to extend the meaning of *turba* until only the *primores civitatis* are commemorated as participating with the clergy when Justinian drew up his law in 546.[55] The *clerici et primores civitatis* mentioned by Justinian were to choose three names and accordingly drew up electoral decrees for the three.[56] Justinian did not further elaborate the procedure, but evidently the prescriptions of Canon 4 of the Council of Nice were to be followed, since the law says: "Sequentes igitur ea quae a sacris canonibus statuta sunt . . ."[57]

The interference of the emperors had the effect of reducing the share of the laity in elections to a still greater extent. Finally, canon 3 of the seventh general council[58]

---

[55]N. 123.

[56]N. 123 and 137.

[57]N. 137, 2.

[58]C. 7, D. LXIII; cf. Schroeder, *Disciplinary Decrees of the General Councils, Text, Translation and Commentary* (St. Louis: Herder, 1937), p. 146; the following is the translation contained in Percival, *The Seven Ecumenical Councils,* The Nicene and Post-Nicene Fathers, 2nd. series, XIV, 557: "Let every election of a bishop, presbyter, or

declared that in accord with canon 4 of the Council of Nice the election of bishops belonged exclusively to the synod of bishops (thus they gave their interpretation of the Nicean canon). The eighth general council repeated this doctrine in canon 22 saying that, "concordans prioribus conciliis", the choice of a bishop belongs to the episcopal college and no lay person whatever may intervene unless invited to do so by the Church, in which case he will conduct himself with all due reverence.[59] By the time of Balsamon in the second quarter of the 12th century the participation of the laity had entirely disappeared and the election of bishops was in the hands of the metropolitan and comprovincials exclusively.[60]

ARTICLE IV. *"Electio per clerum et populum" in the Fifth Century and After.*

Though the people and the local clergy gradually ceased to have any share in elections in the East, the letters of Pope Celestine I (422-432) and Pope Leo I (440-461) show that their influence continued to be important in the West.

In 428 Pope Celestine, writing to the bishops of Gaul, laid down the principle: "Nullus invitis detur episcopus."[61]

---

deacon, made by princes stand null. . . For he who is raised to the episcopate must be chosen by bishops, as was decreed by the holy fathers of Nice in the canon which says: It is most fitting that a bishop be ordained by all the bishops of the province; but if this is difficult to arrange, either on account of urgent necessity, or because of the length of the journey, three bishops at least having met together and given their votes, those also who are absent having signified their assent by letters, the ordination shall take place. The confirmation of what is thus done, shall in each province be given by the metropolitan thereof."

[59]C. 1, D. LXIII; cf. Schroeder, *op. cit.*, pp. 173-174.

[60]Funk, *Abhandlungen*, I, 33.

[61]*Ep.* IV, 5—*MPL*, L, 434. This dictum was repeated in canon 11 of the V Council of Arles (549), which added that the citizens and clergy may not be forced to consent by the mighty.—Harduin, II, 1443.

To the bishops of the province of Vienne in 445 Pope Leo wrote: "Qui praefuturus est omnibus, ab omnibus eligatur." He further elaborated what he meant by "all", saying: "Teneatur subscriptio clericorum, honoratorum testimonium, ordinis consensus et plebis."[62]

The democratic character of the Gallo-Roman municipal regime may have exerted an influence on the election of bishops. The Gauls were accustomed to debate their common interests in orderly assemblies and this custom of civic life fostered participation in the affairs of ecclesiastical life.[63] The accounts of the fifth century show that the clergy and people continued to have part in the election. Perhaps the most vivid descriptions of the actual course of such an election are those contained in two letters of Sidonius Apollinaris. They record two elections in Gaul between the years 470 and 480. At Chalon-sur-Saône there were three worthless candidates. The one had nothing to commend him save the accident of noble birth; the second had sought to curry favor by giving sumptuous banquets; a third had secretly promised to influential persons a share in the goods of the Church. The comprovincial bishops who had assembled passed by all three candidates and decided on a certain John, whom they proceeded to consecrate. This occurred, as Sidonius Apollinaris reports, "stupentibus factiosis, erubescentibus malis, acclamantibus bonis, reclamantibus nullis."[64]

At Bourges on another occasion there were numerous competitors with each one trying to out-bid and out-bribe the other. Sidonius Apollinaris, himself a bishop, brought all parties around to putting the election in his hands and to binding themselves by oath to accept his choice. He then appointed Simplicius.[65]

From these and other contemporary accounts it is clear

[62]*Ep.* X,—*MPL*, LIV, 634.

[63]Imbart de la Tour, *Les Elections*, pp. 55-62; Raynouard, *Droit Municipal*, 1, 182.

[64]*Epistolae Lib.* IV, *ep.* 25—*MPL*, LVIII, 531.

[65]*Epistolae Lib.* VII, *ep.* 9—*MPL*, LVIII, 575-580.

that three factors were still involved in the appointment of bishops—the clergy, the people, and the comprovincial bishops. The juridical value of each factor in designating the candidate is still rather indefinite.

In the instances recorded by Sidonius Apollinaris the bishops prevailed over the laity in the determination of the person of the candidate, but at the election of St. Martin of Tours (374) some of the bishops were opposed to him and nevertheless the wishes of the people prevailed.[66]

In 446 Pope Leo I wrote to the bishops of Africa, blaming them for a bad choice of bishops and accusing them of having been too much influenced by popular clamor, "mirantes tantum apud vos . . . tumultum valuisse popularem. . ."[67] But in the previous year (445) he had written to the bishops of the province of Vienne rebuking them for not heeding the principle: "Qui praefuturus est omnibus, ab omnibus eligatur." That the episcopal electors attend to the voices of the citizens, to the testimony of the populace—this is the custom of those who know the rules of the Fathers.[68] The apparent contradiction between these two letters of Pope Leo I is perhaps explained by a principle contained in the letter of Pope Hilary to Ascanius of Tarragona written in 465. The Pope referred to the "petitions" of the people and, without denying that these wishes were deserving of consideration in the choice of bishop, added that they should not have such weight that in seeking to accede to them the will of God would be transgressed.[69]

From the data at hand it seems impossible to say more than that the "electio per clerum et populum" included a

---

[66]"Mirum in modum incredibilis multitudo non solum ex illo oppido sed etiam ex vicinis urbibus ad suffragia ferenda convenerat . . . Pauci tamen et nonnulli ex episcopis, qui ad constituendum antistitem fuerant evocati, impie repugnabant. . . Nec vero aliud his facere licuit, quam quod populus Domino volente cogebat." *Vita Martini*, c. IX—*MPL*, XX, 165.

[67]*Ep.*, XII, 1-2—*MPL*, LIV, 645.

[68]*Ep.*, X,—*MPL*, LIV, 634.

[69]Harduin, II, 788.

number of elements none of which could be neglected. A choice by popular clamor against the better judgment of the bishops was clearly irregular, but a choice by the bishops alone was scarcely less blameworthy. "No doubt," as Carlyle-Carlyle express it, "the *practice* of the time was often a little uncertain, but the *principles* acknowledged were clear and there was no serious dispute about them."[70]

Practice, as the few accounts cited show, was indeed uncertain and varied. Principles, especially those embodied in the letters of Pope Leo I and Celestine I were clear: "Nullus invitis detur episcopus." "Qui praefuturus est omnibus, ab omnibus eligatur." The conciliar enactments and papal decrees from which these principles were drawn and on which was based the idea of "electio per clerum et populum" were taken up into the "Liber Canonum" compiled by Dionysius Exiguus about 500. A copy of this book was sent by Pope Hadrian I to Charlemagne. It was the law-book of the Middle Ages, one of the most noteworthy fore-runners of the *Decretum Gratiani.*[71] The "Liber Canonum" was violated when the royal authority made episcopal appointments without regard to the wishes of clergy and people. A return to the principles of these ancient canons and decrees was the aim of Gregory VII and the other Popes of the Investiture Struggle.

The history of the legislation on elections enacted between 500 and 1150 will be discussed when treating the background for the *Decretum Gratiani.* At this point a chapter will be inserted showing the history of monastic elections. About the year 530 St. Benedict summarized and digested monastic legislation, just as Dionysius, about 500, had compiled and methodized the general law of the Church.

---

[70]Italics inserted. R. W. Carlyle and A. J. Carlyle, *A History of Medieval Political Theory in the West* (New York, 1922-1928), IV, 25.

[71]Cf. *MPL*, LXVII, 141-316.

CHAPTER THREE

THE INFLUENCE OF MONASTICISM ON CANONICAL ELECTIONS

The Rule of St. Benedict is a landmark in the history of monastic elections, because in its prescriptions it embodies all the wisdom of former monastic rules and is at the same time a model for later legislation. Before drawing up the rule St. Benedict made a close study of previous legislation, both general and particular.[1] At the time of its publication the Rule seems to have influenced Justinian, Caesarius of Arles, and Cassiodorus.[2] It gradually became the common law for the monks of the West and finally its directions concerning elections became an influence throughout the entire Church, even in non-monastic circles when Chapter LXIV was taken up into the *Decretum Gratiani*.[3]

ARTICLE I. *Monastic Elections before St. Benedict (300-530).*

1. *Oriental Rules*

The Oriental rules are almost completely silent about the election of the abbot.[4] The regulations of Pachomius (+346), which are best preserved in the recension of St. Jerome,[5] placed the entire government in the hands of Pach-

[1] John Chapman, *St. Benedict and the Sixth Century* (New York: Longmans, 1929), pp. 33 and 203.

[2] Chapman, *op. cit.*, pp. 194-195.

[3] C. 14, D. LXI.

[4] Henri Lévy-Bruhl, *Etude sur les Elections Abbatiales En France* (Paris, 1913), p. 12.

[5] Max Heimbucher, *Die Orden und Kongregationem*, I, 108, not. 2.

omius and his successors, the archimandrites, who supervised all subordinate monasteries and nominated the abbots without either the counsel or consent of the monks.[6] The so called rule of St. Basil (+379) is a catechism of questions and answers on the virtues and practices of religious life.[7] Since it presupposed the monastery as already constituted, it contained no constitutional prescriptions and, therefore, nothing on the election of the abbot. Lévy-Bruhl assumes that the primitive monasteries practiced a form of election after the analogy of the contemporary episcopal elections[8] and this supposition seems to be borne out by the account of the general election held by the Basilian monks in Palestine in 493, when Theodosius was elected archimandrite of all Palestine, and Sabbas was unanimously named exarch of all the laurae in the Holy Land.[9] The Code of Justinian, in introducing a new method of electing the abbot, implied that formerly the oldest monk by profession, unless obviously unfit or unworthy, was appointed by the bishop without any consultation of the monks.[10] It is vain to search for a general prescription among the ancient monks and their rules,[11] since most of the rules are collections of spiritual maxims with only the briefest statements of practical details;[12] other accounts of monastic life attribute the nomination of superiors to miraculous interventions or even obscure the history with the narration of the boldest legends.[13]

---

[6]Heimbucher, *Die Orden und Kongregationen*, I, III.

[7]*Ibid.*

[8]Lévy-Bruhl, *Elections*, p. 12.

[9]Heimbucher, *op. cit.*, I, 126.

[10]C. (1, 3) 46.

[11]"Il serait vain de chercher une regle generale parmi les plus anciens monasteres connus lorsqu'il s'agit de l'election du superieur." —Henri Leclercq, *Dictionaire d'Archaeologie Chretienne*, IV-2, 2611.

[12]Cuthbert Butler, *Benedictine Monachism*, 2 ed. (London: Longmans, 1924), p. 164.

[13]Henri Leclercq, *Dictionaire d'Archéologie Chrétienne*, IV-2, 2611.

2. *Western Rules*

According to the rule of St. Columban the abbot was nominated by his predecessor.[14] The *Regula Magistri,* which was probably a monastic code for certain monasteries in Gaul during the VII century, directed that the abbot choose his successor just before his death.[15] The rule which Caesarius of Arles (+542) laid down for the nuns of his diocese allowed the members of the monastery to elect the abbess.[16]

ARTICLE II. *Elections in the Rule of St. Benedict (c. 530).*

It is generally assumed that Chapter LXIV of the Rule of St. Benedict ordains that the abbot be elected by the monks of the community.[17] Dom Chapman, however, has shown that this choice of the monks was not a canonical election, but rather the presentation of a name or a manifestation of the community's desires which was made to the diocesan bishop.[18] Subjection of the monasteries to the bishop was the general law of the Church at the time,[19] a law which was repeated by local councils during the decades before and after the composition of the Rule.[20] St Bene-

---

14Lévy-Bruhl, *Elections*, p. 14.

15*Holstenii Codex Regularum Monasticarum et Canonicarum . . . a Mariano Brockie* (6 tomi in 3 vol., Augustae Vindobonorum, 1759). I, 288.

16Holstenius-Brockie, *op. cit.*, I, 361.

17Cf. text in *Sancti Benedicti Regula Monachorum* (Editio Critico-Practica, ed. Cuthbertus Butler, Friburgi Brisgoviae: B. Herder, 1912), p. 111.

18*St. Benedict*, p. 60, n. 1; see also Butler, *Benedictine Monachism*, p. 408.

19Council of Chalcedon (451), canon 4—Harduin, II, 602.

20I Council of Orleans (511), canon 19—Harduin, II, 1011; V Council of Arles (554), canon 2—Harduin, III, 327.

dict had neither the intention nor the authority to withdraw the abbot's appointment from the power of the diocesan bishop. Since, however, Gregory the Great instructed the bishops to appoint as abbot none other than the one chosen by the monks, the joint presentation of the local community soon came to have the effect of a decisive election.[21]

St. Benedict desired that the community should be unanimous in its choice of superior *(concors congregatio)*.[22] Though this was highly desirable, it was neither necessary nor sufficient. It was not sufficient because the unanimity might be the result not of the Holy Spirit, but of the evil spirit. The entire community might unite in choosing a person who would connive at their vices.[23] Complete unanimity was not necessary, because often opinion would be divided and the better judgment might rest with a minority.[24] The principle of majority-rule seems very simple and obvious to moderns, but this principle entered the realm of ecclesiastical law at a comparatively late date.[25] At any rate, it was not admitted by St. Benedict.[26] Chapter LXIV of the Rule embodies the principle enunciated by Pope Leo in his letter to Anastasius of Thessalonica (a. 446): "Is alteri praeferatur qui majoribus et studiis juvatur et meritis."[27] In other words, votes are to be weighed rather than counted.

---

[21]Lateran synod of 601—Harduin, III, 538-539.

[22]*Regula Monachorum*, cap. LXIV.

[23]*Regula, loc. cit.*, "Quod si omnis congregatio vitiis suis. . . consentientem personam pari consilio elegerit. . . "

[24]*Regula*, cap. LXIV, ". . . sive omnis concors congregatio . . . sive etiam pars quamvis parva congregationis saniore consilio elegerit."

[25]Lévy-Bruhl, *Elections*, p. 18.

[26]The final decision rested with the diocesan bishops, neighboring abbots, etc. *Regula*, cap. LXIV.

[27]Nikolaus Hilling, "Zur Abtswahl der Benediktinerregel", *AKKR*, CII (1922), 55-57.

ARTICLE III. *The Effect of St. Benedict's Electoral Ordinance.*

1. *Its Effect on Conciliar Legislation (530-821)*

Pope Gregory the Great frequently quotes the *Regula Monachorum* and takes it for granted that there is but one rule for monks.[28] He probably had the Rule of St. Benedict in mind when he decreed in 601 that the successor of a deceased abbot should be elected freely and unanimously by the brethren of the congregation.[29] Since Gregory in other passages[30] admitted that the diocesan bishop had the right to install and bless the new abbot, it would seem that the decree of 601 had for its purpose to protect the monks from all undue episcopal interference.[31] An earlier African synod at Carthage (535 or 534) had granted the monks even greater exemption from the diocesan bishop. It directed that when the abbot died the whole community should elect a new abbot and the bishop should not claim this right of election. If a dispute occurred among the monks concerning the election, the other abbots were to settle it. If the scandal continued, the matter was to be brought before the Primate.[32]

The prescription of this African council regarding the part taken by the other abbots is very similar to Chapter LXIV of the Rule, but the exclusion of the diocesan bishop is not contemplated in the Rule of St. Benedict. Probably, as Lévy-Bruhl supposes,[33] this African enactment owed its

---

[28] Chapman, *St. Benedict*, p. 197-203.

[29] Harduin, III, 538.

[30] See e. g., *Epistolae Lib.* III, *ep.* 23—*MPL*, LXXVII, 622.

[31] Thomas F. Reilly, *The Visitation of Religious* (Washington: Catholic University, 1938), pp. 38-39.

[32] "Et quando ipsi abbates de corpore exierint, qui in loco eorum ordinandi sunt, judicio congregationis eligantur: nec officium sibi hujus electionis vindicet aut praesumat episcopus."—Harduin, II, 1177.

[33] *Elections*, pp. 24 and 77.

inspiration to the spirit of St. Augustine, which continued to dominate the African Church long after his death and which was always favorable to monasticism.

More in accord with canon 4 of the Council of Chalcedon (451),[34] which subjected the monks of town and countryside to the diocesan bishop, and with canon 2 of the V Council of Arles (554), which declared that the discipline of monks and monasteries pertained to the bishop of the territory,[35] the prescription of canon 51 of the IV Council of Toledo (633) gave to the bishop the right: to encourage the monks to a holy life, to *institute abbots* and other officials, and to correct violations of the rule.[36] Institution (*instituere*) probably meant installation accompanied by abbatial blessing.[37] Since the whole tendency of the canon was to safeguard monastic liberty,[38] the appointing (*instituere* or *constituere*) on the part of the bishop did not exclude a previous choice (*eligere*) by the monks.[39]

Over five hundred years later Gratian[40] saw a direct conflict between the words of this canon of the IV Council of Toledo and the decree of Gregory the Great. He attempted to solve the difficulty by observing that the Toletan decree was directed at monks "indomitae cervicis et effrenatae superbiae", such as those who tried to poison St. Benedict. Against this type, likewise, canon 4 of the Council of Chalcedon (451) was directed. Probably the truth of

---

[34]Harduin, II, 602.

[35]Harduin, III, 327.

[36]Harduin, III, 585.

[37]Lévy-Bruhl, *Elections*, p. 27.

[38]Some bishops, the synod found, used the monks for work, as though they were slaves, and they regarded the monasteries as their private property. Cf. Harduin, III, 585.

[39]Chapman, *St. Benedict*, p. 60, n. 1; Lévy-Bruhl admits the possibility of a previous election by the monks, but inclines to the view that *instituere* here means a right of nomination in the fullest sense. —*Elections*, p. 29.

[40]C. 1, C. XVIII, q. 2.

the matter is that the movement in favor of exemption, as evidenced by the decree of 601 as well as in other documents of the period,[41] was not yet strong enough to set aside the traditional subjection to the diocesan bishop.

The Council of Estiennes (743) aimed at spreading the observance of the Rule of St. Benedict,[42] but no special mention was made of St. Benedict's ruling on elections. The tendency to reduce the power of the bishop over monastic elections was observable in canon 17 of the Council of Frankfort (794) and in a conciliar law of 821. The canon of the Council of Frankfort[43] spoke of the *jussio regis* and the *consensus episcopi*. The law of 821[44] declared that, since a monastery evidently could not exist without an abbot of the same order, one was to be chosen with the consent of the bishop of the city. The legislation, in its wording, is quite different from the law of the Council of Toledo (633). Over a period of two hundred years an evolution in the status of abbeys is noted. The monasteries were gradually withdrawn from subjection to the bishop; they were temporarily dominated by the royal authority, and finally they achieved full exemption, in elections as well as in other matters, when the papacy of the eleventh century undertook its struggle against state dominance. This line of development can be traced even in the scanty conciliar legislation of the period. It is more clearly evident from the history of actual practice.

---

[41]Co. 2, 3, 4, C. XVIII, q. 2.

[42]*MGH, Capitularia Regum Francorum* (ed. Boretius), I, 28.

[43]*Ibid.*, p. 76; Harduin, IV, 903.

[44]Canon 10: " . . . eligendus est inter eos vir modestus et prudens una cum consensu episcopi civitatis . . . "—*MGH, Concilia Aevi Karolini*, (ed. Werminghoff), II-2, 591; compare this enactment with the prescription of an English synod in 787 (probably held at Chelsea), which directed that when an abbot dies another is to be elected from that monastery with the consent of the bishop."—Harduin, III, 2072.

2. *The Effect of the Regula Monachorum on Electoral Practice during the Merovingian Period (530-752).*

The spread of the Benedictine electoral practice encountered many obstacles during the Merovingian period. Bishops apparently continued to make direct appointments.[45] Many of the old rules, especially that of St. Columban, continued to survive and there are evidences of abbots being appointed by their predecessors.[46] The greatest obstacle was the proprietary system which was dominant at the time. The founder of an abbey and his successors were regarded as the proprietors of the foundation and one of the principal rights of such a proprietor was that of nominating the abbot.[47] The system, however, indirectly furthered the spread of free election. Since the proprietor, and not the bishop, had the right—according to the ideas of the period—to appoint the abbot, the proprietor was also able to accord the monks electoral freedom. This was often done,[48] and the phrases used in the documents such as ". . . secundum regulam Sti. Benedicti . . . abbatem ibi constituant" or "ipsa congregatio elegerit sibi secundum sanctam regulam. . ." show how the Rule influenced these privileges. The king, during the Merovingian period, was a founder and proprietor like other great persons in the kingdom and seems not to have exerted greater rights.[49] The bishops, too, in Spain and in France tended to exercise pro-

---

[45]*Vita Sancti Germani—MGH, Auctores Antiquissimi,* (ed. Krusch), IV-2, 12; *Vita Droctovaei Abbatis Auctore Gislemaro,—MGH, Scriptores Rerum Merovingicarum,* (ed. Krusch), III, 543.

[46]*Vita Walarici Abbatis Leuconaenensis—MGH, Scriptores Rerum Merovingicarum,* (ed. Krusch), IV, 163-164.

[47]"Dana les circonstances normales, lorsqu'il s'agit simplement de pourvoir au remplacement d'un abbe pendant le cours de l'existence d'une abbaye, le principe subsiste: le proprietaire nomme l'abbe."—Lévy-Bruhl, *Elections,* p. 53.

[48]Mansi, XVIII b (Baluzzius) 580 and 582.

[49]Lévy-Bruhl, *Elections,* p. 190.

prietary rather than episcopal rights,[50] though they granted some privileges of election.[51] The proprietors, whether these were lords, kings, or bishops, had control of the appointment of most abbots[52] during the Merovingian period and free election was a privilege rather than a right deriving from the common law.

3. *The Effect of the Regula Monachorum on Electoral Practice during the Carolingian Period (752-c. 900).*

During the Carolingian period the action of the king took on much more importance in the administration of abbeys. The *tuitio regis* was greatly extended and independent abbeys disappeared. The abbots became valuable agents of the central power. Often they were the *missi regis*. Where the Merovingian abbot was an ascetic, the Carolingian abbot was often a functionary.[53] In the synod at Aix-la-Chapelle in 802 Charlemagne ordered the adoption of the Rule of St. Benedict by all the monks of the empire.[54]

Charles used his power to the advantage of monasticism, but he and his successors were also anxious to have control over these strategic posts of government. The synod of Paris in 846 assured a free election to the monastery of Corbie in accordance with decrees of Louis the Pious, Lothar and also of Emperor Charles.[55] At a synod near Toul in 859 Charles the Bald was petitioned to grant to the abbey of Fleury the exercise of its privilege of free

[50]II Council of Seville (619), canon 10—Harduin, III, 561; see also canon 51 of the IV Council of Toledo—Harduin, III, 585.

[51]Pardessus, *Diplomata*, II, 221, n. 423, cited by Levy-Bruhl, *op. cit.*, p. 54.

[52]There are some instances of direct election in abbeys that seem not to have had a proprietor, cf. e. g., *De Virtutibus Sanctae Gertrudis*, c. 6—*MGH, Scriptores Rerum Merovingicarum*, (ed. Krusch), II, 467.

[53]Lévy-Bruhl, *Elections*, p. 192.

[54]Hefele, *Conciliengeschichte*, III, 693.

[55]Harduin, IV, 1501.

canonical election.[56] These conciliar decrees, scanty though they are, show that election still continued to be regarded as a privilege, but when it took place the procedure was according to the Rule of St. Benedict. In England, where the abbeys did not as yet figure as part of the civil polity, a synod of London in 816 said that a bishop could elect abbots and abbesses in his diocese with the consent of the monastic family.[57]

Conditions in the kingdom of Louis the German appear to have been about the same as those in the realms of his two brothers, Charles the Bald and Lothar.[58] The royal rights attained such dominance in episcopal elections that the claims of canon law were reduced to a mere formality. Louis exerted an even stronger control over the election of abbots. Though he dispensed numerous electoral privileges to monasteries and confirmed others, he never hesitated to break through these restraints when it was to his own advantage.[59]

Under the later Carolingians the king still had the right to confirm the elections of abbots, though in general canonical elections took place in virtue of privilege. Schur notes fully 45 instances of new grants and confirmations of monastic rights to free election between 876 and 918.[60]

4. *The Effect of the Regula Monachorum on Electoral Practice from 918 to 1056.*

By the end of the Carolingian period forces were gathering which were to change and perfect many institutions in the Church. Though in general the elevated standards of

---

[56]Canon 11—Harduin, V, 487.

[57]" . . . cum consensu et consultu familiae. . "—Harduin, IV, 1219.

[58]Johannes Schur, *Königthum un Kirche im Ostfränkischen Reiche vom Tode Ludwigs des Deutschen bis Konrad I* (Paderborn, 1931), p. 17.

[59]Schur, op. cit., p. 18.

[60]*Ibid.*, p. 92.

monastic life were at low ebb in the tenth century, it was during this same century (in 910) that the abbey of Cluny was founded, from which were to go forth Leo IX and Gregory VII. From this time on the history of monastic elections became merged in the greater question of free election for all church offices. In 952, at a synod at Frankfort, Emperor Otto the Great forbade abbeys which possessed the right of free election to surrender this to anyone; only for those abbeys which did not possess such an electoral right could the king provide abbatial incumbents.[61] In line with this same tendency to maintain free election wherever it existed, a synod of London in 970 or 971 decreed that the privilege of free election which King Edgar (959-975) had granted to the monastery of Our Lady of Glastonbury should be maintained.[62]

When elections took place during this period the monks were not the only ones who took part in the proceedings. Mention was made of soldiers and layfolk.[63] Little is known of the formalities observed at the actual voting.[64]

Leo IX (1049-1054) granted the privilege of free election to many abbeys, among them Lorsch,[65] Cluny,[66] Corvey[67] and Beneventum.[68] In all the privileges granted by Pope Leo he directed that the election be performed according to the Rule of St. Benedict. Other contemporary descriptions

---

[61]The synod enacted but two decrees, of which this is listed in second place—Mansi, XVIII a, 435.

[62]Canon 4—Mansi, XIX, 23.

[63]Joannes E. Polzin, *Die Abtswahlen in den Reichsabteien von 1024 bis 1056* (Greifswald, 1908), pp. 45-47.

[64]"Über die Art der Stimmenabgabe, ob sie mündlich oder schriftlich erfolgt ist, können wir nichts genaueres mitteilen. . . "—Polzin, *op. cit.*, p. 48.

[65]"Vor seiner Abreise aus Mainz erliess Papst Leo noch mehrere Bullen zu Gunsten einzelner Klöster und Kirchen, bestätigte insbesondere dem Kloster Lorsch das Recht der freien Abtwahl. . . "—Hefele, *Conciliengeschichte*, IV, 699.

[66]Mansi, XIX, 683.

[67]*Ibid.*, 685.

[68]*Ibid.*, 688.

of monastic elections used phrases like "concors totius congregationis electio"[69] which are identical with the words of the Rule and imply that even outside the privileged monasteries the Rule was being followed. In the privilege given to the abbey of Fulda in 1039, the words "salvo consensu regis" are inserted and this may have been presupposed in all.[70]

It appears from the foregoing that monasticism exerted no lasting influence on canonical elections until the coming of St. Benedict. After the publication of the Rule three forces successively dominated the monastic institution, and accordingly, as one or the other held sway, the choice of the monks had more or less decisive effect.

As long as the monasteries were directly subject to the bishops, the choice of the monks tended to be merely advisory, the bishop retaining the right of nomination.

During the Merovingian period the king and other proprietors withdrew the monasteries from the sway of the bishops and often gave them privileges of free election. Though the royal power, especially after Charles Martel and his successors won supremacy, acted through the semblance of a free local election, when the era of royal dominance had passed the memory of a truly free election survived.

The third force which interested itself in the question of monastic elections was the Papacy. From the time of Gregory the Great the Popes favored the freedom of the monasteries. The action of kings and princes in withdrawing abbacies from episcopal control opened the road for the Popes—at the time of the investiture struggle—to give to the monasteries *libertas Romana* (as exemption was called), especially in the matter of abbatial elections. The *Regula Monachorum* contributed to Canon Law the idea of a fixed electoral college, the *congregatio*. The Rule also

---

[69]*Gesta Abbatum Gemblacensium*, c. 47—*MGH*, *Scriptores*, (ed. Pertz), VIII, 542.

[70]Polzin, *Die Abtswahlen*, p. 50 ff.

embodied the idea of exalting the *sanior pars* above the *maior pars*. The Rule of St. Benedict on abbatial elections is not the unique source of these two ideas, but it is a very ancient embodiment of electoral principles. Both before and after its inclusion in the *Decretum Gratiani* Chapter LXIV of the Rule of St. Benedict influenced Canon Law.

CHAPTER FOUR

TRANSITION FROM "PRIMITIVE" ELECTIONS TO "DECRETAL" ELECTIONS

ARTICLE I. *Background for the Study of Elections in the Decretum Gratiani.*

1. *The Law from Primitive Times until the 12th Century*

The ancient ecclesiastical election of a bishop by the clergy and people with the co-operation of the metropolitan and the comprovincial bishops remained the general law until the twelfth century.[1] The neglect of canonical election was never recognized as legal.[2] Whenever an effort was made to return to a strict ecclesiastical election, the conciliar decrees speak of "electio per clerum et populum".[3]

The decrees of Pope Leo the Great seem to have been regarded as the best formulation of the law regulating this election by clergy and people. These decrees are contained in the Liber Canonum of Dionysius Exiguus,[4] the law book of the early Middle Ages. They form the basis of the law

---

[1]Philipp Hofmeister, *Bischof und Domkapitel* (Württemberg: Funk, 1931), p. 64.

[2]"Diese Art der Einsetzung [neglecting canonical election] ist freilich niemals als rechtmaessig anerkannt worden. . . "—Bonin, *Die Besetzung der deutschen Bistümer in den letzten 30 Jahren Heinrichs IV, 1079-1106* (Jena, 1889), p. 10, n. 1; similarly, A. Scharnagl, "Der Begriff der kanonischen Wahl in den Anfängen des Investiturstreits", *ZSS* (kan. Abth.) XVI (1927), 443.

[3]Council of Aix-la-Chapelle (817), can. 2—Harduin IV, 1213.

[4]*MPL*, LXVII, 141-316.

for papal elections established by Pope Nicholas II in 1059.[5] Gratian, too, cites them frequently in his treatise on canonical elections.[6] They may have been neglected in practice, but they seem never to have been revoked.

2. *Royal Interference Reduced Elections to a Mere Formality*

The first legal recognition of royal consent in an episcopal election is found in the V Council of Orleans (549). Before the time of King Clovis (481-511) the principle formulated by Pope Celestine I[7] and restated by Pope Leo I, namely, "Nullus invitis detur episcopus", had been followed in the churches of Gaul.[8] Clovis did not deprive the Church of its liberty, but his wise policy was not followed by his successors.[9] Interferences with elections by the royal authority became frequent. Finally the Council of Orleans (549) tried to regulate abuses by allowing a reasonable participation on the part of the king. Canon 10 directs that no one should acquire a bishopric for a price or by gifts, but with the consent of the king; after an election by clergy and people in accordance with the old canons, the candidate should be consecrated by the metropolitan or his delegate together with the comprovincials.[10] Canon 8 of the Council of Paris (557) seems to be an early reaction against this concession of the Council of Orleans. The canon stresses once more the principle of Popes Leo and Celestine, saying: "No city is to be forced to take a bishop, if he has not been freely chosen by clergy and people. He shall not be ap-

---

[5]Can. 1, D. XXIII: "Certus vero atque legitimus hic electionis ordo perpenditur, si . . . illa B. Leonis . . . sententia recolatur."

[6]C. 1, D. LXII; cc. 19, 27, 36, D. LXIII; cc. 5, 8, D. LXI.

[7]"Nullus invitis detur episcopus, cleri, plebis, et ordinis consensus et desiderium requiratur" (a. 428) Celestine I, *ep.* IV, 5—*MPL*, L, 434.

[8]Boucharlat, *Les Elections*, p. 121.

[9]*Ibid.*, pp. 61-70.

[10]" . . . cum voluntate regis, juxta electionem cleri ac plebis, sicut in antiquis canonibus tenetur scriptum. . . "—Harduin, II, 1443.

pointed at the command of a prince against the will of the metropolitan and comprovincials."[11]

Though reactions did come from time to time, the successors of Clovis became the lords and tyrants of the Church rather than its protectors.[12] Charles Martel ignored the sacred character of the episcopacy and disregarded the prescriptions of canon law, principally because the guardians of ecclesiastical rights, the bishops themselves, were frequently not faithful to their trust and failed to command the respect which their predecessors had inspired in Clovis. It required the genius of Pepin and Charlemagne to understand the civilizing mission of the Church and to restore the moral force of the episcopacy.[13] But a restoration of free election did not keep pace with the restoration of episcopal dignity. The Carolingian bishop was a royal functionary like the count. He was an organ of government, and the king who named the count also named the bishop. That which had been recognized in the sixth and seventh centuries as an abnormal and irregular fact became in the eighth century an institution.[14]

There was a movement of opposition against this denial of free election. Forces kept the old idea alive. In the synod of Aix-la-Chapelle (817 or 818) a canon was enacted directing that bishops were to be elected by clergy and people without simony and according to worthiness.[15] There is nothing to prove that this canon was ever observed.[16] In the reform synod of Paris (829) canon 22 is addressed to the Emperors Louis and Lothar admonishing them to be very careful in the appointments of bishops and pastors.[17] A similar admonition is repeated in 844.[18]

---

[11]Harduin, III, 338.

[12]Boucharlat, *Les Elections*, p. 122.

[13]*Ibid.*, p. 124.

[14]Imbart de la Tour, *Les Elections*, p. 105.

[15]Can. 2—Harduin, IV, 1213.

[16]Imbart de la Tour, *Les Elections*, p. 178.

[17]Lib. III, can. 22—Harduin, IV, 1289-1360.

[18]Can. 2 of the synod of Diedenhofen—Harduin, IV, 1466.

Prescriptions similar to the canon of the Council of Orleans (549) can be found in the conciliar legislation of Spain. In the beginning the Visigothic kings apparently did nothing to hinder free canonical election by clergy and people,[19] but in the course of the seventh century their influence over elections grew[20] and finally reached its climax in canon 6 of the XII Council of Toledo (681). The canon declared it lawful for the bishop of Toledo to appoint those bishops "quoscumque regalis potestas elegerit", provided the bishop deems the candidates worthy.[21]

Throughout the later Carolingian period and during the feudal period the royal influence became so dominant that canonical election was either reduced to a mere formality or disappeared entirely.[22] Where elections took place they were held in virtue of privilege rather than in virtue of the common law.

In the tenth century the election by clergy and people was little more than an approval of the king's choice.[23] Ratherius of Verona gives a very full description of his own election during the reign of Otto I (936-973). He describes his election in the royal palace of Aix-la-Chapelle on Ember Wednesday of September, "electus . . . non solum ab his quorum intererat specialius, sed et ab episcopis, abbatibus, comitibus, totiusque regni primoribus. . ." Then, on the following Sunday he was "elected" by the people.[24] This

---

[19]Phillips, Kirchenrecht, VIII, 179.

[20]Funk, *Abhandlungen*, I, 36.

[21]Harduin, III, 1715.

[22]"[Des Königs] Recht . . . war so sehr in Übergewicht, dass es die Ansprüche des kanonischen Rechts bis zur reinen formalen Wahl herabsinken lassen, oder ganz ausschalten konnte."—Schur, *Königthum und Kirche*, p. 17; cf. also Imbart de la Tour, *Les Elections*, p. 360.

[23]"Hanc enim hujus temporis episcoporum eligendorum methodum fuisse, ut, quem princeps vellet, clerus et populus eligeret . . . "—Ballerini Brothers, foreword to *Opera Ratherii Veronensis—MPL*, CXXXVI, 16.

[24]"Rursum electus." Cf. Ratherius Episcopus Veronensis, *Phrenesis—MPL*, CXXXVI, 365.

second election was the *laudatio* which some would regard as a survival of the original "electio per clerum et populum" and a necessary condition for every canonical election.[25]

Ratherius seems eager to show that the prescriptions of law were faithfully carried out. He uses the very words of Pope Leo: ". . . *electus* . . . non solum ab his quorum intererat specialius, sed et ab . . . totius regni primoribus *expetitus* . . . *judicio* et consilio provincialium . . . constitutus."[26] He also received "*subscriptionem* septem tam venerabilium antistitum. . ."[27]

But even if the formularies of Leo I and Celestine I were carried out to the letter, their spirit was dead. The people might give their acclamations to the announcement from the pulpit: "Si vobis ista electio placeat, dextris in coelum levatis significate."[28] They might give their consent to the threefold: "Placet vobis? Vultis eum? Laudatis eum?",[29] but they really had nothing to do with the designation of the candiate. This was done either by the king or by a select group of lay and clerical notables under the king's supervision.[30]

There were probably no instances in the eleventh century where the consent of clergy and people was denied, but normally this was a mere ceremony. Thus, in 1013 when Henry II gave the see of Hamburg to his chaplain,

---

[25]"Die Gemeinde gab durch die 'laudatio' ihren consensus zu der geschehenen Wahl . . . Eine Wahl konnte noch immer für Kanonisch gelten, so lange der ursprüngliche Wahlakt, die "electio cleri et populi" stattfand; fiel die letztere fort, so war sie nicht mehr kanonisch." —Gerdes, *Die Bischofswahlen*, pp. 59-60.

[26]Ratherius, *Phrenesis*, I—*MPL*, CXXXVI, 365; compare Leo, Ep. CXLVII, 1: "Nulla ratio sinit ut inter episcopos habeantur qui nec a clericis sunt *electi*, nec a plebibus *expetiti*, nec a comprovincialibus episcopis cum metropolitani *judicio* consecrati."—*MPL*, LIV, 1203.

[27]Ratherius, *De Contemptu Canonum*, I, 36: compare Leo: " . . . teneatur *subscriptio* clericorum. . . "—*MPL*, LIV, 1199.

[28]Ratherius, *Phrenesis*, 11—*MPL*, CXXXVI, 378; cf. Gerdes, *Die Bischofswahlen*, p. 60.

[29]Gerdes, *op. cit.*, p. 60.

[30]Gerdes, *op. cit.*, p. 42.

Unwann, the chronicler notes that the appointment was acknowledged "cum laude advenientium etsi non spontanea".[31]

The king handed over the episcopal office and his consent gave the *jus ad rem.* In the view of later canon law, as Bernheim says,[32] this is monstrous; but to deny the fact that this monstrosity once existed can be to the interest of no party, even the most extreme, because thereby one would completely obscure the justification and even the intelligibility of the passionate entry of the Gregorian party into the struggle for "free canonical election".

3. *The Struggle for a Restoration of "electio per clerum et populum"*

The conflict between Gregory VII and Emperor Henry IV was "the result of a different view of what constituted ancient law and custom, and what was merely long-standing but none the less insufferable abuse."[33]

The ancient right of "electio per clerum et populum" had never been surrendered. Throughout the entire period of royal dominance the ancient forms had survived. The forms of ecclesiastical freedom had kept alive the memory of freedom itself.

It was not an innovation when Leo IX in 1049,[34] Nicho-

---

[31]A. Scharnagl, "Der Begriff der kanonischen Wahl in den Anfängen des Investiturstreits", *ZSS* (kan. Abth.), XVI (1927), 443.

[32]Investitur und Bischofswahl im 11. und 12. Jahrhundert", *ZKG*, VII (1884), 303.

[33]Geoffrey Barraclough, *Papal Provisions* (Oxford: Blackwell, 1935), p. 129; cf. Beyer, *Die Bischofs-und Abtswahlen in Deutschland unter Heinrich IV in den Jahren 1056-1076* (Halle, 1881), p. 24: "Was man jetzt Misbrauch nannte war früher königliches Recht oder doch durch die Gewohnheit zum Recht geworden; man hatte den Misbrauch nicht gesehen, weil überhaupt die Zeit zu einem Rechtsbegriff in diesen Dingen noch gar nicht gekommen war."

[34]Can. 1 of synod of Rheims—Harduin, VI, 1006.

las II in 1059,[35] and finally Gregory VII in 1078 and 1080[36] began the struggle for free canonical election. The date of victory is usually fixed at 1122, when Pope Calixtus II (1119-1124) concluded the Concordat of Worms with Henry V (1106-1125).[37] The concordat did away with the royal consent and confirmation after the election, and placed the influence of the civil power before the completion of the election, namely, during the preliminary deliberations.

The Concordat of Worms, however, was not completely satisfactory. Hinschius is essentially correct when he says[38] that the Gregorian party used the slogan "electio per clerum et populum" as a description of their immediate objective, namely, freedom from royal control, but their ultimate goal was complete freedom from lay interference. The Papal authorities did not really wish to restore the imperfect electoral system of third-century Africa or fifth-century Gaul. It was precisely this vague and uncertain procedure which had opened the way for the tyranny of secular powers.[39]

Towards the middle of the twelfth century ecclesiastics were endeavoring to exclude from canonical elections every lay influence[40]—including that granted by the Concordat of

---

[35]Can. 1 of synod of Tours—Harduin, VI, 1063.

[36]Can. 6 of Roman synod of 1080—Mansi, XX, 533.

[37]Mansi, XXI, 273.

[38]*System*, II, 602.

[39]Giovanni Baptista Montini *(Note Scolastiche per la Storia della Diplomazia Pontificia* [Romae: Apollinaris, 1934] p. 16) says that the troubles concerning papal elections (and they were the same as any other episcopal election for the first centuries) were " . . . generate dall' imperfetto sistema elettivo. . . " and "Questo guaio derivava principalmente dall' imperfezione delle disposizioni giuridiche che regolavano l'elezione . . . " Cf. Gerdes, *Die Bischofswahlen*, p. 71.

[40]See, e. g., Placidus of Nonatula, *De Honore Ecclesiae*, c. 81: "Vere enim haec fictio disciplinae est, cum quisque ideo se putat sacrandum, quia a populo electus et a rege investitus est, cum disciplina spiritus sancti sit, unumquemque pastorem sollummodo pro salute animarum pure et simpliciter ab omnibus clericis eligi, quibus consentire omnes filii illius ecclesiae . . . debent." *MPL*, CLXIII, 652.

Worms—and to limit the participation of monks and clerics who were not members of the cathedral church. The tendency was to place the entire election in the hands of the cathedral chapter.[41] It was at this period that the *Decretum Gratiani* appeared.

ARTICLE II. *Elections in the Decretum Gratiani.*

In Distinction LXII Gratian analyzes a canonical election in three short canons. Canon 3, a statement of Pope Calixtus II in the I Council of the Lateran (1123), is the fruit of the Investiture Struggle: "No one may be consecrated bishop unless he has been 'canonically elected'." In describing a canonical election Gratian departs from the traditional, vague statement of "electio per clerum et populum" and declares: "Electio clericorum est, petitio plebis."[42] This is proved by canon 1, a text of Pope Leo I: "Nulla ratio sinit, ut inter episcopos habeatur, qui nec a clericis sunt electi, nec a plebibus expetiti. . ." The action of the people is further interpreted by canon 2, the dictum of Pope Celestine I: "Docendus est populus, non sequendus. . ." The clergy elect and the people request. That is Gratian's announced thesis, but he does not prove it. By the end of Distinction LXIII, a really important "petitio plebis" has been eliminated, and in its essence, election is restricted to definite clerics, the cathedral canons.

Gratian is aware that the question is not as simple as might appear from Distinction LXII. Therefore, in Distinction LXIII he faces the tangled maze of conflicting laws, devoting 36 canons to a clarification of his position. He marshals all the important texts on the subject from the time of the Council of Laodicea (370-380) to the II Council of the Lateran (1139), but he handles them not so much

---

[41]Johann Baptist Sägmüller, *Die Bischofswahl bei Gratian* (Köln, 1908), pp. 12-13.

[42]Dictum ad D. LXII.

from the viewpoint of a legal historian, as of a practical twelfth-century lawyer.

First, he enumerates 8 canons which show that the laity, whether princes or simple faithful, are to have nothing whatever to do with elections. He cites principally the VII[43] and VIII[44] General Councils, the Council of Laodicea which excluded the tumultuous crowd from elections,[45] and the synod of Paris (557) which reacted against the synod of Orleans (549) by declaring that any bishop who achieves his dignity by royal appointment is not to be received by his fellows.[46] It is a formidable array of texts, beginning with the law of the VIII General Council: "Nullus laicorum principum vel potentum semet inserat electioni . . . cujuslibet episcopi."[47] "His omnibus auctoritatibus," he concludes, "laici excluduntur ab electione sacerdotum, atque iniungitur eis necessitas obediendi, non libertas imperandi."[48]

After this presentation of one side of the question, Gratian introduces the other side with, "Contra vero scribit B. Gregorius. . ."[48a], followed by 17 canons showing the influence of the people and especially of the king. There is a text of Pope Gelasius I (492-496) in which the distinction between the respective rôles of clergy and people is no clearer than in the letters of St. Cyprian: the bishops are to convoke the priests, deacons, and the whole multitude [of the people] so that one worthy of the episcopacy may be chosen not according to any individual's liking, but by the unanimous agreement of all.[49] A letter of Pope Leo I says that a metropolitan is to be appointed "omnium clericorum

---

[43]C. 7, D. LXIII.
[44]C. 1, D. LXIII.
[45]C. 6, D. LXIII.
[46]C. 5, D. LXIII.
[47]C. 1, D. LXIII.
[48]Dictum ad c. 8, D. LXIII.
[48a]Dictum ad c. 9, D. LXIII.
[49]C. 11, D. LXIII.

atque civium voluntate discussa. . .[50] The pseudo-privileges[51] of Hadrian I (772-795) to Charlemagne[52] and the grants of Leo VIII (963-965) to Otto I[53] are cited together with the canon of the XII Council of Toledo (681), which allowed the bishop of Toledo to appoint "quoscumque regalis potestas elegerit".[54]

Having set forth the two groups of apparently conflicting canons, Gratian endeavors to work out their harmonization. He reduces the part of the laity to acclamation and consent, saying that, even if the laity are told to be present at an election, it does not follow that they are commanded to perform the election,[55] but to consent to it. An election is duly performed in the Church when the people acclaim him whom the clergy have elected. This statement is supported by the letter of Pope Celestine I: "Cleri, plebis et ordinis consensus et desiderium requiratur"[56] and the decree of Pope Leo I which speaks of "Vota civium, testimonia populorum. . .", but "electio clericorum. . ."[57]

It is more difficult to set aside the participation of kings and princes on account of the privileges which the compiler believes to be genuine. However, he shows that the privileges were accorded them on account of heresies and schisms. They were to lend their aid so that the clergy might duly elect, but this necessity had ceased and, moreover, these same princes had renounced their privileges.[58]

The final conclusion is: ". . . praemissis auctoritatibus, cunctis liquet electionem clericorum tantummodo esse. . ."[59]

---

[50]C. 19, D. LXIII.

[51]Hefele, *Conciliengeschichte*, III, 579.

[52]C. 22, D. LXIII.

[53]C. 23, D. LXIII.

[54]C. 25, D. LXIII.

[55]" . . . non praecipitur advocari ad electionem faciendam . . . "—Dictum ad c. 25, D. LXIII.

[56]C. 26, D. LXIII.

[57]C. 27, D. LXIII.

[58]Dictum ad c. 28, D. LXIII.

[59]Dictum ad c. 34, D. LXIII.

One more question remains for determination: Among the clergy, does the election belong to the clergy of the cathedral (*majoris ecclesiae*) only, or also to others? This question is answered by canon 28 of the II Council of the Lateran (1139). The canons of the episcopal see perform the election, but they may not, under pain of invalidity, exclude the advice of the monks. Indirectly, this canon goes far to establish the exclusive right of the cathedral chapter. The monks must be admitted, but only to a consultative vote. Only their entire exclusion subjects the election to invalidity. The exclusion of the laity has no legal effect upon the election. Therefore, the law implicitly fostered the growing tendency to restrict the election to the cathedral canons.[60]

Gratian ends this distinction with a canon on the form and procedure of the election. If the votes of the electors are divided, which section is to be preferred? The question is answered by a letter of Pope Leo I to Anastasius of Thessalonica, saying that the judgment of the metropolitan is to choose that candidate "qui majoribus et studiis juvatur et meritis".[61] Complete unanimity is not absolutely necessary, because a divided vote, as the interpolation in Leo's letter says, "nec reprehensibile, nec irreligiosum judicamus". The metropolitan who has the right of confirmation will choose the better candidate. Thus, the canon forms a foundation for the *collatio votorum* of the Decretals.

Beginning with the ancient decrees which gave to the Gregorian party their slogan of "electio per clerum et populum", Gratian in his legal analysis followed the changes of history to an "electio per clerum tantummodo". Though the exclusion of all but the cathedral canons was met with

---

[60]Sägmüller, *Die Bischofswahl,* pp. 12-13; F. Geselbracht, *Das Verfahren bei den deutschen Bischofswahlen in der zweiten Hälfte des 12. Jahrhunderts* (Leipzig, 1905), p. 136 ff.

[61]C. 36, D. LXIII.

resistance, the *Decretum* was a powerful influence in consolidating the victory of the Investiture Struggle and bringing into being a new form of election, viz., one by the cathedral chapter.[62]

---

[62]Cf. c. 4, X, *de postulatione praelatorum*, I, 5: In 1205 certain suffragan bishops claimed the right by privilege of electing with the cathedral chapter; c. 50, X, *de electione et electi potestate*, I, 6: Between 1227 and 1234 twenty clerics and fourteen chaplains were admitted under protest to vote with the eighteen canons and three abbots of the church of Como, whose right to vote was not questioned; c. 56, X, *de electione et electi potestate*, I, 6: Gregory IX during the first years of his pontificate (1227-1234) found it necessary to issue a decree forbidding lay persons to join with the canons in the election of a bishop. Cf. also, Haentzsche, "Die Entstehung des ausschliesslichen Wahlrechts des Domkapitels zu Hildesheim", *AKKR*, LXXI (1894), 3-12.

CHAPTER FIVE

Elections in the Decretals

ARTICLE I. *Elections from the Decretum Gratiani (1150) to the IV Lateran Council (1215).*

1. *The Exclusive Electoral Right of the Chapter is Strengthened*

Both legislation and the teaching of canonists had the effect of placing elections more securely in the hands of the cathedral canons. At the III Lateran Council (1179) Alexander III placed the papal election in the control of the cardinals alone. The example of the supreme See of Christendom apparently served as a model for elections in the other cathedral churches of Europe.[1] The canons elected to the exclusion of all other clerics. This right was not won in a day nor in a decade, but by the end of the twelfth century it was a fairly entrenched canonical doctrine.[2]

Thus Bernard of Pavia, writing between 1191 and 1198, raised the question in his *"Summa"* as to whether the canons must convoke the other city and rural clergy in accord with the rule: "ille qui praeest, ab omnibus quibus praeest sit eligendus." He answered that this dictum must be interpreted as meaning that those who are *specially* respon-

---

[1]C. 6, X, *de electione et electi potestate*, I, 6; Sägmüller, "Die Papstwahl durch das Kardinalscollegium als Prototyp der Bischofswahl durch das Domkapitel," *Theol. Quartalschrift*, XCVII (1915), 321.

[2]In 1200 Innocent III wrote to the archbishop and canons of Sutri: " . . . secundum statuta canonica electiones episcoporum ad cathedralium ecclesiarum clericos regulariter pertinere noscantur. . . "—C. 3, X, *de causa possessionis et proprietatis*, II, 12.

sible to the bishop must be convoked, otherwise every cleric in the world would have to vote for the Pope, instead of the cardinals alone, as the law provided. Furthermore, he said that the vote of the canons prevailed over the "religiosi viri" of C. 35, D. LXIII.[3]

2. *Closer Attention is Given to Formalities*

The decretal "*Quia propter*" of the IV Lateran Council was enacted *propter diversas electionum formas* followed by the various chapters during the decades before 1215. Celestine III (1191-1198) had prescribed a form[4] according to which the electors were to convene in one place. After invoking the Holy Spirit they were to proceed to nominate a person on whom all or the *maior pars sanioris consilii* could agree. Bernard of Pavia in his "*Summa de Electione*" indicated that there were various methods of nominating the person. Those who had the right to elect could do so either directly or by means of "electors". If they chose to act directly, then one of the seniors asked each one singly concerning his choice of candidate. If they acted by means of electors, there were two possibilities: either the electors had full freedom of choice and might select a worthy candidate without regard to the various opinions of the chapter; or the electors were obliged to discover the wishes of the capitulars and then select him whom all or the greater part desired to have selected as a candidate for office.[5]

Bernard of Pavia does not use the word "*compromissum*", nor does he speak of "*compromissarii*", but there is little difference between the electors with full freedom of choice and the "*compromissarii*" as described in c. 8, 30, 32, 33, X, *de electione et electi potestate*, I, 6.

---

[3]Bernardus Papiensis, *Summa Decretalium* (ed. E. A. Th. Laspeyres, Ratisbonae, 1860), p. 309.

[4]C. 14, X, *de electione et electi potestate*, I, 6.

[5]Bernardus Papiensis, *Summa*, p. 317-318.

The second type of electors, namely, those who must determine the wishes of the capitulars, are similar to the tellers of c. 42, X, *de electione et electi potestate,* I, 6. They must elect him whom the greater part of the chapter desires. A decretal of Innocent III in 1199 shows that the Chapter of Capua chose three of their number to interrogate the capitulars as to their choice of candidate.[6] The Chapter of Toulouse chose two canons who in turn were to select five others who finally would nominate a candidate.[7] The Chapter of Cremona committed the election to four members of the chapter and three clerics of the city with the understanding that the minority would accede to the choice of the majority.[8] These were some of the "divers forms", as the decretal *"Quia propter"* expressed it, "which some have endeavored to discover." In an age of strict law, when great attention was paid to formalities, such diversity had to be regulated.

Bernard of Pavia was preoccupied with the formalities of election. Not only did he clearly classify the forms into certain general divisions, but he raised such questions as the necessity for a signed document of election, the precise right acquired by election, the duty of the confirming superior. He did not judge the written document of election to be substantially necessary; before confirmation the election remained *suspensa et infirma,* but the superior was obliged to confirm the election without delay, unless a just and reasonable cause could be urged against confirmation.[9]

Election, as described by Bernard of Pavia, was a general method of summoning a person to an ecclesiastical post.[10] It applied, as far as was practicable, to a monas-

[6]" . . . ut vota singulorum seriatim perquirerent. . . "—C. 19, X, *de electione et electi potestate,* I, 6.

[7]C. 30, X, *de electione et electi potestate,* I, 6.

[8]C. 36, X, *de electione et electi potestate,* I, 6.

[9]*Summa,* pp. 318, 320, 322.

[10]"Est autem electio alicuius personae ad religiosam domum, praebendam, dignitatem vel administrationem canonice facta vocatio." —*Summa,* p. 307.

tery, a prelacy, or a prebend. The canons spoke principally of the elections of prelates, "quod autem de praelati electione dicitur, in aliorum electionibus ad consequentiam est trahendum. . ."[11]

ARTICLE II. *The Regulations of the Decretal "Quia propter", 1215.*

> *Quia propter* diversas electionum formas, quas quidam invenire conantur, et multa impedimenta proveniunt, et magna pericula imminent ecclesiis viduatis, statuimus, ut, quum electio fuerit celebranda, praesentibus omnibus, qui debent, et volunt et possunt commode interesse, assumantur tres de collegio fide digni, qui secrete et sigillatim vota cunctorum diligenter exquirant, et in scriptis redacta mox publicent in communi, nullo prorsus appellationis obstaculo interiecto, ut is collatione habita eligatur, in quem omnes, vel maior et sanior pars capituli consentit. Vel saltem eligendi potestas aliquibus viris idoneis committatur, qui vice omnium ecclesiae viduatae provideant de pastore. Aliter electio facta non valeat, nisi forte communiter esset ab omnibus, quasi per inspirationem, absque vitio celebrata. Qui vero contra praescriptas formas eligere attentaverint, eligendi ea vice potestate priventur. § 1. Illud autem penitus interdicimus, ne quis in electionis negotio procuratorem constituat, nisi sit absens in eo loco, de quo debeat advocari, iustoque impedimento detentus venire non possit, super quo, si opus fuerit, fidem faciat iuramento, et tunc, si voluerit, uni committat de ipso collegio vicem suam. § 2. Electiones quoque clandestinas reprobamus, statuentes, ut, quam cito electio fuerit celebrata, solemniter publicetur.[11a]

The foregoing decretal definitely confined the elections "in ecclesiis viduatis" to the chapter of canons. At the same time its clear regulations concerning electoral procedure were followed in the elections of both canons and

---

[11] *Ibid.*, p. 308.

[11a] C. 42, X, *de electione et electi potestate*, I, 6, See Schroeder, *Disciplinary Canons*, p. 265, for an English Translation of this Canon.

monks.[12] This chapter is the *forma concilii*—as Gregory IX calls it[13]—according to which all elections are judged.

1. *Analysis of the Decretal "Quia propter"*

The IV Lateran Council limited the forms of election to three: a) acclamation; b) compromise; c) scrutiny. The use of any other form invalidated the election. Acclamation took place if the chapter, without previous deliberation—and as if moved by the Holy Spirit (*quasi-inspiratio*)—decided to elect a certain man. Since one dissenting voice was enough to invalidate this method of procedure, its use was infrequent.[14] The method of compromise also called for a high degree of unanimity, since all had to agree to surrender their rights to the *compromissarii*. In practice, therefore, the method of scrutiny was the most popular of the three forms. An election by scrutiny was conducted as follows: When an election was to be celebrated —so canon 24 of the IV Lateran Council directed—three members of the chapter were selected in the presence of all the electors. These three tellers secretly, singly, and diligently investigated the votes of all, put these votes down in writing, and then published the votes immediately. Thereupon he was declared elected who, after due comparison, was found to have the consent of the greater and more discerning part of the chapter. As soon as the election was celebrated it was solemnly published. Clandestine elections were reprobated.[15]

Laurence of Somercote, a canon of Chichester, who wrote a treatise on elections in 1254, says that the form of

---

[12]"Processus Electionis Abbatum S. Albani"—*Monasticon Anglicanum* (ed. Ellis and Bandinel), II, 191, note.

[13]C. 55, X, *de electione et electi potestate*, I, 6.

[14]Laurence of Somercote, *Tractatus de Electionibus*—*Lincoln Cathedral Statutes* (ed. Bradshaw and Wordsworth, Cambridge, 1897), II, cxxx.

[15]C. 42, X, *de electione et electi potestate*, I, 6.

scrutiny is the ordinary form of election, although it is subject to "infinite dangers". In enumerating these legal pitfalls, he offers a good analysis of the decretal *"Quia propter"*: There are six points so necessary for the election, that if any of them are passed over the election is rendered null by the law itself. The first is that the votes of all be investigated secretly; the second, that this be done singly; the third, that they be set down in writing; the fourth, that they should be immediately published in common; the fifth, that there be a threefold comparison, namely, number compared with number, merits with merit, zeal with zeal; the sixth, that a general or common election follow.[16]

The treatise of Laurence of Somercote is interesting because it was written as a practical guide for actual elections. He describes how the tellers (as they later came to be called) would interrogate the capitulars in a corner of the chapter room, setting down the voter's name and his choice, so that later the comparison of zeal and merit could be made in order to determine who had been chosen by the more discerning section of the chapter. This treatise also offers formulas for decrees of election and for petitions of confirmation.

2. *Influence of the Decretal "Quia propter"*

Even in the nineteen years that intervened between 1215 and the publication of the Decretals of Gregory IX, the decretal *"Quia propter"* was the guide for papal decisions in disputed elections, and these decisions in turn served to round out the law of elections.

First of all, the decretal *"Quia propter"* contemplated a definite college of electors, acting in a collegiate manner (*collegialiter*). One act of election only was produced by this group, because it had to be a common election, as Greg-

[16] *Lincoln Cathedral Statutes*, II, cxxxvi.

ory IX said.[17] It was not deemed sufficient for each to consent singly. Group action was required.

Therefore, it followed that a legitimate act of *convo-*
I. *cation* was very important and was regulated by law.[18]

Flowing from the significance and importance of legitimate convocation were the frequent[19] *actiones de contemptu* on the part of canons who had been passed over in the act of convocation. If it was possible to call a capitular and the chapter failed to do so, chapter 28 of the title "*de electione et electi potestate*" declared that this voter could have the election nullified even after confirmation. But, unless he brought suit, the election stood. If those who were summoned neglected to come, the election was conducted by those actually present.[20] Later canonists[21] were to determine that two thirds of the chapter had to be summoned before an election could take place.

The electoral college was a definite moral person with-
II. in itself and therefore as a further consequence *ex-*
cluded all outsiders, such as members of another abbey,[22] suffragan bishops,[23] other clerics,[24] and layfolk, particularly when their presence interfered with canonical freedom.[25]

Besides those who had to be excluded from the elec-
III. toral college because they were not members, there
were also certain members whom it was unnecessary

---

[17]C. 55, X, *de electione et electi potestate*, I, 6.

[18]C. 14, 35, 36, 42, 55, X, *de electione et electi potestate*, I, 6.

[19]C. 28, 36, 55, X, *de electione et electi potestate*, I, 6.

[20]C. 19, 28, 35, 42, X, *de electione et electi potestate*, I, 6.

[21]Cf. Hostiensis, *de electione*, n. 11; cf. also Michiels, *De Personis*, 11, 379, 4.

[22]C. 8, X, *de consuetudine*, I, 4; c. 47, X, *de electione et electi potestate*, I, 6.

[23]C. 4, X, *de postulatione praelatorum*, I, 5.

[24]C. 50, X, *de electione et electi potestate*, I, 6.

[25]C. 43, 50, 51, 56, X, *de electione et electi potestate*, I, 6.

or unlawful to summon because they lacked *the requisite qualifications.* Such were: heretics,[26] those who had been suspended,[27] and those who had been deprived of the power of electing.[28]

The decretal *"Quia propter"*, by its prescription of
IV. "statuimus. . . ut is eligatur, in quem omnes, vel maior
et sanior pars capituli consentit", helped to develop the *method of determining the collegiate choice.* Modern law[29] accepts the principle of numerical majority in virtue of which the moral person as a whole is deemed to express its will by means of the majority of its members: "Quod maior pars facit, totum capitulum facere videtur."[30] This principle was slow in finding adoption by the medieval canonists. They were reluctant to equate the *maior pars* with the *sanior pars* and to reduce important decisions to a problem in arithmetic.[31]

Before the III Lateran Council (1179) there seems to have been no text in the law in which the quantitative majority is declared to be sufficient. The texts[32] sought rath-

---

[26]C. 13, X, *de haereticis,* V, 7.

[27]C. 8, X, *de consuetudine,* I, 4; c. 16, X, *de electione et electi potestate,* I, 6; c. 9, X, *de exceptionibus,* II, 25; c. 29, X, *de praebendis et dignitatibus,* III, 5.

[28]C. 7, 20, 23, 25, 40-43, 50, X, *de electione et electi potestate,* I, 6; c. 3, X, *de translatione episcopi,* I, 7. Phrase used in these sources is: *eligendi potestate privatus.*

[29]Can. 101, § 1, n. 1.

[30]Pierre Gillet, *La Personnalite Juridique En Droit Ecclesiastique* (Malines: Godenne, 1927), p. 138; cf. *Glossa* in c. 6, X, *de constitutionibus,* I, 2.

[31]"Non sufficit ad confirmationem electionis, quod sit facta a maiori parte, nisi etiam illa pars sit sanior."—Summarium, c. 57, X, *de electione et electi potestate,* I, 6; M. V. Clarke, *Medieval Representation and Consent,* p. 339; Gillet, *La Personalite Juridique,* p. 139.

[32]E. g., *Regula Monachorum,* cap. LXIV: " . . . pars quamvis parva congregationis saniore consilio elegerit."—ed. Butler, p. 111; Concordat of Worms: "sanior pars"—Mansi, XXI, 273; c. 14, X, *de electione et electi potestate,* I, 6: " . . . maior pars sanioris consilii . . . "

er to apply the rule of Leo the Great which declared that when the votes were divided between two sections, he should be preferred "qui maioribus et studiis juvatur et meritis".[33]

The III Lateran Council declared that a two-thirds majority was necessary and sufficient for the election of the Pope. No question could be raised about the *sanior pars*. The principle of majority prevailed. But in other elections this law itself declared that[34] the opinion of the *maior et sanior pars* must prevail, because whatever doubt might have remained as to which party had the sounder judgment could be resolved by the confirming superior. This very special rule of a two-thirds majority was enacted for the Roman Church, because there no recourse could be had to a superior.[35]

During the decades immediately following the promulgation of the decretal *"Quia propter"*[36] the threefold comparison of the votes (*collatio votorum*) continued, namely, a comparison of number with number, merit with merit, zeal with zeal. This was the rule which Bernard of Pavia said he had learned from his master in law, John of Tournai: "In discensiones partium eligentium circa personas tria sunt attendenda, videlicet numerus et bonus zelus et dignitas vel auctoritas; quaecumque autem pars duobus horum praeeminet, in electione debet obtinere."[37]

Despite the fact that—as canon 1 of the III Lateran Council had declared—the confirming superior could decide which part was *sanior*, this effort to compare votes and to weigh them qualitatively was fraught with many difficulties and inconveniences. Gradually the presumption gained

---

[33]C. 36, D. LXIII.

[34]C. 6, X, *de electione et electi potestate*, I, 6.

[35]*Ibid.*

[36]Cf. Laurence of Somercote, *Tractatus—Lincoln Cathedral Statutes*, II, cxxxviii.

[37]*Summa Decretalium*, p. 315-316.

ground among canonists that the majority usually had the greater discretion on its side.[38] Gregory IX decided that the *maior pars* of the IV Lateran Council meant the absolute majority.[39] This decision served to obviate disputes as to which side was truly *maior*. Gregory X in the II Council of Lyons (1274) decided that no opposition could be raised against a two-thirds majority. A numerical majority of that size was also supposed to have greater reason and discernment on its side.[40] This enactment went far to fix the rule of numerical majority both in legislation and in canonical doctrine. As far as religious were concerned, the Council of Trent,[41] by requiring a strictly secret vote, prevented all comparison between the voters on either side of a divided election and determined the result by number alone.

Besides the method of determining a collegiate choice
V. by means of the votes of all or of the greater and more
discerning part of the chapter, the decretal "*Quia propter*" allowed the electoral college to employ the *method of compromise*. The electors could commit their power of election to one[42] or more fit men, the *compromissarii*, who would elect in the name of all.[43] The Decretals of Gregory IX made little or no change in the method of compromise as described by Bernard of Pavia.[44] The compromise could be either absolute[45] or limited by conditions, for instance, that the *compromissarii* choose him who is seen to be the choice of the greater and more discerning section of the

---

[38] Gillet, *La Personalite Juridique*, p. 140.

[39] C. 55, X, *de electione et electi potestate*, I, 6.

[40] C. 9, *de electione et electi potestate*, I, 6, in VI°.

[41] Sess. XXV, *de regularibus*, c. 6.

[42] C. 8, X, *de electione et electi potestate*, I, 6.

[43] "Vel saltem eligendi potestas aliquibus viris idoneis committatur, qui vice omnium ecclesiae viduatae provideant de pastore."—C. 42, X, *de electione et electi potestate*, I, 6.

[44] *Summa Decretalium*, pp. 317-318.

[45] C. 8, X, *de electione et electi potestate*, I, 6. In this instance the electors enjoyed full freedom of choice—called "*plenum arbitrium*" by Bernard of Pavia.

chapter.[46] The form of compromise did not admit of much legal development. Particular conditions could be imposed in each case. These conditions, provided they were not contrary to law, might range from the obligation of choosing the bishop-elect from among the clerics of the local church[47] to the necessity of arriving at a choice before a certain candle had burnt out.[48]

After an election had been duly conducted and the
VI. chapter had arrived at a choice, the person elected did
not immediately enjoy full rights over his office. The election required *confirmation.* Before that was given, the election remained "suspensa et infirma", as Bernard of Pavia says,[49] and the elected person was forbidden to administer his office.[50] The necessity of confirmation was clearly indicated in the decretals,[51] but it was not so clear who was the confirming superior. Previous to decretal law bishops were confirmed by the metropolitan and suffragans,[52] and the metropolitan by all the bishops of the province.[53]

The Popes of the twelfth century gradually vindicated unto themselves the right to confirm all metropolitans.[54]

---

[46]C. 32, X, *de electione et electi potestate,* I, 6. This is what Bernard of Pavia called the "*pars sollicitudinis.*" It was practically the same as the *scrutinium mixtum* of later canonists, i. e., a compromise in which the *compromissarii* act in the manner of tellers and proceed otherwise as at an election. "It is used," says Reiffenstuel (Lib. I, tit. 6, n. 77), "because it is simpler, quicker, and subject to less invalidating formalities than the simple scrutiny."

[47]C. 32, X, *de electione et electi potestate,* I, 6.

[48]" . . . usque ad consumptionem cuiusdam candelae . . . "—C. 52, X, *de electione et electi potestate,* I, 6.

[49]*Summa Decretalium,* p. 320.

[50]C. 7, *de consuetudine,* I, 4; c. 18, X, *de praebendis et dignitatibus,* III, 5.

[51]C. 11, X, *de electione et electi potestate,* I, 6; c. 1, *de translatione episcopi,* I, 7.

[52]C. 1, D. LXII.

[53]C. 1, D. LXVI.

[54]CC. 18, 28, X, *de electione et electi potestate,* I, 6; cf. Hinschius, *System,* II, 577, 590, 600, where he shows that by the end of the twelfth century the pope was exercising the right to confirm and consecrate metropolitans throughout Germany, France, England and Italy.

The right of the metropolitan to confirm a suffragan bishop was still admitted in the Decretals of Gregory IX,[55] but the tendency was to place this power also in the hands of the Roman Pontiff. "What has been called the *Metropolitanverfassung*" of the Church, a system which had served its purpose in time past, now became obsolete. The actual law was for the most part not altered; but a new practice grew up, and a new age—one of vigorous practical centralization—began. From now on the active part taken by the papacy in the direction of administration—above all in nomination to major benefices—was developed on a scale which previous popes had not countenanced."[56]

Although the chapter had the right to name the pastor for the vacant church, conciliar canons and decrees took care that this right did not hinder the welfare of the flock. Besides laying down qualifications for candidates, repeated enactments required that the election be not delayed longer than three months.[57]

If the chapter neglected its duty, then the right to
VII. name the pastor *devolved upon* the next higher superior.[58] In the case of archbishops the law of devolution followed the same line of development as the law of confirmation. An archbishop had no superior save the Pope and therefore the election of an archbishop devolved upon the Pope, if the chapter was negligent. With regard to bishoprics, a distinction was at first made between negligence and other causes. In the case of negligence the arch-

---

[55]C. 32, X, *de electione et electi potestate*, I, 6.

[56]Geoffrey Barraclough, "The Making of a Bishop in the Middle Ages", *Cath. Hist. Rev.*, XIX (1933), 289.

[57]C. 11, D. L. (Greg. I, 597); c. 35, D. LXIII (II Conc. Lat., 1139); c. 41, X, *de electione et electi potestate*, I, 6 (IV. Conc. Lat., 1215).

[58]" . . . qui eligere debuerant, eligendi potestate careant ea vice, ac ipsa eligendi potestas ad eum qui proxime praeesse dignoscitur, devolvatur."—C. 41, X, *de electione et electi potestate*, I, 6.

bishop could provide. In all other cases, e. g., in the election of an unworthy candidate, in loss of the power of electing on the part of the chapter, in disputed elections, the Holy See had the right of devolution.[59] All doubt, however, in the matter of confirmation and devolution was to be swept away in the system of reservations[60] which gradually concentrated all power over bishoprics in the hands of the Pope.

ARTICLE III. *Elections in the Sext and in Later Decretals.*

The law of elections seems to have developed with unusual rapidity. There is hardly a trace of capitular elections before 1100. In the *Decretum Gratiani* there is no mention of capitular procedure, save for the bare statement of a principle in C. 36, D. LXIII, and even that principle has no immediate bearing on a capitular election, unless it is read in connection with the preceding canon which speaks of elections by the monks and cathedral canons. And still the period between 1150 and 1215 saw such a complete unfolding of the institute of elections, that later decretals did little more than clarify certain principles and round out particular provisions of the law.

Thus the Sext of Boniface VIII made further deter-
I. minations with regard to the *qualifications* of the electors. A canon below the age of puberty did not have
to be called to an election, because he was presumed to lack

---

[59]This was first clearly stated in c. 18, *de electione et electi potestate*, I, 6, in VI°, but c. 23, X, *de electione et electi potestate*, I, 6 stated in the summary: "Si omnes privati sunt [scil. potestate eligendi] devolvitur ad Papam in ecclesiis cathedralibus." This question seems to have remained doubtful until settled by a constitution of Alexander IV (1254-1261), which was the ruling on which c. 18, *de electione et electi potestate*, I, 6, in VI° was based. Cf. Barraclough, *Cath. Hist. Rev.*, XIX (1935), 290.

[60]C. 2, 34, *de praebendis et dignitatibus*, III, 4, in. VI°; c. 4, *de electionibus*, I, 3, in Extravag. Com.

the necessary discretion.[61] In religious houses those who were not yet professed, were not to be admitted to vote with the professed, and in the churches of regulars the *conversi* (the lay brothers) were not to be admitted to elections with the clerics.[62] There were further enactments regarding penal deprivations of the right to vote,[63] and the employment of a proxy was closely regulated.[64]

As to the *voting* itself, Innocent IV in the I Council of
II. Lyons (1245) reprobated all conditional, alternative,
and uncertain votes.[65] Gregory X in the II Council of Lyons (1274) enacted a number of decrees concerning disputed elections and the appeals against elections. It was into this setting that the law was placed concerning the presumption that a two-thirds majority had right and reason on its side. This majority could never be attacked on any grounds less than those of a plea of complete invalidity.[66]

Moreover, Boniface VIII settled a dispute which had
III. arisen among canonists concerning the possibility of
limited compromise, i. e., a compromise in which the *compromissarii* were bound to investigate the desires of the chapter and then to nominate and elect him who was seen to be the choice of the majority. Some canonists declared that this form had been outlawed by the decretal "*Quia propter*". Canon 29, *de electione et electi potestate*, I, 6, in VI°, declared that the form of limited compromise described in the decretal "*Quum dilectus*"[67] was not revoked by the IV Council of the Lateran. If, however, this form was used, then the *compromissarii* had to elect him on

---

[61] C. 32, *de electione et electi potestate*, I, 6, in. VI°.

[62] C. 32, 43, *de electione et electi potestate*, I, 6, in VI°.

[63] C. 7, *de electione et electi potestate*, 1, 6, in VI°; c. 1, *ut lite pendente nihil innovetur*, II, 8, in VI°; c. 18, *de sententia excommunicationis suspensionis et interdicti*, V, 11, in VI°.

[64] C. 46, *de electione et electi potestate*, I, 6, in VI°.

[65] C. 2, *de electione et electi potestate*, I, 6, in VI°.

[66] C. 9, *de electione et electi potestate*, I, 6, in VI°.

[67] C. 32, X, *de electione et electi potestate*, I, 6.

whom the absolute majority (and not merely the relative majority) had agreed.[68]

The Sext gave legal recognition to a formality on
IV. which thirteenth-century canonists appear to have set great store, namely, the *electio communis*. Election (so the reasoning seems to have proceeded) is an act of a moral person, the electoral college. The moral person, though, is distinct from the individual members. Therefore the formal election must be distinct from the single votes of the members. Someone must be commissioned to act in the name of the college and pronounce the formal election for the moral person which is unable to act.[69]

In 1254 Laurence of Somercote wrote regarding election by scrutiny: "Iniungant singuli eorum *alicui* de seipsis, quod nominatum eligat per haec verba . . . Nisi enim fieret haec *electio generalis sive communis*, ipso iure nihil omnino videretur actum esse quantumcumque solemnitates aliae servarentur."[70]

This reasoning (note the word "*videretur*") was probably a conclusion from the statement of Gregory IX: ". . . non tamen debet subsequi electio singularis sed *communis* . . ."[71] At any rate Boniface VIII[72] admitted that after a choice by scrutiny ". . . est per unum pronuncianda et facienda communis electio secundum canonica instituta . . ." and he ordered the same rule to be followed in the event of compromise. Otherwise, even if all the *compromissarii* were unanimous in their choice, the election would be invalid. Therefore this law of the Sext was as follows: In order that an election may be evidently single and common, one person in the name of all must pronounce the elec-

---

[68]C. 23, *de electione et electi potestate*, I, 6, in VI°.

[69]Alfred von Wretschko, "Die Electio Communis bei den kirchlichen Wahlen im Mittelalter," *Zeitschrift für Kirchenrecht*, XI (1901), 321-392.

[70]*Lincoln Cathedral Statutes*, II, cxxxix.

[71]C. 55, X, *de electione et electi potestate*, I, 6.

[72]C. 21, *de electione et electi potestate*, I, 6, in VI°.

tion in the singular number (scil., *eligo*) and this rule was to be followed whether the chapter proceeded by way of scrutiny or by way of compromise.[73]

The act of *confirmation* was also more carefully regu-
V. lated by the II Council of Lyons (1247). If the elected person meddled in the affairs of his office before confirmation, the law immediately deprived him of all right acquired through his election.[74] The electors were to notify the elected one of his election as soon as possible. He in turn had to give his consent within a month under pain of deprivation of all acquired right, and after giving his consent he had to apply for confirmation within three months, likewise under pain of nullification of the election.[75]

The law of *devolution* was still further determined by
VI. Boniface VIII[76]. But, as was noted above, the system of reservations soon concentrated all power over bishoprics in the hands of the Pope. As a result elections were confined to the internal affairs of chapters and of religious houses. As Barraclough notes, ". . . it is hardly an exaggeration to say that the common law [esp. with regard to the election of *bishops*] was scarcely defined before it was obsolete. At any rate, the period during which it held unchallenged sway was a remarkably short one. . . (The system of reservations prevented) an election from taking place, conferring instead the power of direct nomination on the pope. . . It is only essential to grasp how wide was the use to which the system, already in the thirteenth century, was put. As early as 1249 the pope took control of the whole of Germany by inhibiting elections 'absque nostra licentia speciali' . . . and apart from general orders of this

[73]" . . . ut censeatur evidentius unica et communis, est ab uno vice omnium, sive per compromissum sive per scrutinium procedatur, electionis pronunciatio per verba singularis numeri facienda."—C. 4, *de sententia et re iudicata,* II, 14, in VI°.

[74]C. 5, *de electione et electi potestate,* I, 6, in VI°.

[75]C. 6, *de electione et electi potestate,* I, 6, in VI.°

[76]Cc. 18, 37, *de electione et electi potestate,* I, 6, in VI°.

sort, innumerable single churches throughout the period in question were reserved for the single occasion. All this papal activity was at the expense of capitular election and of the 'jus commune'. It was a new system which for a time ran parallel with the old, but rapidly came to replace it. After the middle of the thirteenth century, the 'electio communis' was fighting a losing battle: its full and unchallenged practical importance definitely fell within the period before the death of Innocent IV (1254).[77]

---

[77]"The Making of a Bishop in the Middle Ages", *Cath. Hist. Rev.*, XIX (1933), p. 284-285; see the same author, *Papal Provisions* (Oxford: Blackwell, 1935), p. 129 ff.

CHAPTER SIX

Recent Developments in Canonical Elections From the Council of Trent to the Code

The law of elections as contained in the Decretals remained substantially unchanged until the time of the Council of Trent. The Council legislated concerning the elections of regulars and nuns, and these prescriptions had their influence on the general law of elections as contained in the Code. After the Council of Trent there were no important enactments on elections save a succession of decrees affecting the abuse of electoral capitulations, namely, the custom of having the candidates swear to uphold certain rights and customs of the chapter.

To avoid repetitions it will be best, as each point of Tridentine and post-Tridentine legislation is considered, to focus thereon the opinions of representative authors who wrote after the Council of Trent and before the enactment of the present law of the Code. Since there are few important differences in the canonical teachings on elections in the three centuries and a half here to be considered, this era will be regarded as one period of legal history.

ARTICLE I. *The Council of Trent and Elections.*

1. *A secret vote*

Although the decretal *"Quia propter"* had demanded that the tellers inquire about the capitular's vote in a secret manner, the voting was not really secret, since a comparison had to be made between the relative zeal and merit of the electors. From certain decretals it is clear that the chapter often knew quite well for whom each member had voted.[1] The Council of Trent, however, required such secrecy in the elections of all regular superiors of whatever kind that the names of the electors should never be revealed.[2] The reason given by the Council is that the election be performed without fraud. Secrecy was an aid to freedom, a protection against all undue influence, chief of which was subornation. Severe penalties against those guilty of subornation were inflicted by Pius V in 1571[3] and by Clement VIII in 1599.[4]

From this conciliar ordinance regarding secrecy, canonists began to draw various conclusions affecting electoral procedure. First, the *comparison of votes* on the basis of zeal and merit was held to be a violation of secrecy and was therefore omitted, the resulting election being decided by *numerical majority* alone. Reiffenstuel said indeed that the comparison of votes was to be omitted in the elections of regulars, but rejected the reasoning which derived the rule from the Council of Trent. He said it was rather because religious have left all things for Christ and are presumed to proceed according to their best judgment in the election.[5] Wernz, however, said the omission of this comparison was "propter legem de secretis suffragiis" and, though this law was enacted for religious, the advantages of omitting all comparison of votes made this the common law before the Code.[6] Piat, likewise, attributed the omission of the ancient *collatio* to the rule of the Council of Trent regarding secrecy.[7]

It was further concluded that the forms of compromise and acclamation were forbidden to regulars on account of

---

[1]Cf., e. g., c. 50, X, *de electione et electi potestate*, I, 6.

[2]Sess. XXV, *de regularibus*, c. 6.

[3]Const., *"Pastoralis Officii"*, 28 maii, 1571, § 4—*Bullarium Romanum*, VII, 917.

[4]Const., *"Nullus Omnino,"* 25 iulii, 1599, § 22—*Bullarium Romanum*, X, 665.

[5]*Jus Canonicum Universum* (Monachii, 1702), Lib. I, tit. 6, n. 136.

[6]*Ius Decretalium* (Romae, 1906), II, n. 371.

[7]*Praelectiones Iuris Regularis* (Tornaci, 1890), II, 45.

the prescription of absolute secrecy. This conclusion was not admitted by all and therefore was regarded as a disputed point down to the time of the Code.[8] Thus Rodericus held that religious were permitted to use the form of compromise, since the rule of the Council of Trent regarding secret votes applied only to the form of scrutiny.[9] Laurence de Peyrinis in a note to the Constitution *"Exponi Nobis"* of Gregory XIII, August 15, 1580, declared that compromise for religious was abolished by the Council of Trent.[10] Ferraris,[11] Reiffenstuel,[12] and Piat[13] admitted that important authors denied the abolition of compromise and of acclamation but they could not see how such denial could be reconciled with the law of the Council of Trent.

Most authors[14] held that the secrecy required by the Council of Trent did not demand the use of a written ballot. This opinion was confirmed by the following chapter in the same XXV session of the Council of Trent which, in adverting to the bishop's part in the election of abbesses, specifies: ". . . vota singulorum *audiat*, vel accipiat."[15]

2. *A free vote*

As was said above, the Council of Trent insisted on a secret ballot to avoid fraud and to insure freedom. Ferraris noted various methods of procedure which simultane-

---

[8]Piat, *op. cit.*, II, 8.

[9]*Questiones Regulares et Canonicae* (Venetiis, 1611), Tom. II, q. 51, n. 9.

[10]*Privilegia Regularibus Praesertim Minimis PerSummos Pontifices Sixtum IV usque ad Urbanum VIII Concessa* (Venetiis, 1649), p. 224.

[11]*Prompta Bibliotheca* (Lutetiae Parisiorum, 1865), "Electio", art. IV, n. 28.

[12]Lib. I, tit. 6, n. 348.

[13]*Praelectiones*, II, 8.

[14]Thus, Reiffenstuel, Lib. I, tit. 6, n. 124 and 351; Piat, *Praelectiones*, II, p. 8, n. 5, and others cited by Piat.

[15]Sess. XXV, *de regularibus*, c. 7.

ously violated secrecy and freedom.[16] Thus, if the president of the chapter passed out ballots on which was marked the name of a candidate, the election was null. The same was true if a *"pater praedominans"* handed a marked ballot to one of his henchmen with the direction that this be shown to all the members of his following. The Sacred Congregation of the Council, on May 27, 1623, declared that it was not lawful for a religious prelate to curtail liberty by proposing two or three names from which one was to be elected.[17]

3. *A vote by duly qualified electors*

The Council of Trent declared that in order to be a duly qualified elector in any church, whether cathedral or collegiate, secular or regular, one must have received at least the subdiaconate.[18] Though this text of the Council refers in itself to *churches* only and says nothing about the elections of religious to prelacies within their order, custom interpreted the Council of Trent as meaning to exclude the lay brothers from all elections in accord with c. 36, *de electione et electi potestate*, I, 6, in VI°.[19] But if the Constitutions admitted the lay brothers, they were to be summoned to the chapter, notwithstanding the conciliar law.[20] Thus the Capuchin Order in 1647 obtained a declaration from Innocent X that the lay brothers might be admitted to the chapter "non obstante Concilio Tridentino."[21]

Though the law was most definite that the election was confined to the members of the chapter, who in most cases would be clerics, authors before the Code disputed as to

---

[16]*Bibliotheca* "Electio", art. IV, n. 35-36.

[17]*Fontes*, n. 2441.

[18]Sess. XXII *de ref.*, c. 4.

[19]Piat, *Praelectiones*, II, 11; Rodericus, *Questiones Regulares*, II, q. 51, n. 5.

[20]Ferraris, *Bibliotheca*, "Electio", art. IV, n. 38.

[21]Cf. *Monumenta ad Constitutiones Ordinis Fratrum Minorum Capuccinorum*, ed. Venantius a Lisle en Rigault (Romae, 1916), p. 367; *Bullarium Capucinorum*, I, 103.

whether a vote could be given for a single time to a non-member of the chapter. Wernz thought that the chapter might do so by unanimous consent.[22] Piat declared that it was more probable that this could not be done. Since provincials, abbots, and priors were forbidden by the Council to supply the votes of those religious who were absent, it seemed to Piat that there was all the more reason why these authorities as well as the unanimous chapter should be forbidden to give a vote to one who was not a member of the chapter.[23] De Peyrinis [24] and Reiffenstuel[25] believed that the chapter could confer a vote on an outsider by unanimous consent for a single time. Reiffenstuel argued that since the chapter could make an outsider a *compromissarius*, it could also give him a vote.

Most of the old reasons for *deprivation of vote* remained in force and new ones were introduced at this period. The Council of Trent deprived a religious of his right of active and passive voice in the chapter for two years, if he was found guilty of proprietorship.[26] Paul IV (1555-1559), in response to the needs of the time, issued a decree in which heretics and schismatics were severely interdicted from all participation in elections.[27]

4. *A vote by one present in the chapter*

Under certain conditions the decretal *"Quia propter"* had allowed the appointment of a proxy to take the place of an absent capitular. By forbidding religious superiors to supply the votes of the absent, the Council of Trent raised the question as to whether or not a proxy might be em-

---

[22]*Ius Decretalium*, II, n. 334.

[23]Cf. sess. XXV, *de regularibus*, c. 6; Piat, *Praelectiones*, II, 19 and 22.

[24]*Subditus, Praelatus, ac Formularium* (Venetiis, 1648), I, 122.

[25]Lib. I, tit. 6, n. 160.

[26]Sess. XXV, *de regularibus*, c. 2.

[27]Const. *"Cum ex Apostolatus,"* 15 febr., 1559, § 5—*Fontes*, n. 94

ployed.[28] In accord with the Constitution *"Christifidelium"* of Innocent XII, February 16, 1694, it would seem that the employment of a proxy by religious was forbidden by the Council and therefore the vote of the absent one could not be supplied unless the constitutions allowed some form of proxy.[29] Alexander VII (1655-1667) allowed the members of Capuchin provincial chapters to vote by proxy in those provinces which were devastated by the plague, provided the number of proxies did not exceed one third of those voting.[30] This was a permission which seems to have been granted for a single instance. When in 1723 the Minister General of the Order of Friars Minor of the Observance asked of Pope Innocent XIII the faculty of supplying the votes of the absent missionaries, the Holy Father declined to derogate from the prohibitions in force.[31]

The prohibition of supplying the votes of the absent did not extend to those who were absent from the chapter room but nevertheless present in the house. Canon 168 of the Code is the first clear law which exactly describes the manner of obtaining the vote of one who is sick and unable to be present in the chapter room, but almost the exact wording of the canon is found in many authors who wrote during the time between the enactment of the Council of Trent and the Code. Thus, Reiffenstuel[32] said: "Infirmus [in Monasterio, in quo electio peragitur, vel saltem in Civitate], qui ob infirmitatem personaliter electioni interesse nequit, potest . . . per semetipsum dare votum suum: atque in hoc . . . casu debent scrutatores ad ipsum accedere, et

[28]"Nec in posterum liceat provinciales, aut abbates, priores aut alios quoscumque titulares ad effectum electionis faciendae constituere, aut voces absentium supplere."—Sess. XXV, *de regularibus*, c. 6.

[29]§ 12—*Bullarium Romanum*, XX, 600.

[30]Oct. 20, 1657—*Monumenta ad Constitutiones Capuccinorum*, p. 257.

[31]S. C. Ep. et Reg., *Ordinis Minorum Observantium*, 15 maii, 1723 —*Fontes*, n. 1840.

[32]Lib. I, tit. 6, n. 192; see also, De Peyrinis (1648), *Subditus*, I, 117; Piat (1890), *Praelectiones*, II, 14.

suffragium ipsius recipere . . . In praxi tamen . . . observandas esse speciales consuetudines."

Allied to the question of supplying votes and appointing a proxy is the question whether one could cast more than one vote in any single ballot because of several titles to vote. In answer to a question of the Minister General of the Order of Friars Minor, the Sacred Congregation of Bishops and Regulars declared that a Definitor who was at the same time guardian of a convent could not cast two votes in the chapter.[33] Antecedents for this decision are found as early as the year 1313 in the Constitutions of the Order of Friars Minor, where it is said: No friar in one and the same year shall have more than one vote in the election of a discreet to the chapter. . . The General Chapter held at Lyons in 1518 declared: In no chapter whatever may a friar cast more than one electoral vote.[34]

ARTICLE II. *Post-Tridentine Legislation on Elections.*

1. *Electoral capitulations*

Between 1584 and 1754, three important papal decrees were directed against the abuse of capitulations. The abuse was very old, for Nicholas III (1277-1280), whose constitution on the subject these subsequent decrees renew, recounts the vicious custom which had arisen of forcing prelates, canons, rectors and other officials to swear to uphold divers customs and statutes. Canons and lay people refused to receive certain appointees until they had sworn to these capitulations. Nicholas III declared that these oaths were binding in as far as they referred to licit, possible things, and to matters not injurious to ecclesiastical liberty. Otherwise, they did not bind.[35]

---

[33] S. C. Ep. et Reg., *Ordinis Minorum Observantium,* decr. 11 mart., 1836, ad V.—*Fontes,* n. 1909.

[34] *Monumenta ad Constitutiones Capuccinorum,* p. 357.

[35] C. 1, *de iureiurando,* II, 11, in VI°.

These capitulations often amounted to a full program of government which the bishop or abbot was bound to carry out. In the course of time the extent of these statutes grew. Thus in Constance the number of articles in the capitulations grew from nine in 1294 to thirty-seven in 1491.[36] Canons were admitted to the chapter only on condition that they swear to uphold these ancient rights, statutes and customs. When elections were held, all bound themselves by oath to uphold the capitulations if they were elected. The election was undertaken and executed on this condition.

Gregory XIII (1572-1585) renewed the constitution of Nicholas III (1277-1280), attempting to extirpate whatever was an abuse in these sworn conditions.[37] Innocent XII (1691-1700) went further, interdicting every sort of pact and condition no matter how made. He desired to see the abuse utterly rooted out and he applied the constitution not only to cathedral churches but also to monasteries.[38] Benedict XIV (1740-1758) finally summed up and renewed all preceding constitutions on this question, giving them the greatest possible application and extent. He said that it was profoundly to the interest of the Church to safeguard the objective liberty of election and to exclude all personal ambition and aggrandizement. Therefore, even agreements which would be useful to monasteries and other corporate bodies, and not contrary to natural law, have been forbidden by the sacred canons and Apostolic constitutions. All the former laws were renewed and extended to "monasteria vel capitula, sive collegia mixta ex utriusque sexus personis."[39]

2. *The election of the vicar capitular*

The Council of Trent ordered the chapter to elect a vicar capitular within eight days after the death of the bish-

---

[36]Hofmeister, *Bischof und Domkapitel*, p. 63.

[37]Const. *"Inter Apostolicas,"* 5 sept. 1584—*Fontes*, n. 154.

[38]Const. *"Ecclesiae Catholicae,"* 22 sept. 1695—*Fontes*, n. 259.

[39]Const. *"Pastoralis,"* 15 iul. 1754—*Fontes*, n. 430.

op.[40] During the period after the Council of Trent disputes concerning elections of vicars capitular and consequent decisions by the Sacred Congregation of the Council served to develop and clarify the law of elections.

The decretal "*Quia propter*" was always understood to apply chiefly to the election of a pastor in the strict sense, viz., to the election of a bishop. The law speaks of those prelates, said Reiffenstuel, through whose death the church is regarded as widowed. This applies, of course, to the bishop who is spiritually espoused to his church.[41]

The law applied with equal strictness to those whose relation with their church was similar to that of a bishop. But in the elections of inferior prelates, such as cathedral canons, the full rigor of the law did not have to be observed. So also in the elections to prelacies within their order, regulars were not held to the discriminating niceties and the utmost subtilities of the law.[42]

The Council of Trent, by its insistence on a secret vote, introduced a necessary amount of formality into the elections of regulars, but the election of the vicar capitular was left unregulated.

As late as 1885 the Sacred Congregation of the Council declared that it was not necessary to follow the full rigor of the law in the election of a vicar capitular.[43] The Congregation of Bishops and Regulars had declared the same thing in 1852, saying that it was enough if this election was conducted as a capitular act (*capitulariter*) and if the majority gave their consent.[44]

---

[40]"Item officialem, seu vicarium infra octo dies post mortem episcopi constituere . . . omnino teneatur [capitulum]"—Sess. XXV, *de ref.*, c. 16.

[41]Lib. I, tit. 6, n. 110. cf. Ferraris—art. I, n. 36.

[42]Reiffenstuel, lib. I, tit. 6, n. 112 and 337.

[43]S. C. C., *Veliterna*, 18 apr. 1885—*Fontes*, n. 4267.

[44]S. C. Ep. et Reg., *Gravinen et Montis Pelusii*, 30 iul. 1852—*Fontes*, n. 1963.

There was naturally great diversity in the method of holding the election.[45] The diversity gave rise to disputes which centered, in several cases, around the question of whether a capitular could vote for himself.[46]

In 1912 a consultor of the Congregation of the Council wrote a lengthy study in which he reproduced the history of the jurisprudence on this point. He indicated that the Congregation had in different cases applied the law in a flexible and even divergent manner, apparently hesitant of bringing all cases under one inclusive positive rule and seemingly inclined to the side of equity in handling the separate individual cases. When referring to the codification of Canon Law which was then in progress, the consultor recommended the adoption of that specific legislation which is now contained in canon 170: "Suffragium sibimetipsi nemo valide dare potest."[47]

Sess. XXIV, *de ref.*, c. 16 of the Council of Trent had declared that the appointment of a vicar capitular *devolved* upon the metropolitan, if the chapter neglected to provide within the eight days specified by law; if the vacancy occurred in a metropolitan see then the older of the suffragans had the right of devolution. The Congregations applied this rule throughout the period before the Code.[48]

The election of a bishop, which had been the typical canonical election in decretal law, became the rare excep-

---

[45]"Hic fit electio per suffragia vivae vocis aperte notificando sensum suum; ibi per vota secreta; alibi per scrutinium non quidem solemne sed fere tale; alibi per 'ballotationes'. Nunc sufficit excessus unius voti medii (e. g., quatuor de septem) nunc excessus unius voti (quinque ex octo) . . . "—S. C. C., Laquedonien., 16 mart. 1912—Fontes, n. 4361.

[46]S. C. C., *Armacana*, 12 mart. 1672; S. C. C., *Turritana*, 21 nov., 1722; S. C. C., *Veliterna*, 17 dec. 1881; S. C. C., *Veliterna*, 18 apr. 1865; S. C. C., *Laquedonien.*, 16 mart. 1912.—*Fontes*, n. 2827; 3248; 4254; 4267; 4361.

[47]S. C. C., *Laquedonien.*, 16 mart. 1912, ad. 3—*Fontes*, n. 4361.

[48]S. C. C., *Mazarien*, mense ian. 1587; S. C. C., *Turritana*, 21 nov. 1722; S. C. C., *Turritana*, 20 nov. 1723; S. C. Ep. et Reg., *Sutrina*, 10 jun. 1603—*Fontes*, n. 2168; 3248; 3270; 1620.

tion during the period after the Council of Trent. In the United States as elsewhere the selection of candidates for the episcopacy changed with the growth of the Church. Bishop Carroll by special concession of the Holy See was nominated by the local clergy. Others were chosen at the suggestion of their Metropolitan and fellow suffragans and some had their names presented by individual bishops.[49] From 1884 to 1916 the hierarchy of the United States as well as all Diocesan Consultors and Irremoveable Rectors enjoyed the right of recommending candidates for bishoprics according to a procedure which was somewhat like an election.[50] But these presentations of lists of three names, *dignus, dignior, dignissimus,* were neither elections nor nominations, but merely recommendations. "Nevertheless, the Holy See nearly always appointed one of those suggested and usually the first one on the list if both the priests and the Bishops had made the same first choice."[51] This method called *terna* remained in use until July 25, 1916 when the Sacred Consistorial Congregation issued a decree giving us our present method.[52] This is really not a method of securing appointments to bishoprics, since the law of appointments is contained in can. 329, § 2: "Eos libere nominat Romanus Pontifex", but it is a method of ascertaining—in accord with can. 330—whether candidates are qualified for the office of bishop. The method briefly is as follows.

"Every other year at the beginning of Lent each Bishop is to indicate to his Metropolitan one or two priests whom he deems fit for the episcopal office, stating the name, age, origin, residence and position of each. He may make his

---

[49]S. B. Smith, *Elements of Ecclesiastical Law,* 3 vols., (New York, 1887-1888), I, 51; S. B. Smith, *Notes on the Second Plenary Council of Baltimore,* New York, 1874, pp. 93 and 94.

[50]John D. M. Barrett, *A Comparative Study of the Councils of Baltimore and the Code of Canon Law* (Washington: Catholic University, 1932), p. 56-59, see especially p. 58.

[51]Ibid., p. 58.

[52]AAS, VIII (1916), 400; cf. *Eccl. Rev.* LVI (1917), 58.

choice from any diocese or province, but he must know his candidate personally and very well. Before making his choice he must ask the advice of his Diocesan Consultors and Irremoveable Rectors, not collectively but individually. He may consult other members of the clergy, secular and religious. In no case, however, is he bound to follow the advice given.

"When the Metropolitan has received all these names, he adds his own and draws up a general list in alphabetical order. A copy of this he sends to each of his suffragans that they may make opportune investigations. All this is to be done prudently and cautiously so as not to break the strict secrecy of the proceedings. After Easter on a day and a time fixed by the Archbishop, the Bishops meet, without any solemnity to avoid drawing attention, for a serious but moderate discussion of the candidates proposed. After this discussion the Bishops vote on each candidate in alphabetical order. No vote need be taken on the one or ones unanimously disqualified. For the voting three ballots are used, one white, one black and one colored, signifying respectively approbation, rejection and abstention from voting. The candidates are then listed in the order of merit. If several receive the same number of votes, the bishops may by written ballot determine who is to be given the preference.

"A report of the proceedings is to be sent to the Holy See with whatever information may help in the selection of the best fitted person. This a bishop may do also by private letter to the Consistorial Congregation or to the Pope."[53]

Similar instructions have been issued by the Sacred Consistorial Congregation for Canada and Newfoundland,[54]

---

[53]Barrett, *op. cit.*, pp. 58-59.

[54]March 19, 1919—*AAS*, XI (1919), 124.

Scotland,[55] Brazil,[56] Mexico,[57] and for bishops of the Latin rite in Poland.[58]

Despite this share in designating the person of candidates for bishoprics which is enjoyed by bishops and priests in the United States and elsewhere, it still remains true that since the Council of Trent episcopal elections were the rare exception. Other ecclesiastical elections were not strictly held to the forms of the decretal *"Quia propter"*. Yet, decisions of the Congregations in disputed elections indicated that in reference to the law of elections there could be drawn from decretal law a "jus commune" which was to be applied to all elections of whatever kind. The Code brought uniformity into this matter by drawing up an article on elections in general—Canons 160-182—and by directing that with regard to the election of the vicar capitular,[59] ". . . constitutio fieri debet per actum capitularem ad normam can. 160-182," and that with regard to the elections of religious, ". . . servetur ius commune de quo in can. 160-182. . ."[60]

Historical Summary

From the foregoing chapters it appears that, although a form of election in which clergy and people shared was known from the very beginning of the Church, the first traces of canonical election as described in canons 160-178 of the Code of Canon Law are not found before the development of the cathedral chapter in the twelfth century.

Underlying all the requirements of canons 160-178 is the idea of a clearly defined electoral college which proceeds according to rigid formalities. Election as based upon these conditions cannot be discovered in the early ages of the

[55]November 20, 1920—*AAS*, XIII (1921), 13.
[56]March 19, 1921—*AAS*, XIII (1921), 222.
[57]April 30, 1921—*AAS*, XIII (1921), 379.
[58]August 20, 1921—*AAS*, XIII (1921), 430.
[59]Can. 433, § 2.
[60]Can. 507, § 1.

Church. The only semblance of it is found in the collegiate action of the provincial bishops, as described in canon 4 of the I Council of Nice and in the monastic elections as specified in Chapter LXIV of the Rule of St. Benedict, although in neither of these two cases can we speak with definiteness concerning the formalities of procedure.

The primitive election "per clerum et populum" involved a heterogeneous assemblage of persons. The principles of ecclesiastical liberty—especially the principle, "Ille qui praeest ab omnibus quibus praeest eligatur"—were stressed rather than juridical methods of voting. This type of election survived until the twelfth century. After the royal power had reduced the election "per clerum et populum" to a mere formality, Gregory VII fought for the restoration of the primitive election. The Investiture Struggle resulted in a victory for the Church.

The *Decretum Gratiani* is the bridge between the primitive election "per clerum et populum" and the capitular elections of the Decretals.

The IV Lateran Council (1215) in the decretal *"Quia propter"* laid down rules for canonical elections which influenced decretal law throughout the thirteenth century and led to the formulation of electoral law as we know it today. The main elements in the electoral law of the Code, viz., the convocation of the electors (cans. 162-163), the exclusion of all outsiders (cans. 165-166), stringent qualifications for voting (can. 167), formal electoral procedure (cans. 164, 168-174), a clearly defined legal result, namely a *ius ad rem* to be followed by confirmation (cans. 175-178), all these points were substantialy evolved by the Popes and canonists of the thirteenth century.

The canonical doctrine on elections was modified by the Council of Trent and clarified by the authors who wrote between 1563 and 1918, but canons 160-178 of the Code set forth in all essentials the law of Innocent III. The next section of this study presents a critical commentary of these canons which constitute the modern law of canonical elections.

PART TWO

CANONICAL COMMENTARY

CHAPTER SEVEN

The Code Law in Relation to Special Electoral Prescriptions

Canon 160

Romani Pontificis electio unice regitur const. Pii X VACANTE SEDE APOSTOLICA, 25 Dec. 1904; in aliis electionibus ecclesiasticis serventur praescripta canonum qui sequuntur, et peculiaria, si qua sint, pro singulis officiis legitime statuta.

ARTICLE I. *Specific Elections Governed by Canons 160-178.*

The *election of the Roman Pontiff* is not regulated by canons 160-178 and is therefore excluded from the scope of this dissertation. However, the Constitution *"Vacante Sede Apostolica"*,[1] which governs papal elections, may be usefully consulted as an analogical norm for other elections. Historically, the election of the Holy Father has been the prototype for the elections of inferior prelates[2] and at the present time the papal electoral law should be consulted whenever there is a lacuna in the general law of elections.[3]

In all *other ecclesiastical elections* the prescriptions of canons 160-178 must be followed. Therefore, the following specific elections are governed by these norms: a) the elec-

---

[1]Pius X, Dec. 25, 1904—C. I. C., Documentum I.

[2]See, for instance, Saegmueller, "Die Papstwahl durch das Kardinals-collegium als Prototyp der Bischofswahl durch das Domkapitel", *Theol. Quartalschrift,* XCVII (1915), 321.

[3]Cf. can. 20.

tion of bishops as well as of abbots and prelates *nullius*;[4] b) the election of the vicar capitular or diocesan administrator and of the capitular econome;[5] c) all elections in religious institutes which take place in the chapters (as distinguished from appointments made by vote of the superior and his council);[6] d) the election of officers in lay confraternities and associations.[7]

The term "ecclesiastical election" in canon 160 seems to have a broad meaning as well as a stricter signification. Before the Code an ecclesiastical election was a canonical process which could be performed only by clerics and had for its object, the appointment to an ecclesiastical prelacy or benefice.[8] This meaning seems to be retained as the primary significance of the word in the context of canons 145-195, the title on ecclesiastical offices. The Code, however, draws under the heading of ecclesiastical elections the electoral appointments of all religious, and even those of associated lay people, by directing these groups to follow the procedure of canons 160-178.[9]

Whenever a strictly ecclesiastical office is to be filled by an election it would seem that canons 160-178 must be

---

[4]Cans. 329, § 3; 321.

[5]Cans. 432-433; cf. Jaeger, *Administration of Vacant and Quasi-Vacant Dioceses in the United States*, p. 112-130.

[6]Cans. 506-507. In order to determine which superiors are elected, the constitutions must be consulted. The highest superior of an institute is almost always elected; also, the superiors of independent monasteries whether of men or of women. Frequently the intermediate or provincial superiors, especially in institutes of men, are chosen by election. Recently the Holy See approved the constitutions of a congregation of women which provided that the provincial superiors be elected by the province. In the Order of Friars Preachers even the local priors are elected by the community. Besides the actual superiors, the counsellors, procurators, and secretaries are often chosen by election. Finally, delegates to the provincial and general chapters are canonically elected.

[7]Can. 697, § 2; 715, § 1.

[8]Cf. Schmalzgrueber, Lib. I, tit. 6, n. 5; Fagnanus, Lib. I, tit. 6, n. 56.

[9]Cf. cans. 507, § 1 and 697, § 2.

followed, even if there is no explicit prescription for this in the Code. Therefore, if the statutes of a seminary would provide that the rector be elected by the professors, such choice is an ecclesiastical election because the rectorship is an ecclesiastical office.[10] The appointment must, accordingly, be governed by the canons on elections.

ARTICLE II. *Other Electoral Prescriptions.*

A. *In the General Law*

Specific elections besides being regulated by the general norms of canons 160-178 are also governed by *other prescriptions lawfully enacted.* Some of these prescriptions are enacted by the *general law* of the Code. Thus, the election of a vicar capitular must take place within eight days,[11] notwithstanding canon 161 which grants three months as a time limit beyond which the election to an office must ordinarily not be deferred. The elections of bishops and of prelates or abbots *nullius* require an absolute majority of votes,[12] whereas the general law of canon 174 (cf. can. 101, § 1, n. 1) declares that a relative majority is sufficient on the third ballot.

B. *In Particular Law*

Other prescriptions controlling elections are derived from *particular law.* This is evident, for instance, from canon 507, § 1 which directs that in the elections performed in the chapters of religious institutes, the constitutions of the institute must be followed in all things that are not contrary to the common law. These constitutions are particular laws.

When it is said that the constitutions of religious institutes form a body of particular law, this statement can have

---

[10]Cf. cans. 1358 and 1368.

[11]Can. 432, § 1.

[12]Cans. 321; 329, § 3.

divers significations. Particular law may derive either from the Apostolic See or from inferior legislators. The Apostolic See enacts particular law when it legislates, not for the universal Church, but for a special group within the Church. Inferior legislators, such as local ordinaries or the General Chapters of exempt clerical institutes, create particular law when they legislate for their subjects. Therefore, the "constitutions" mentioned in canon 507, § 1, form a body of particular law which derives both from the Apostolic See and from inferior legislators.

Constitutions may derive from inferior legislators because it is not necessary that all constitutions be approved by the Holy See. Since the beginning of the nineteenth century the constitutions of new congregations of pontifical right are always examined and, when fully satisfactory, are approved by the Holy See.[13] But even before their approval by the Holy See, the approbation given by the local ordinary[14] makes them particular law for the institute and such constitutions are included in canon 507, § 1, as norms which the religious must follow in their elections. Institutes which arose in the sixteenth century were expressly given the authority to frame their own statutes and constitutions without further recourse to the Holy See. This is true of the Barnabites,[15] Theatines,[16] and Jesuits.[17] Still older Orders such as the Dominicans, the Discalced Carmelites, and the Augustinians drew up constitutions without the intervention of the Holy See and the legislative authority in these institutes still enjoys the right to change and

---

[13]*Normae*, S. C. de Rel., March 6, 1921, n. 8, d) and n. 19-21—*AAS*, XIII (1921), 312-319; cf. Orth, *Approbation of Religious Institutes*, p. 65-73 and 154-157.

[14]*Normae* of 1921, n. 8, d); cf. can. 492.

[15]Clement VII, const. *Vota*, Feb. 18, 1533, § 3—*Bullarium Romanum*, VI, 160.

[16]Clement VII, const. *Exponi Nobis*, June 24, 1524, § 4—*op. cit.*, VI, 73.

[17]Cf. Suarez, *De Religiosis*, Tr. X, Lib. I, c. 4, n. 11—*Opera Omnia*, XVI, 580.

develop their constitutions.[18] Thus the term "constitutions" in canon 507, § 1, refers to the particular enactments of inferior legislators as well as to particular laws deriving their force from the Apostolic See. If the constitutions are contrary to the Code, then the law of the Code must prevail, but the *electoral prescriptions not contrary to the Code* must be followed.

It is to be noted that constitutions are not contrary to the Code:

a. If they are *stricter than the Code;* if, for instance, they require for active voice not only perpetual profession[19] but also a number of years spent in the institute after taking perpetual vows.[20]

b. If the general law contains a *clause permitting an exception.* Clauses such as, "unless the law ordains otherwise", are used ten times within the nineteen canons of the article on elections.[21] With regard to the manner, place, and time of convoking the voters,[22] the method of obtaining the vote of an infirm elector present in the house[23] the procedure followed by the tellers in opening and counting the ballots,[24] the Code either explicitly permits the *constitutions* to be followed if they prescribe a method different from that of the Code, or directs that the details of the constitutions be followed where the Code is rather general.

In determining the appointment of tellers,[25] the reasons for depriving a person of active voice,[26] and the method

---

[18]Cf. Larraona, "Commentarium Codicis," *CpR,* IV (1923), 138, n. (384). See also Wernz, *Ius Decretalium,* Lib. III, n. 596, not. 46; Bouix, *Tractatus de Iure Regularium,* I, 193.

[19]Can. 578, n. 3.

[20]Cf., e. g., *Constitutiones Capucoinorum,* art. 140.

[21]Cf. cans. 161, 162, § 1; 163; 167, § 1, n. 5; 168; 171, § § 1, 2; 172, § 1; 174 (cf. can. 101, § 1, n. 1); 177, § 4.

[22]Can. 162, § 1.

[23]Can. 168.

[24]Can. 171, § 2.

[25]Can. 171, § 1.

[26]Can. 167, § 1, n. 5.

of deciding by how many votes and on what ballot the election is completed,[27] the Code allows "particular law" to extend or modify the general law.

In three instances[28] the Code says simply "unless the law ordains otherwise", without explaining whether this refers to the common law of the Code or to particular law, but since the term is general and all-inclusive, it seems right to conclude that both general and particular law are meant.[29]

In one instance in this article the Code uses the phrase *nisi lege peculari aliud caveatur,*[30] and some canonists[31] have stressed the meaning of *peculiaris,* insisting that only a special indult of the Holy See will allow of this exception. The phrase, however, does not differ from the other phrases already discussed, since *lex peculiaris* in canon 163 has the same meaning as *praescriptum peculiare* in canon 160 and is equivalent to *lex propria* or *particularis.*

c. The body of particular law admitted and safeguarded by these phrases may comprise statutes legitimately enacted either *before* or *after* the Code. With regard to laws legitimately enacted before the Code, these safeguarding clauses prevent their abrogation and expressly maintain them in effect.[32] A doubt may arise as to the power of legislators after the Code. The Apostolic See may, of course, ratify statutes even when these are directly contrary to the Code,[33] but what of the power of other legislators?

---

[27]Can. 174 (cf. 101, § 1, n. 1).

[28]Cans. 161; 172, § 1; 177, § 4.

[29]"Contra eum qui legem dicere potuit apertius, est interpretatio facienda", Reg. 57, R. I. in VI°; cf. Larraona, "De Electionibus Religiosorum," *CpR,* VIII (1927), 179, not. 6.

[30]Can. 163 forbidding a vote by proxy or by letter.

[31]E. g., Ayrinhac, *General Legislation,* p. 332; Maroto, *Institutiones,* I, 746.

[32]Canon 6, n. 1.

[33]Thus the electoral regulations of the Dominicans, in as far as they were contrary to the canons, were expressly confirmed by the Holy See after the Code.—Cesterle, *Praelectiones Iuris Canonici,* I, 255.

May a local ordinary in drawing up constitutions for a diocesan institute regard these phrases in the law as empowering him to institute regulations differing from the Code? Theoretically, it would seem that he could. Canon 163, for instance, forbids a voter to employ a proxy, "unless a special law provides otherwise." The framers of new constitutions are directed to use the canons as their guiding norms.[34] Therefore, when faced with this direction of canon 163 a local ordinary might argue that the Code here admits a contrary disposition enacted even by an inferior legislator and, in directing him to follow this canon in framing legislation, the Holy See implicitly allows him to insert a law permitting a proxy. Whatever value this reasoning has in theory, it would be most unwise to follow this course of action in practice. The Sacred Congregation of Religious, in laying down norms for framing new constitutions, desires that the positive dispositions of the canons and not the exceptions be followed. It is the ultimate aim of a diocesan congregation to have its constitutions approved by the Holy See and it is improbable that the Sacred Congregation would approve arrangements which are admittedly exceptional.

However, the general chapter of an established institute which still has the power of changing its constitutions without intervention of the Holy See,[35] could take advantage of the exceptions permitted by canon 163 and other canons and, even after the Code, pass the special law permitting a proxy, or enact other dispositions authorized by these phrases.

---

[34] *Normae* of 1921, n. 1—*AAS*, XIII (1921), 312.

[35] Larraona, "Commentarium Codicis." *CpR*, IV (1923), 138, not. (384), observes that many institutes have lost the right to change the constitutions without such intervention, because after once submitting the constitutions for the approval of the Holy See their laws become reserved to the Holy See.

C. *Customs*

Besides the special rules governing individual elections, *legitimate customs* in conformity with the Code should also be followed.[36] Special customs are explicity safeguarded by three canons of the article on elections.[37] Customs that are contrary to the Code may be tolerated, provided they are centenary and immemorial and cannot well be suppressed.[38]

D. *Privileges*

In one canon on elections the Code expressly safeguards privileges.[39] *Other privileges* in the matter of elections that were granted by the Apostolic See to physical or moral persons and were still in use and unrevoked at the time of the Code remain intact and may still be followed, since nowhere in the article on elections does the Code revoke privileges.[40] Vermeersch[41] says that privileged constitutions prevail over the Code. It would have to be very clear that these are truly privileged, since the mere fact that the Holy See has confirmed the constitutions even *in forma specifica* does not change their nature to the extent of making them privileges.[42]

The present chapter may be summarized as follows: in order to obtain the complete law for a specific ecclesiastical election, the general law of canons 160-178 must be considered in connection with other prescriptions of the Code and of particular law. It is necessary also to consider legitimate customs and privileges.

The electoral practice of older religious institutes will seldom be found to conflict with the Code. Canons 160-

[36]Can. 29.

[37]Cans. 162, § 1; 168; 171, § 2.

[38]Can. 5.

[39]Can. 165.

[40]Cf. can. 4.

[41]*Epitome*, I, 360.

[42]Cf. Larraona, "Commentarium Codicis", *CpR*, IV (1923), 139, not. (390).

178 agree very substantially with the old law on elections and hence the works of pre-Code authors who commented on the elections of regulars[43] may still be usefully consulted. Before the Code it was maintained that religious were not bound to observe the full rigor of the law in holding their elections.[44] This was because a canonical election in the strict sense was the election of a bishop. All other elections were merely imitations of this prototype of canonical elections. Now, however, there is a common law of elections which all are bound to observe with equal care.

[43]E. g., Passerini, O. P., *De Electione Canonica;* Piat, O. M. Cap., *Praelectiones Iuris Regularis;* Ferraris, O. F. M., *Bibliotheca,* v. "Electio"; Reiffenstuel, O. F. M. *Ius Canonicum Universum;* Schmalzgrueber, S. J., *Ius Ecclesiasticum.*

[44]Cf. Reiffenstuel, Lib. I, tit. 6, n. 112 and 337.

CHAPTER EIGHT

Remote Preparations for an Election

The necessary preparations for an election are both remote and proximate. The proximate preparations for an election include the examination of the credentials of voters, the appointment of tellers and other formalities which take place immediately before the election. These will be treated later. The principal remote preparation is the act of summoning the voters to the place of the election. Since the summons must set a definite place and time for the election, it will be necessary to consider first the time-limit within which the voters must perform an election.

ARTICLE I. *The Time-limit for the Holding of an Election.*

Canon 161

Si cui collegio sit ius eligendi ad vacans officium, electio, nisi aliud iure cautum fuerit, nunquam differatur ultra trimestre utile computandum ab habita notitia vacationis officii; quo termino inutiliter elapso, Superior ecclesiasticus, cui ius confirmandae electionis vel ius providendi successive competit, officio vacanti libere provideat.

A. *Offices Affected by This Canon*

Many offices are excluded from the full scope of this canon by the phrase, "unless the law ordains otherwise".

The law to which the canon refers may be (as explained in the foregoing chapter) either a prescription of the general law, or a particular regulation such as an article in the constitutions of a religious institute. Thus, the general law ordains that the office of vicar capitular be filled within eight days.[1] The particular law of the Dominican Order requires that the local prior be chosen within one month,[2] but permits the office of provincial to remain vacant for more than six months.[3]

The former law did not expressly allow these exceptions, but canonists held that religious were exempt from the rule of a three month time-limit.[4] The present law admits exceptions, provided they are expressly contained in the legislation of religious. If the constitutions are silent on this point, then all vacancies must be filled within three months.[5] Augustine says that the common law "admits religious constitutions only in so far as they do not conflict with the present canon" and he concludes that "privileges granting an extension of time to certain institutes are now without effect."[6] The common law, however, explicitly admits an exception, and this canon in no way derogates from privileges safeguarded by canon 4.

B. *Reckoning the Time*

The three months within which a group of voters must complete their election is reckoned, not from the moment the office actually becomes vacant, but from the time that the voters learn of the vacancy. If, for instance, a chapter of canons has the right to elect the bishop, the time-limit

---

[1]Can. 432, § 1.

[2]Fanfani, *De Iure Religiosorum*, p. 110.

[3]Passerini, *De Electione Canonica*, XIII, 21.

[4]Cf. e. g., Ferraris, *Bibliotheca*, v. "Electio", IV, 76.

[5]Vermeersch, "De utili tempore faciendae electionis," *Periodica*, XIII (1924) (71)-(72).

[6]*Commentary on Canon Law*, II (4th ed., 1923), 124.

of three months is not counted from the moment of the bishop's death, but from the time that the chapter becomes apprised of the fact. The three months are computed in accordance with canon 34, § 3, n. 3.[7] If the canons learn of the bishop's death on the 4th of September, this day is not counted as part of the interval during which the election is to be held. The interval of three months would in this case comprise the days falling between September 5th and December 4th, both of these dates being figured inclusively. In other words, the election would have to be completed by the end of December 4th.

Is it necessary that the entire board of electors or at least a majority of them receive notice of the vacancy in order to mark the beginning of the three months during which the election must be held? Coronata[8] (in discussing the month granted for a new election after the voters learn of the elected person's refusal to accept the office) speaks of "collegiate knowledge". He says that to have collegiate knowledge it is not sufficient that the president or a few members of the electoral college obtain this knowledge. The notice must be either received by the assembled voters, or communicated to each of them by the president, or printed in an official publication.

But canon 161 does not expressly say that the electoral *college* must learn of the vacancy; it simply says that the three month interval begins from the moment the vacancy becomes known. Questions of knowledge do not depend on majorities. A fact is said to be known in a certain locality even if, here and now, relatively few know of it. It is public property and it will soon be a matter of general knowledge. Thus, it seems sufficient if the one charged with convoking the members of the board receives notice that the

---

[7]See the example there cited: "octiduum a vacatione sedis episcopalis."

[8]*Institutiones*, I, 284, not. 9.

office is vacant in a purely informal manner.[9] The Code says *ab habita notitia vacationis* instead of *a tempore vacationis* in order to safeguard the rights of the voters, but their rights are sufficiently safeguarded if they are certain of being summoned to the election.

The period of three months is to be computed as a period during the entire lapse of which there is a really available time for action *(tempus utile)*.[10] Those days on which hindrances obstruct the use of the right are not to be counted as part of the time during which the right or duty is to be exercised. The available time here in question is measured in reference to the opportunity enjoyed by the chapter as a whole, and not with respect to the possible action of the individual electors who compose the chapter. Still, it might happen that a third or even one half of the individuals enjoying the right to vote are *indefinitely* hindered and obstructed in the use of their right. They may be serving as chaplains in time of war or may be otherwise prevented from exercising their right, possibly for a year or more. Is the election, therefore, to be indefinitely postponed? This might seem to be an unreasonable use of time designated as available for action. Canonists before the Code solved the difficulty by placing the interest of the Church before the interest of the individual voter. They held that a person who could not be present and vote within the time given by law could not be considered a voter for practical purposes.[11] In the concrete, the chapter was regarded as be-

---

[9]Compare Fontanella, *Resolutiones de Iurepatronatus*, Lib. VI, q. 11, "Citatio [ad litem] facienda collegio, sufficit fieri maiori de collegio. . . [vel si sit facienda] universitati, sufficit si fiat Syndico Universitatis. . . " The notice given to the president of the electoral college may be informal, as stated in the text, but it must of course be certain.—Cf. Larraona, "De Electionibus Religiosorum", *CpR*, VIII (1927), 293.

[10]Can. 35; cf. Cicognani, *Canon Law*, p. 695.

[11]" . . . non sint computandi nisi qui debent et volunt et possunt commode interesse."—Reiffenstuel, Lib. I, tit. 6, n. 120; cf. Barbosa, Lib. I, tit. 6, c. 42; Ferraris, *Bibliotheca*, v. "Absens", I, 10.

ing composed of those voters who were able to exercise their right on some date within the legal time-limit. The basis for this doctrine was found in the phrase *praesentibus omnibus qui . . . possunt commode interesse* of c. 42, X, *de electione et electi potestate,* I, 6. Before the Code, if a chapter was composed of fifteen voters and six of these were indefinitely hindered from voting, then those six were not considered voters for practical purposes. In the concrete, the chapter was composed of the nine voters who were able to vote within the legal time-limit. In how far this principle may still be followed will be more fully discussed in the next article of this chapter. Here it may be briefly stated that the clause *qui commode possunt interesse* is not contained in the Code; that part of the old law together with its interpretations seems to have been suppressed. Today impediments to voting which affect more than half the individual voters may be said to affect the chapter and as long as these impediments continue the time-limit for holding an election will be indefinitely prolonged. Therefore, if eight out of fifteen voters are stricken with illness for two weeks, fourteen days may be added to the three month period. If the time-limit was to have expired on December 4th, it does not now expire until December 18th.[12]

The impediments to action must be extraordinary, such as war or pestilence. Time consumed by the ordinary delays of issuing convocatory letters and while travelling to the place of the chapter may not be deducted from the continued passing of the three month period, because this is the very reason why three months are granted.[13]

C. *Sanction Placed on Failure to Elect*

The chapter must *complete the election* within the time-limit. If the three months expire without action or are spent in fruitless balloting, all right of election is lost and

[12]Cf. Passerini, *De Electione Canonica,* XIII, 24.

[13]Schmalzgrueber, Lib. I, tit. 6, n. 35.

the appointment devolves upon the superior who had the right to confirm the election or, if the election was such as to require no confirmation, upon the one who would have the next right to fill the office. This superior can be determined by deciding which official would have power to remove the person from office or to accept his resignation.[14]

The Code does not expressly say that the chapter loses the right of electing upon the expiration of three months, but the higher superior's right of appointment effectively extinguishes the chapter's right of election.[15] If the constitutions are more rigid than the Code and allow only one month for an election, the subjects may not argue that the Code forbids superiors to appoint until *three* months have expired. The phrase "unless the law ordains otherwise" applies to the entire canon, to the power of the superior as well as to the time-limit of the chapter. The fact that the Code says the superior is free to make an appointment does not exempt him from consulting his council if this is required by law for the making of such an appointment at any other time.

ARTICLE II. *Summoning the Voters.*

Canon 162

§ 1. Salvis peculiaribus constitutionibus vel consuetudinibus, collegii praeses, statuto modo, loco ac tempore electoribus convenienti, convocet omnes de collegio; et convocatio, quando personalis esse debet, valet, si fiat vel in loco domicilii aut quasi-domicilii vel in loco commorationis.

---

[14]Cf. can. 161. See also Maroto, *Institutiones*, I, 756.

[15]Ferraris, *Bibliotheca*, v. "Electio", IV, 78; Vermeersch, "De tempore utili electionis faciendae", *Periodica*, XIII (1924), (72).

§ 2. Si quis ex vocandis neglectus et ideo absens fuerit, electio valet, sed ad eius instantiam debet, probata prateritione et absentia, a competente Superiore irritari, etiam secuta confirmatione, dummodo iuridice constet recursum saltem intra triduum ab habita notitia electionis fuisse transmissum.

§ 3. Quod si plures quam tertia pars electorum neglecti fuerint, electio est ipso iure nulla.

§ 4. Defectus convocationis non obstat, si praetermissi nihilominus interfuerint.

§5. Si agatur de electione ad officium quod electus ad vitam retinet, convocatio electorum ante officii vacationem nullum habet iuridicum effectum.

The authoritative act of summoning the electors to meet in a definite place and at a definite time is called the act of convocation.[16] Since it is a substantial requirement that the voters be gathered together in one place, a summons indicating the place and time is necessary. Normally the voters will not be assembled at the same place and time, unless a summons is issued.

A. *The Official Who Summons the Voters*

The Code says that the voters are to be convoked by the president of the electoral college, who will often be a different person from the official who presides at the election. The president of the college mentioned in canon 162, § 1, is the superior of the persons who compose the chapter; he is the president of the voters as opposed to the president of the voting. This distinction has been definitely established by a decision of the Sacred Congregation of Religious, July 2, 1921.[17] This decision held that in diocesan congre-

[16]"Intimatio auctoritativa electionis, qua ipsius tempus, locus, adiunctave vocalibus communicentur et ut ad electionem ipsi concurrant invitantur."—Larraona, "De Electionibus Religiosorum," *CpR*, IX (1928), 329.

[17]*AAS*, XIII (1921), 481. Compare canons 171, § 2, and canon 506, § 4.

gations of women the bishop of the place where the election is held presides at the voting for a new superioress general, but it is the right and duty of the existing superioress general, as superior of the voters, to determine the place and time of the election.

The superior who convokes the electors must observe all that the constitutions and particular customs require. These may demand, for instance, that the general superior's permission be obtained before holding a provincial chapter.[18] The local ordinary must be seasonably informed when there is question of the election of the highest superior of a monastery of nuns or of an institute of religious women.[19]

If the official charged with convoking the chapter refuses to do so, then the right to summon the voters passes to the next ranking member of the electoral body. If the time-limit is close to expiration and all efforts to obtain a legitimate act of convocation have failed, the voters can come together without formal convocation, lest they be deprived of their right to vote.[20]

B. *The Persons to be Summoned*

Canon 162, § 1, directs the president to summon *omnes de collegio*. Throughout the article on elections the assembly of voters is called a *collegium*. This is not to be understood as meaning a *persona moralis collegialis* as described in canon 99.[21] At times the college of voters will be materially identical with a collegiate moral person, as when a chapter of canons holds an election, nevertheless the board

---

[18]Cf. *Constitutiones Capuccinorum*, art. 144.

[19]Cf. can. 506, § § 2, 4; when a monastery of nuns is subject to a regular superior, the nuns notify the regular superior and he in turn must notify the local ordinary.—Cf. Bachofen, *Compendium*, p. 212.

[20]Cf. can. 162, § 4; see also Maroto, *Institutiones*, I, 734.

[21]Cf. Mörsdorf, *Die Rechtssprache des Codex Iuris Canonici*, p. 123-124; Larraona, "De Electionibus Religiosorum", *CpR*, IX (1928). 335, not. 97.

of electors is always formally distinct from the moral person. Often the voters merely represent one or more moral persons as in the provincial and general chapters of religious. *Collegium* in the phrase, *omnes de collegio,* signifies the group of individuals who enjoy the right to vote in a given election.

Before the Code the president of the chapter was not bound to summon *all* the voters, but only those *qui debent et volunt et possunt commode interesse.*[22] In other words, he was not bound to summon those who had lost their right to vote, or who had renounced their vote, or who were so far distant from the place of the election that it could be foreseen that they would not be able to arrive in time for the election. Some canonists maintain that this doctrine of the old law continues in force.[23] Larraona[24] says that the president need not summon those who are physically or morally impeded from coming, but he admits that at the present time this opinion is rather difficult to maintain. Ayrinhac[25] sees a definite change in the law. "All who have a right to vote must be convoked," he says. "Ancient canonists added, provided they can conveniently come, but no such restriction is expressed or implied in the present law." Augustine[26] and Toso[27] seem to hold the same view that a change has been made in the law.

If the old law has not been changed or even if it is doubtful whether a change has been made or not, the pre-Code legislation and its classic interpretation must be regarded as binding today.[28] But when canon 162, § 1 is com-

[22]C. 42, X, *de electione et electi potestate,* I, 6; cf. Barbosa, Lib. I, tit. 6, c. 42; Passerini, *De Electione Canonica,* XI, 33-40; Fagnanus, Lib. I, tit. 6, c. 42; Ferraris, *Bibliotheca,* v. "Absens", I, 1.

[23]Cf. Maroto, *Institutiones,* I, 734; Goyeneche, *Iuris Canonici Summa Principia,* I, 193; Coronata, *Compendium,* I, 286; Sipos, *Enchiridion,* p. 136; Wernz-Vidal, *Ius Canonicum,* II, 267, not. 23.

[24]"De Electionibus Religiosorum," *CpR,* IX (1928), 336.

[25]*General Legislation,* p. 331.

[26]*Commentary,* II, 125.

[27]*Commentaria Minora, Liber II De Personis,* I, 131.

[28]Can. 6, nn. 2, 4.

pared with c. 42, X, *de electione et electi potestate,* I, 6, a definite change seems to have been made. Indeed, the viewpoint of the two laws is quite different. Canon 162, § 1, is concerned with the process of assembling the voters. The old law sees the voters already assembled at the place of the election (*praesentibus omnibus qui debent* etc.) and is concerned with the manner in which the voting is to take place. The old law says nothing about the process of convoking the voters. The act of convocation is the very gist of canon 162, § 1. Therefore, all voters whom it is possible to reach should be summoned. It will then be left to the discretion of the voters themselves whether to accept the invitation or decline it.

All voters must be summoned, but is it lawful for a voter to decline to answer the summons? May one renounce the right to vote? Perhaps a distinction may be made between a vote which is given to be exercised for the public good and one that is a private benefit.[29]

Most of those who vote in the provincial and general chapters of religious enjoy this right not for their own advantage but for the common good. Thus the *Normae* of 1901 decree that the voters in the general chapter of an institute not yet divided into provinces include all superioresses of houses in which at least twelve religious dwell as one delegate from each house of twelve religious.[30]

Such a superioress cannot renounce her right to vote because the exercise of this right is one of the duties of her office. It is a right given for the public good. Likewise, a delegate who has accepted her election must exercise the right committed to her. Number 214 of the *Normae* allows the institute to grant a perpetual right to all former superioresses general. This would seem to be a private right, which the voter is free to renounce. Likewise, all who vote

---

[29]Cf. Piat, *Praelectiones*, II, 19.

[30]N. 215.

in the local election to choose a delegate from the local community are said to exercise a private right which they may renounce.

Passerini,[31] however, does not admit the distinction between a vote given for the public good and one which is a private benefit. He says that the right of election is always given to be exercised for the common good. In the cases cited, where reference is made to the former superioress general, it is probable that the commuunity desires the former superioress' knowledge and experience.

There may be times when one is gravely bound to participate in an election and the law of a religious institute may insist that all vote who have a right to do so,[32] but ordinarily no one should be forced to vote unless his absence and neglect will seriously harm the Church or the community.[33] Practically, then, a voter may renounce his vote.

Particular law may leave it to the discretion of the superior to decide whether to restore active voice to the one who has renounced it.[34] But, in general, one may reassume his vote, because voting is both a right and a duty; even if at times this duty may be declined without guilt, one may always reconsider and decide to perform the duty.[35]

Law may demand in some cases that each voter be summoned personally, in which case it is enough to send the letter of convocation to the person's place of domicile, quasi-domicile or actual residence. For religious the notice may be sent to their actual stopping place or to the house to which they are assigned.[36]

---

[31]*De Electione Canonica,* XI, 17-18.

[32]Larraona, "De Electionibus Religiosorum", *CpR,* X (1929), 56.

[33]Schmalzgrueber, Lib. I, tit. 6, n. 22; Ferraris, *Bibliotheca,* v. "Electio", III, 4; Maroto, *Institutiones,* I, 743; Passerini, *De Electione Canonica,* XI, 28.

[34]Cf. *Ordinationes O. M. Cap.,* n. 167.

[35]Passerini, *De Electione Canonica,* XI, 77; 83.

[36]Cf. Ayrinhac, *General Legislation,* p. 331; Fanfani, *De Iure Religiosorum,* p. 117.

C. *Nature of the Summons*

The superior is bound to determine for the election a place and a time which will be convenient for the voters. The purpose of the summons is to acquaint the voter with the place and the time so chosen. If the voter already knows of this without formal summons, nothing further is required. He who is already well-informed need not be informed further.[37]

Any method of convocation selected by the president will be valid provided there is moral certainty that the voter will be able, if he wishes, to arrive in due time for the election. The *Normae* of 1901 prescribe that a circular letter be issued.[38] For the proximate call to the actual voting the ringing of a bell may be employed, provided the voters have been informed that this will be the signal for the election.

If the summons sets a date which does not give the voters sufficient *time* to appear, the convocation is regarded as invalid. The summons should note, not only the *day* but also the *hour* of the election. If no hour is stated it is presumed that the election will be held at the hour customary in the organization, e. g., in the morning after Mass.[39]

The *place*, also, must be convenient for the voters. If the place of the election is designated in the constitutions, this may not be changed by the voters, unless the group actually has the power to modify the constitutions. Where no law fixes the place of the election the advantage of the voters should be consulted. In a certain election where half the voters lived in Ireland and the other half in England, Innocent III suggested that the Irish voters go to England

---

[37]"Eum qui certus est, certiorari ulterius non oportet"—Reg. 31, R. J. VI°.

[38]N. 211.

[39]Hostiensis, *de Electione*, n. 11; Mocchegiani, *Iurisprudentia*, I, 687; Fanfani, *De Iure Religiosorum*, p. 117.

for the election if it was inconvenient for the English to come to Ireland.[40]

Once a day and hour have been set, they can be changed as often as necessary, provided the voters are informed and provided also that the postponement does not place the election beyond the time-limit allowed by law.[41]

D. *The Juridical Effect of the Summons*

One of the principal juridical effects of the summons can be seen in the declaration of canon 163,[42] which states: After a lawful summons has been issued the right to vote belongs [exclusively] to those who are present on the day set in the summons. There is an important contrast between the effect produced by a lawful summons, and the legal requirements when no summons precedes an election. If no summons is issued to the absent, then *two thirds* of the voters must assemble before a valid election can be performed. Once a legal summons has been issued, even *one voter alone* can perform the election on the day fixed if he alone appears.[43]

What constitutes a *legal summons*? This has already been indicated to some extent in the preceding number. A lawful act of convocation must clearly indicate the day, hour, and place of the election. This place and time must be convenient for the voters and must be intimated to all

---

[40]C. 28, X, *de electione et electi potestate*, I, 6; Schmalzgrueber required a two-thirds vote to change the place of the chapter from the accustomed spot.—Lib. I, tit. 6, n. 30.

[41]Cf. Maroto, *Institutiones*, I, 732.

[42]This canon (163) will be considered in the next chapter from a slightly different viewpoint.

[43]" . . . quodsi ad tempus congruum considerata distantia et aliis circumstantiis assignatum, absentes non venerint, extunc praesentes eligant et hoc per prima iura . . . intelligo, si citatio facta fuerit congruo tempore, alias, contra. . . "—Hostiensis, *De Electione*, n. 11; "Potest totum ius collegii venire in unum"—Barbosa, Lib. I, tit. 6, c. 1. This is the common law. Particular statutes, as will be noted in the next chapter, may make other provisions.

the voters. Everyone capable of voting in a given election has the right to be summoned and the deliberate neglect of this right is a violation of justice. The validity of the election, however, does not suffer, unless more than a third of the voters are slighted.[44]

If the chapter consisted of 12 persons, but only 8 were summoned, the election would be valid if 5 of the 8 cast their votes for a certain person. But if only 7 were summoned and 5 were slighted, the election would be utterly invalid.[45]

What *legal remedy* is given to a voter whom the president neglects to summon? The election, of course, is valid if the voters who have been slighted do not make up more than a third of the chapter. For the sake of peace, therefore, a voter may simply consent to the election which has been performed by the others; but, if he chooses to contest the election the law gives him a very powerful remedy. If he can prove that he was slighted and, consequently, was absent from the election, the competent superior must annull the election even after it has been confirmed.[46] This remedy is called an *actio de contemptu* and is a personal action which can be prosecuted by anyone of those not called, but by no one else.[47] The question may be settled in an administrative manner and need not be presented in judicial fashion.[48] The superior before whom the appeal or recourse is brought is the one who had the right to confirm the election or, if the election was such as to require no confirmation, the official capable of removing the incumbent from office. The injured party must prove two things:

---

[44]Can. 162, § 3. "Quod si plures quam tertia pars electorum neglecti fuerint, electio est ipso iure nulla."

[45]"Si essent duodecim electores et quatuor contempti, valeret electio facta a quinque ex octo praesentibus; secus, si essent contempti quinque, quia tunc non essent ibi duae partes ex tribus."—Fagnanus. Lib. I, tit. 6, c. 42.

[46]Canon 162 § 2.

[47]Passerini, *De Electione Canonica*, XI, 120.

[48]Cf. Maroto, *Institutiones*, I, 736.

1) that his absence was caused by not being summoned;[49] 2) that he put in his claim for the annullment within three days after hearing about the election. If he neglects to institute proceedings within three days he is presumed to have ratified the election, and the election can never again be attacked on this ground.

The chapter, on its side, can exclude the claim by proving either that the voter actually was summoned or that the neglect was purely accidental. In order to hinder unjust claims against elections prudence may dictate, in some cases, that the electoral summons be sent by registered mail. If it is no fault of the chapter that the summons did not reach the voter, there can be no action on grounds of "contempt".[50] If it is evident that the president has sent the summons in good faith and that in spite of his best efforts the summons has miscarried, then the absent voter has suffered no injustice at the hands of the chapter and the other voters cannot be made to suffer for something beyond their control.

If the election is to be held for an office that is given for life, such as a bishopric, the summons has no juridical effect until the office is vacant.[51] If, for instance, a canon is summoned to the election of a bishop before the death of the episcopal incumbent, such summons is without legal effect. If the election is held after the death of the bishop without a second summons being sent to the absent canon, he may have the election annulled on grounds of contempt, because the first notification was entirely illegal.[52]

When elections are held for offices which become vacant by the lapse of a specified time it is customary and perfectly legal to summon the voters before the office be-

---

[49]The mere fact that one did not receive a formal summons gives no right to have an election annulled if the voter was nevertheless present at the election.—Can. 162, § 4.

[50]Cf. Passerini, *De Electione Canonica*, XI, 129.

[51]Cf. can. 150, § 1; 183, § 1; 430, § 1.

[52]Cf. c. 36, X, *de electione et electi potestate*, I, 6, where this case is fully described.

comes vacant. The offices in many religious institutes are held for a term of years, the time being reckoned from chapter to chapter. Since the office of superior does not become vacant until the new chapter meets, it is evident that by the very nature of the case the letters of convocation will always be issued before the vacancy of the office.[53]

As a final summary of this chapter it may be stated that in regulating the remote preparations for an election the law endeavors to safeguard both the welfare of the Church and the rights of the individual voter. During the age when the law of election was being developed and perfected there was usually great danger in delaying the election. Reiffenstuel mentions the dangers of schism, sedition, usurpation, secular interference, and other evils.[54] An early election was important and a period of three months was regarded as the extreme time-limit. The interest of the Church was given chief consideration. In consequence of this customs developed according to which it was not necessary to summon or await the arrival of a voter if he was more than twenty miles away from the place of election.[55]

There were, of course, even in ancient times milder customs which gave more heed to individual rights; but the general tendency was to place the public interest first and foremost. At the present time canon 162, § 1, stresses the individual rights of the single voters who compose the chapter. All must be summoned. If more than half of the voters are legitimately impeded from holding the election, the time-limit (in accordance with canon 161) may be extended beyond the canonical period of three months. A definite change has been made in the law.

---

[53] Cf. Larraona, "De Electionibus Religiosorum", *CpR*, VIII (1927), 285.

[54] Lib. I, tit. 6, n. 119.

[55] Passerini, *De Electione Canonica*, XI, 36.

CHAPTER NINE

THE VOTERS

After discussing the remote preparations for a canonical election, the Code proceeds to set forth the requirements and qualifications of those who actively participate in the election, namely, the voters. The first requirement is that they appear in person at the place and time determined in the electoral summons.

ARTICLE I. *Physical Presence in the Electoral Assembly.*

Canon 163

Convocatione legitime secuta, ius eligendi pertinet ad eos qui praesentes sunt die in convocatione statuto, exclusa facultate ferendi suffragia non solum per epistolam, sed etiam per procuratorem, nisi lege peculiari aliud caveatur.

A. *Physical Presence in General*

It is essential that an election be conducted as a collegiate act. Hence the right to vote pertains to those who have assembled on the day set in the official summons. If this summons has been sent out to all voters and has definitely determined the place and hour of the voting, then the full right to proceed with the election belongs to those who are actually present, regardless of how small this number may be.[1] Even if only one voter is present, he may proceed with the election.[2] This is the common law. Particular law, however, may require the presence of a definite number. The *Normae* of 1901 declare: For the validity of the acts of the General Chapter the *presence* of at least two thirds of the voters is required.[3] According to Canon 162, § 3, the acts of the chapter are valid if two-thirds of the voters have been *summoned,* even if only a small number are present, but constitutions that are modelled on the *Normae* may require the physical presence of two-thirds of the voters before the chapter can act.

The rule contained in No. 223 of the *Normae* is quite similar to the rule of a quorum in Anglo-American parliamentary procedure. This rule requires a definite number to be present before a vote can be taken. No such rule exists in general Canon Law. When the day set in the letters of convocation arrives then those who are present, no matter what their number, are not obliged to await the arrival of the absent, even though it is known that they will arrive in a short time, and even though they are legitimately detained.[4] If, for example, a group of 20 are notified that they are to hold an election on December 15th, then even if only 4 are present on that date these may hold the election, notwithstanding the fact that a severe snow storm has prevented the arrival of the other 16 and it is known that they will be able to come on the following day. In strict justice, the 4 who are present may hold the election. They can, of course, postpone the vote, but they are not obliged to do so.[5]

If some of the voters who are present withdraw after the chapter has convened, the effect of their leaving de-

---

[1]Maroto, *Institutiones,* I, 747; Coronata, *Institutiones,* I, 255; cf. Passerini, *De Electione Canonica,* XI, n. 86; cf. others cited in chapter VIII.

[2]"Potest totum ius collegii venire in unum."—Barbosa, Lib. I, tit. 6, c. 1.

[3]N. 223.

[4]Cf. Maroto, *Institutiones,* I, 747.

[5]Cf. Coronata, *Institutiones,* I, 255.

pends on the prescriptions of the constitutions. If the general law alone is followed, then those voters who remain, no matter how small their number, have full power of election because canon 163 says without restriction that the right to elect belongs to those who are present.

If the constitutions require a quorum (e. g., two-thirds) for the validity of every act of the chapter—as n. 223 of the *Normae* of 1901 seems to imply—then the loss of a quorum will suspend the chapter. But if the constitutions require a quorum only to *begin* the chapter, the departure of a number or even of a majority has no effect once the chapter has been opened. Those who remain have legitimately begun the election and have, therefore, a perfect right to complete it.[6]

Frequently, however, it will be lawful for a majority of the voters to postpone the election even after the chapter has assembled.[7] For this postponement a majority vote seems to be sufficient, but the decision in all probability must be made by a formal vote. It will not suffice for the majority simply to get up and leave. Reiffenstuel,[8] indeed, says that if most of the voters leave it is presumed that they desired to dissolve the chapter, but canon 101, § 1, n. 1, implicitly requires that a formal vote be taken on all collegiate decisions.

If the chapter has no power to transfer the date of the election[9] or if the day of the meeting is the last day within the legal time-limit, even a formal vote of the majority would not avail to postpone the election. The full voting power would rest with those who remain.

The requirement of physical presence excludes the employment of a proxy as well as the right to send a vote by letter, unless particular law or custom permit these procedures. The particular law (as explained in a foregoing

---

[6]Cf. Reiffenstuel, Lib. I, tit. 6, n. 201.

[7]Passerini, *De Electione Canonica,* XI, 103.

[8]Lib. I, tit. 6, n. 202.

[9]Cf. *Constitutiones O. F. M.*, n. 460.

chapter) may be an enactment either of the Holy See or of an inferior legislator, promulgated either before or after the Code. The phrase *lex peculiaris* is the same as that used in canons 160 and 162, § 1, and has no greater force than the phrase *lex particularis.* Canon 163 admits an exception for particular law; therefore, special enactments (even though deriving their authority from a source inferior to the Holy See) may be followed.[10]

Augustine[11] denies that a contrary custom can permit the employment of a proxy or a vote by letter, but the canon makes no distinction between written law and customary law; consequently, a legitimate custom may be followed.[12]

When it is stated that even an inferior legislator may pass a law admitting a proxy, this must be understood as meaning a stable act of legislation. An institute enjoying the abstract right to pass such a law cannot admit proxies as the need arises if no authorizing statute has been passed. In particular instances recourse must be had to the Holy See. Thus the Capuchins obtained permission from the Sacred Congregation for Religious to appoint two proxies in place of delegates who could not come to the General Chapter from Communist Spain.[13]

If the electoral laws of the institute are contained in constitutions which may not be changed without the intervention of the Holy See,[14] then the Holy See must be petitioned for indults allowing the employment of a proxy or

---

[10]Cf. Coronata, *Institutiones*, I, 256; Larraona, "De Electionibus Religiosorum", *CpR*, X (1929), 270; Michiels, *Ius de Personis*, I, 392-393. Maroto (*Institutiones*, I, 746) and Ayrinhac (*General Legislation*, p. 332) say that the Holy See may permit exceptions to this general rule, but not inferior legislators.

[11]*Commentary on Canon Law*, II, 128.

[12]Cf. authors just cited (not. 10) with whom Maroto (*Institutiones*, I, 746) agrees.

[13]Rescript n. 1986/38, May 6, 1938—*Analecta O. M. Cap.*, LIV (1938), 125.

[14]Cf. *Constitutiones O. F. M.*, n. 706; *Constitutiones O. M. Cap*,. art. 249.

admitting a vote by letter. The Friars Minor obtained permission for commissaries and guardians in America and Asia to send their vote to their respective provincial chapter in Europe.[15]

Where it is customary to elect a delegate-alternate who will vote if the delegate is impeded, this elected substitute is not a proxy and a law or custom which provides for this arrangement is in full accord with canon 163.

B. *A Voter Who is Ill, but is Present in the Place of Election.*

Canon 168

Si quis ex electoribus praesens in domo sit in qua fit electio, sed electioni ob infirmam valetudinem interesse nequeat, suffragium eius scriptum a scrutatoribus exquiratur, nisi aliter particularibus legibus vel legitimis consuetudinibus fuerit constitutum.

If a voter is ill, but is present in the house of the chapter, he is regarded as physically present for purposes of the elections even though he is unable to come to the chapter room. The phrase "present in the house" may here be taken in the broad sense that is attached to the words by canonists when commenting on canon 514.[16] Even if the infirmary is a separate building, the sick voter may still be regarded as "present in the house" if the infirmary forms a moral unit with the house of the chapter. The voter may, of course, renounce his vote, but if he does not do so and is

---

[15] *S. C. de Rel.*, March 12, 1928—*Acta Minorum*, XLVII (1928), 94-95.

[16] "Intra septa monasterii"—Cf. Coronata, *Institutiones*, I, 649.

in good mental health the tellers not only may but must obtain his vote in every ballot that is cast.[17]

The manner in which the tellers will obtain the vote of the sick voter may be further determined by particular law or custom. The Code requires that the tellers receive his written ballot, but even if the sick man is unable to write he may communicate his vote orally to the tellers who will immediately set it down in writing.[18]

In the election of the abbess in monasteries of nuns, two priests act as tellers. Since these are forbidden to enter the enclosure,[19] it is evident that canon 168 cannot be literally followed in the case of a nun who is ill within the house. But in this event it seems permissible in virtue of canon 20 for the president of the chapter to appoint two nuns who will obtain the vote of the sick nun just as the tellers do according to canon 168.[20] In other elections time may be gained by appointing two additional tellers who will secure the votes of the sick. Warrant for this procedure may be found in the constitution *Vacante Sede.*[21]

ARTICLE II. *One Vote for Each Voter*

Canon 164

Etsi quis plures ob titulos ius habeat ferendi nomine proprio suffragii, non potest nisi unicum ferre.

---

[17]The obligation of obtaining the vote of a sick voter is to be interpreted in the light of the rule: "Odia restringi, et favores convenit ampliari." (Reg. 15—R. I. in VI°.) The strict obligation of obtaining the vote is limited to the actual building in which the chapter is held. If too great delay would be caused by obtaining the vote from another building "intra septa monasterii" the chapter would not be obliged to do this.

[18]The possibility of *oral* voting under the present legislation will be discussed more at length in the chapter on the form of election.

[19]Canon 506 § 2.

[20]Cf. Mocchegiani, *Iurisprudentia,* I, 260; Fanfani, *De Iure Religiosorum,* p. 115.

[21]Pius X, Dec. 25, 1904, n. 62—Documentum I, *C. I. C.*

Should one of the voters present be personally entitled to vote on a twofold ground, e. g., as an elected delegate and as a former Superior General, canon 164 forbids him to cast two votes. Several reasons for being able to vote in one's own name do not increase the number of votes one may cast, but if one of the voters serves as proxy for an absent voter he has the right to cast two votes, one in his own name and the other in the name of the person whom he represents.

Coronata[22] and Vermeersch[23] declare that the canon forbids the casting of several votes because of several titles, (*plures ob titulos*), but does not forbid the casting of two or more votes by reason of one title (*unum ob titulum*), so that if the constitutions would, for instance, grant the provincial the right to cast two votes in every election by reason of his single title of provincial this would not be contrary to canon 164.

Although this reasoning has something to commend it, the conclusion seems to be excluded by bringing into relief the main command of the canon. The dispositive part of the law seems to be: [*Elector*] *non potest nisi unicum* [*suffragium*] *ferre,* and the law adds further: *Etsi quis plures ob titulos ius habeat suffragandi. . .* No voter can cast more than one vote. This is forbidden under all circumstances, even if a voter has several titles to vote.

ARTICLE III. *Persons Excluded.*

A. *The Exclusion of Outsiders*

Canon 165

Nullus collegio extraneus admitti potest ad suffragium, salvis privilegiis legitime quaesitis; secus, electio est ipso facto nulla.

---

[22]*Institutiones,* I, 257.

[23]"Quaesita de Religiosis", *Periodica,* XII (1924), (15)-(16).

An election is always to be performed by an assembly of qualified voters. Thus all non-voters and all disqualified voters must be excluded. The non-voters are excluded in virtue of canon 165; the disqualified voters, in virtue of canon 167, § 1. A non-voter is *collegio extraneus*, an "outsider", a term which has received scant attention from canonists who have written since the promulgation of the Code.[24]

The precise meaning of the term, *extraneus*, is necessarily dependent upon the extension of the term, *collegium*. Suppose an election to take place in a religious community. Three groups of persons may be considered with reference to this election:

Group One: members of the community who are voters.

Group Two: members of the community who are not voters, because (e. g.) not yet perpetually professed.

Group Three: all non-members of the community: lay persons, members of other religious institutes etc.

In its strictest sense *collegium* may be taken to mean the assembly of the voters (Group One). Hence, anyone who is not a voter is an outsider, even though he belongs to the community for which the election is being conducted.[25] This meaning would exclude as *extranei* not only Group Three but also Group Two.

But apparently the Code is not rigid in attaching the same meaning to *collegium* whenever it occurs in the article on elections. In canon 162, § 1, for instance, *collegii praeses* has been construed as meaning the superior of the community for which the election is being held and not the

[24]Cf., e. g., Schäfer, *De Religiosis*, p. 218; Chelodi, *Ius de Personis*, p. 236; Wernz-Vidal, *Ius Canonicum*, II, 264; Cappello, *Summa*, I, 348; Vermeersch-Creusen, *Epitome*, I, 190; Coronata, *Institutiones*, I, 257.

[25]Maroto, *Institutiones*, I, 778; Larraona, "De Electionibus Religiosorum", *CpR*, IX (1928), 335.

superior of the actual election,[26] but in canon 174 the same phrase means the presiding officer of the election. The contrast between the two meanings becomes sharp when one considers the election of the highest superior in a diocesan congregation of women; in canon 162, § 1, *praeses collegii* means the superioress general; in canon 174 it means the local ordinary.

Perhaps *collegium* in canon 165 has the same meaning which the Sacred Congregation for Religious gave to the term when interpreting canon 162, §1. In this case, outsiders are all non-members of the community for which the election is being held (Group Three, but not Group Two). Under the term, "outsider", would be included laypersons, members of other religious communities and others who have not even a seeming right to assist at the election. In a religious institute the members of another institute would be outsiders. Non-voting members of the same institute would not be considered outsiders.

There are several reasons favoring this latter interpretation: 1) The old legislation which Cardinal Gasparri (as a canonist of great authority) lists as the source of canon 165 is not concerned with the members of a moral person who happen to lack the right to vote, but refers to outsiders who have no connection with the moral person conducting the election.[27] 2) The admission of an outsider invalidates the entire election. An effect so drastic should be limited as far as may be reasonable, in accord with the rule: *odiosa restringenda.*[28] 3) According to some interpreters[29] canon 167, §1, n. 5, includes within its scope members of a moral person who lack the right to vote, such as the temporarily professed religious.[30] Canon 165, therefore, should be lim-

---

[26]S. C. de Rel., July 2, 1921.—*AAS*, XIII (1921), 481.

[27]E. g., c. 2, C. XVIII, q. 2; c. 8, X, *de consuetudine*, I, 4; c. 50, X, *de electione et electi potestate*, I, 6.

[28]Reg. 15—R. I. in VI°.

[29]This point will be more fully discussed *infra* p. 126.

[30]Can. 578, n. 3; cf. Michiels, *De Personis*, II, 383; Cappello, *Summa*, I, 348.

ited to those who have no connection with the moral person which is entitled to conduct the election.

Against this interpretation is the clear definition of an *extraneus* given by Passerini.[31] The legislator in employing the term knew that it would be understood according to the terminology of the classic authors and in the matter of elections the work of Passerini is outstanding.[32]

An *extraneus,* says Passerini, is one who is not a voter even though he is a member of the convent or church for which the superior is being chosen. Thus, if he is a canon, but not yet a subdeacon, he is an outsider with reference to the election of the bishop. If he is a religious, but not yet professed, or not yet in major orders, or (as in the Order of Preacher) not yet a priest, he is an outsider with reference to the elections of religious superiors. Therefore, it may be stated as a general principle that an outsider is one who lacks some quality or condition requisite for active voice.[33]

This definition certainly does not offer a final interpretation of canon 165, but in contrast to the inferences which lend some support to the other view, this is a clear statement from a reliable source. Even when more modern canonists fail to discuss the definition of *extraneus* in their text, they refer to Passerini's definition in the margin.[34]

It cannot be urged that non-voting members of the institute are covered by canon 167, § 1, because (as will be shown below) canon 167 refers solely to those who are voters (members of Group One, above). Those comprised under canon 167 enjoy the right to vote *in actu primo,* but are

---

[31]*De Electione Canonica,* III, 17.

[32]"Tractatus celeberrimus"—Maroto, *Institutiones,* I, 111; cf. can 6, n. 2.

[33]*De Electione Canonica,* III, 17: "Omnis ille cui deficit aliqua qualitas, seu conditio ex illis quae de iure sunt necessariae ad eligendum, est extraneus a Collegio eligentium."

[34]Cf. Wernz, *Ius Decretalium,* II, n. 353; Wernz-Vidal, *Ius Canonicum,* II, 264; Appeltern, *Compendium,* p. 343; Maroto, *Institutiones,* I, 778 (also discussed by Maroto in the text).

hindered from exercising this right *in actu secundo* either because they are incapable of a human act or have publicly joined an heretical sect or have been otherwise deprived of active voice. Thus, canon 165 refers to non-voters; canon 167 refers to impeded voters.

The admission of an outsider to a vote nullifies the entire election. By the term "entire election" is meant the canonical call described in Chapter One. If an outsider votes, then the entire process in which he is permitted to have a part is without legal effect. Therefore, the single ballotings which aim to achieve an election-result with the participation of an outsider are necessarily void. However, if the chapter expels the outsider after a number of inefficacious ballotings have taken place, it would seem that the chapter could start afresh, disregarding the void ballotings, and achieve a valid election. Moreover, if several canonical elections take place at one meeting of the voters and the outsider is expelled during the course of the meeting, those elections in which he took part are void but the subsequent canonical elections are not affected. In other words, the participation of an outsider invalidates the election, but the chapter itself (as will be shown in Chapter Twelve commenting on canon 178) may repent of its violation of the law, may expel the outsider and then correct the invalid election.

Some authors before the Code did not believe that the admission of an outsider would nullify the entire election.[35] They applied to outsiders the rule which the Code in canon 167, § 2, restricts now to impeded voters. The vote of the outsider was invalid, but the election was not invalid unless the outsider's vote was decisive. The question was disputed, but is now solved by the Code in favor of the stricter view.

The participation of an outsider in an election by the mere casting of his vote does not of itself suffice to nullify the election. There has to be an act whereby he was ad-

[35]Cf. Appeltern, *Compendium*, p. 343; Passerini, *De Electione Canonica*, III, 36; Pirhing, Lib. I, tit. 6, n. 13.

mitted to the vote by the greater part of the chapter. In canon 165 the Code gives an answer to the question which was invariably asked by canonists before the time of the Code: *An capitulum possit admittere extraneum?*[36] The Code answers: *Nullus collegio extraneus admitti potest.* The prohibition affects the chapter. The capitulars may not admit an outsider. If they do so, their election is invalid. But if an outsider votes against the will or without the knowledge of the chapter, the election is not invalid.

Before the Code it was admitted that extern clerics who had been accorded voting privileges by a chapter could by means of legal prescription obtain the strict right to vote after forty years.[37] Centenary and immemorial possession of such a right establishes the presumption that a privilege was granted,[38] and all privileges with reference to outsiders remain intact. The saving clause in canon 165 refers not only to the right of an individual non-member to cast his vote, but also to the acquired right of a chapter to admit an outsider in accordance with their customs. An electoral assembly may have the custom, founded upon a centenary and immemorial privilege, of being able by unanimous consent of the chapter to grant the honor of voting for a single time to a non-member. Such a custom and privilege is safeguarded by canon 165.

B. *Exclusion of Lay Persons*

Canon 166

Si laici contra canonicam libertatem electioni ecclesiasticae quoquo modo sese immiscuerint, electio ipso iure invalida est.

---

[36]Passerini, *De Electione Canonica,* XIV, 24; Reiffenstuel, Lib. I, tit. 6, n. 161-164; Wernz, *Ius Decretalium,* II, n. 354; Appeltern, *Compendium,* p. 343.

[37]Schmalzgrueber, Lib. I, tit. 6, n. 7.

[38]Can. 63.

In the second place the Code with special emphasis excludes lay persons. The term "lay persons" does not include lay religious; it refers only to secular persons.[39] The canon does not only forbid lay persons to vote, but seeks to hinder any lay interference which is prejudicial to ecclesiastical liberty. The old law and its interpretations as well as circumstances will determine what forms of conduct are prejudicial to liberty. It might be ill-advised, but it is not illegal, to admit a lay person to act as stenographer or notary at an election.[40] To cast a vote, to attend the election on the pretext of lending "protection", to demand that one's consent be asked, to exercise a power of veto, all these are instances of acts forbidden to a layman by canon 166.[41] If these acts are no more than attempts and produce no effects whatever on the voters, they can be simply ignored. If, however, the layman's veto or his presence has an effect on even a small number of the voters the election is invalid. The terms of the law are sweeping. It is not required that the coercion or interference with liberty affect a majority of the voters, since the law says: "if lay people interfere in any way whatever." This ruling favors ecclesiastical liberty and is therefore to be given a broad interpretation.[42]

C. *Those Laboring under Disabilities*

In canon 167, § 1, the Code enumerates a list of persons who are under various disabilities which prevent them from voting.

Canon 167, § 1.

a. **Nequeunt suffragium ferre:**

1. **Incapaces actus humani;**

---

[39]Pirhing, Lib. I, tit. 6, n. 18.

[40]Schmalzgrueber, Lib. I, tit. 6, n. 5.

[41]Cf. Piat, *Praelectiones*, II, 58.

[42]Cf. Laymann, *Quaestiones de electione praelatorum*, q. 20 (cited by Pirhing, Lib. I, tit. 6, n. 18.)

Those may not vote who are incapable of placing a human act. This is quite evident from the nature of an election. It follows that those who are habitually deprived of the use of reason or who lack the use of reason at the time of the election are unable to vote.

b. **[Nequeunt suffragium ferre:]**

2. **Impuberes;**

Those who have not yet attained the age of puberty, which is fourteen years of age for boys and twelve for girls,[43] may be mentally capable of voting, but are prevented from doing so by the positive law. The old law presumed that they lacked the necessary discretion.[44]

In most elections those below fourteen will be indirectly prevented from voting by the lack of other canonical requirements, for instance, the age for religious profession.[45] The rule may become practical in lay confraternities which must hold elections in accordance with canons 161-178,[46] for such confraternities may include in their membership a number of persons below the age of twelve or fourteen years.

c. **[Nequeunt suffragium ferre:]**

3. **Censura vel infamia iuris affecti, post sententiam tamen declaratoriam vel condemnatoriam.**

Those who are excommunicated,[47] suspended,[48] under personal interdict,[49] or affected with legal infamy,[50] are dis-

---

[43]Canon 88.

[44]C. 32, *de electione et electi potestate*, I, 6, in VI°.

[45]Sixteen years—Canon 573.

[46]Canon 697, § 2.

[47]Can. 2265, § 1, n. 1 and § 2.

[48]Can. 2283.

[49]Can. 2275, n. 3.

[50]Can. 2294, § 2.

qualified from voting in canonical elections after a condemnatory or declaratory sentence has been inflicted. Before sentence has been inflicted (and the same is true of all who are prohibited from exercising the *actus legitimi* listed in canon 2256, n. 2) they are forbidden to vote,[51] but if they disregard this prohibition their vote is valid.[52] Canon 167, § 1, n. 3 applies to all clerics and religious as well as to voters in the elections of lay associations; after sentence has been passed none of these can vote validly. But canon 2265, § 1, n. 1 which forbids every excommunicated person to vote in ecclesiastical elections must be interpreted strictly as applying only to elections to offices in the strict sense of canon 145, § 2. Therefore, if a member of a confraternity would, for instance, be excommunicated for reading a forbidden book he could, nevertheless, validly and licitly vote for the lay officers of his confraternity. The same would hold true in the elections of Sisters.[53]

d. **[Nequeunt suffragium ferre:]**

4. **Qui sectae hereticae vel schismaticae nomen dederunt vel publice adhaeserunt.**

Immediately after the promulgation of the Code some authors interpreted this section of canon 167 to mean "those who have once belonged to a non-Catholic sect", including even converts who were members of a non-Catholic sect unwittingly and in good faith.[54] It appears that the Sacred Congregation of Religious also followed this interpretation.[55] On the 16th of October, 1919, the Commission for interpreting the Code gave an interpretation of the phrase *qui sectae*

---

[51]Cans. 2263 (see also can. 2256, n. 2), and 2265.

[52]Can. 2265, § 2.

[53]Cf. supra p. 6; see also, Vermeersch-Creusen, *Epitome* (5 ed., Romae: Dessain, 1933), I, 241.

[54]Cf. Papi, *Government of Religious Communities* New York: Kennedy, 1919), p. [81], not. 1.

[55]*Periodica*, X (1922), 101.

acatholicae adhaeserunt in can. 542, n. 1.[56] There is little doubt that the interpretation applies also to the similar phrase in canon 167.[57] The Commission declared that the words do not refer to those who came into the Church from the heresy or schism in which they were born, but solely to those who fell away from the faith and joined a non-Catholic sect, either by placing their names on the official register or by publicly professing their allegiance to such a sect.

A later interpretation of the Commission declared that atheistic sects were equivalent to non-Catholic sects.[58] Apostates who join atheistic leagues or associations contract the same juridical effects as those who join a non-Catholic sect. There is no doubt whatever that this interpretation applies also to canon 167, because the Commission expressly extends its answer to "all juridical effects".[59]

e. **[Nequeunt suffragium ferre:]**

5. **Carentes voce activa . . . ob legitimam iudicis sententiam. . .**

The sentence of a judge deprives of active voice all those who are under censure or legal infamy. Besides this immediate consequence of a declared or judicially imposed censure, deprivation of active voice can also be inflicted as a vindictive penalty.[60] Certain crimes require that this penalty be imposed. The following must be deprived of the right to vote and that by judicial sentence: Religious who are guilty of falsifying letters, decrees, or rescripts of the Apostolic See or who knowingly make use of such forger-

---

[56] *AAS*, XI (1919), 477.
[57] Vermeersch, *Epitome*, I, 190.
[58] July 30, 1934—*AAS*, XXVI (1934), 494.
[59] Cf. *Periodica*, XXIII (1934), 145-146.
[60] Can. 2291, n. 8 and n. 11.

ies,[61] all who are guilty of sollicitation,[62] religious who violate the liberty of the Church by co-operating in the passage of laws, or who directly or indirectly impede the exercise of ecclesiastical jurisdiction whether of the internal or external forum, likewise religious who join a masonic sect,[63] religious who violate common life,[64] religious who admit women to the cloister,[65] religious who conspire against the authority of the Roman Pontiff or his legate, or against their own ordinary or the legitimate orders of any of the foregoing, or who incite subjects to disobedience.[66] The sentence of a judge must always intervene if these penalties are to have their effect.[67] If, for instance, a religious admits a woman to the cloister and incurs the penalty of excommunication, he may repent of his act and can then be absolved from the censure. His crime does not perpetually or temporarily deprive him of active voice, unless this vindictive punishment is inflicted by a judge.

f. **[Nequeunt suffragium ferre:]**

5. **Carentes voce activa . . . ex iure communi aut particulari.**

Some commentators seem to limit this number to *penal* deprivations of the right to vote whether these derive from the common or from particular law.[68] There is, however, some reason for giving to the phrase, *carentes voce activa,* a non-penal meaning also. Canon 629, § 2, says of the member of a religious institute who has served as cardinal or

---

61Can. 2360, § 2.

62Can. 2368, § 1.

63Can. 2336; cf. cans. 2334, 2335.

64Can. 2389.

65Can. 2342, n. 2.

66Can. 2331, § 2.

67Cf. Coronata, *Institutiones*, I, 261.

68Cf. Coronata, *Institutiones*, I, 261; Maroto, *Institutiones*, I, 740; Wernz-Vidal, *Ius Canonicum*, II, 265.

bishop and now lives in a house of his institute: *caret voce activa*. And of the temporarily professed canon 578, n. 3, remarks: *voce activa . . . carent*. One might well be led to regard these two cases as being comprised in the wording of canon 167, § 1, n. 5, namely, *carentes voce activa . . . ex iure communi*. Moreover, this canon is the only place in article on elections where the Code could include the non-penal regulations for voters enacted by particular law, for the canon points to the vote as being invalid when it is cast by such as are designated *carentes voce activa . . . ex iure particulari*. Finally, certain commentators by referring to canon 578, n. 3, in connection with canon 167, § 1, n. 5, impliedly hold that *carentes voce activa* has a non-penal as well as a penal meaning.[69] In endeavoring to decide whether "*caret*" in this canon has a penal or a non-penal meaning, no solution can be found in the word alone. The word in other places certainly has a non-penal meaning, as is evidenced in canons 578 and 692. In other words, it does not always mean "to be deprived of", but *can* mean simply "to lack." It is equally true that *caret* frequently does have a penal meaning.[70] In the former legislation which is listed in the Code as source-material for this canon, the word, *caret*, is twice used and that in a penal sense.[71] The remaining source-material cited by Cardinal Gasparri in connection with canon 167, § 1, generally reflects a penal character, for which purpose the word, *privari*, is employed.[72] In none of these sources is there reference to one who merely lacks qualities or conditions required for voting.

The principal objection to the view that canon 167, § 1, n. 5, reflects legislation of a purely penal character is the

---

[69]Michiels, *De Personis*, I, 383; Chelodi, *Ius de Personis*, p. 236 Cappello, *Summa*, I, 348.

[70]Cf. cans. 2259, § 1; 2275, n. 4; 2385.

[71]C. 41, 43, X, *de electione et electi potestate*, I, 6.

[72]C. 7, 23, 25, 40-43, 50, X, *de electione et electi potestate*, I, 6; c. 3, X, *de translatione episcopi*, I, 7; c. 7, 18, *de electione et electi potestate*, I, 6, in VI°; c. 1, *ut lite pendente nihil innovetur*, II, 8, in VI°; Conc. Trident., sess. XXV, *de regularibus*, c. 2.

very similar terminology used in canons 578, n. 3 and 629, § 2, which are certainly not of a penal character. But apart from this objection the context of canon 167, § 1, seems to restrict n. 5 to a penal meaning.

Those who cannot vote, the canon implies, are such as are hindered by nature or by law. The natural law (further determined by the positive law) says that those incapable of a human act and those who are under age cannot vote. The positive law hinders from voting: those who have been declared or condemned as censured or infamous, those who have apostatized or joined a non-Catholic sect and those who have been deprived of the right to vote. The context of n. 5 taken with numbers 3 and 4 seems to require the penal sense. But a still stronger argument is found in the context of n. 5 itself. Two phrases depend on the one word *carentes,* namely, *carentes ob legitimam sententiam* and *carentes ex iure communi.* The word, *carentes,* is not repeated and must, therefore, bear the same meaning in both cases; but those who have no vote because of a judicial sentence are certainly "penally deprived". Therefore, those who have no vote because of common or particular law are such as are penally deprived by common or particular law.

A) The following are *deprived of active voice by the common law:* a) One who is exclaustrated, for as long as his indult of exclaustration lasts;[73] b) an apostate religious who returns to his institute;[74] c) those deprived of active voice *for reasons connected with elections:*

1. Those who are deprived of the right to vote "for this instance". The meaning is this: because of some action of the voters an election is invalid and as a punishment they are not permitted to correct the invalidity by proceeding to a new election. Instead. "for this present instance", they must accept an appointee of the higher superior. When

[73]Can. 639.

[74]Can. 2385.

the office again becomes vacant the voters may hold an election as usual. The voters incur this penalty in the following cases:

1) If they fail to hold the election within the prescribed time.[75]

2) If they fail to send a postulation to the proper authority within the prescribed eight days.[76]

3) If they request or legitimately cooperate in a violation of canon 166, namely, if they cooperate in lay interference with ecclesiastical liberty.[77]

4) If they knowingly elect an unworthy or unsuitable candidate.[78]

5) If they presume to confer an ecclesiastical office, benefice or dignity after slighting and passing by the authority of the superior in whose hands rests the right of confirmation or institution.[79]

2. Those who are deprived of the right to vote "at the pleasure of the Apostolic See". The single case is this: if the voters co-operate in a violation of canon 176, § 3, namely, if they allow the person elected to meddle in the affairs of his office before he has been confirmed therein.[80]

3. Finally, those who either individually or collegiately are deprived of the right to vote "for all time to come" because of the crime of simony perpetrated by them in reference to ecclesiastical offices, benefices, or dignities.[81]

B) Those deprived of the right to vote by particular law.

The laws of religious institutes as well as the statutes of cathedral chapters or other electoral bodies may contain penalties which deprive the voters of their right to vote. The Council of Trent prescribed the deprivation of active

---

[75]Can. 178.
[76]Can. 181, § 2.
[77]Can. 2390, § 2.
[78]Can. 2391, § 1.
[79]Can. 2393.
[80]Can. 2394, n. 3.
[81]Can. 2392, n. 2.

voice for those religious who were guilty of proprietorship.[82] This is not expressly contained in the Code, but canon 2389 embraces a wider field and prescribes that deprivation of active voice be inflicted for violations of the common life. Religious constitutions may more exactly define this and other causes for deprivation of vote.

Canon 167 § 2

> **Si quis ex praedictis admittatur, eius suffragium est nullum, sed electio valet, nisi constet, eo dempto, electum non retulisse requisitum suffragiorum numerum, aut nisi scienter admissus fuerit excommunicatus per sententiam declaratoriam vel condemnatoriam.**

The first paragraph of canon 167 established which voters should be excluded from the election because of natural or legal impediments. The second paragraph considers the juridical effects on the election, if despite the prohibition a disqualified voter is admitted.

If any of the persons described in nn. 1-5 are admitted the vote of that individual is null and void, but the election is valid, except in two cases which will be noted immediately. Therefore, there is a great difference between the admission of an outsider or of a lay person, and the admission of a disqualified voter. The deliberate admission of an outsider automatically nullifies the entire election. The admission, even deliberate, of a disqualified voter ordinarily does not affect the validity of the proceedings.

The two exceptions to the rule just stated are as follows:

1. If the vote of the disqualified person is decisive.

In this case the election is null. This is an obvious consequence of declaring that such a person's individual vote is null and void. If in an assembly of eleven voters, six votes are cast for A and five for B, A is not elected if it

[82] Conc. Trident., sess. XXV, *de regularibus*, c. 2.

can be shown that the decisive vote in his favor was cast by a disqualified voter. A valid election requires a majority of valid votes. That is the reason why the Code says: if a disqualified voter is admitted to the election and it is evident that, if his vote was deducted, the one elected would not have received the requisite number of votes, then the entire election is invalid.

How will it become "evident" that the disqualified elector's vote was decisive? If the presence of the disqualified person is discovered before the ballots are burned, the tellers may call upon him to identify his ballot (in the manner to be described in the next chapter, p. 148). If it is found that his was the decisive vote, the election is invalid. If the question arises after the ballots have been burned, the election is doubtful. Some authors hold that it should be repeated.[83] The wording of the canon, however, would seem to render this unnecessary. The Code declares that an election in which a disqualified voter participates is valid, unless it is *evident (nisi constet)* that he cast the deciding vote. If the doubt cannot be cleared up, the law supplies for the possible invalidity.

2. If a person who has been excommunicated by condemnatory sentence or one who has been juridically declared as excommunicated is knowingly admitted to the election.

In this case also the election is null. The admission of such an excommunicated voter must be done knowingly and wilfully. Therefore any mitigating circumstance which would diminish the culpability of the chapter will save the election from invalidity.[84] If the disqualified voter is admitted against the will of the majority, he cannot be said to be admitted by the chapter.

In dealing thus with a person who has been excommunicated by condemnatory sentence or who has been declared as excommunicated, canon 167, § 2, takes the excom-

---

[83]Reiffenstuel, Lib. I, tit. 6, n. 171; Coronata, *Institutiones*, I, 261.

[84]Can. 2229, § 2.

municated person from the list of those included in canon 167, § 1, n. 3 and places them almost on the same level as the *extranei* of canon 165, the only difference being that canon 167, § 2, employs the word *scienter* which is not found in canon 165.

In order that the excommunication affect the election it is necessary that the declaration or condemnation continue in its effect *at the time* of the election. Augustine[85] states: "If one commits a crime deserving of declaratory sentence even though only declared after the election, his vote is null and void." This statement would necessarily imply that a declaratory sentence passed after the election will nullify votes (and, consequently, also elections) which were formerly valid. It is true, of course, that canon 2232, § 2, states that a declaratory sentence is retroactive to the moment when the crime was committed, but this general statement in no way derogates from the declaration of canon 2265, § 2, which declares that the acts of those excommunicated persons who have not yet been sentenced are valid. Hence, an election will stand even though it later transpires that some of the voters were excommunicated at the time, and even though sentence has now been declared.

D. *Exclusion of Persons Who Lack Active Voice.*

Persons who are not voters and not members of the chapter are *extranei* and are excluded by canon 165, but at this point, those persons lacking active voice will be more specifically determined.

a. Those lacking active voice *by reason of the general law.*

The temporarily professed members of religious institutes do not enjoy active voice, unless the constitutions expressly accord them this right.[86] The *Normae* of 1901 prescribed that all members of the community, even those with

---

[85]*Commentary on Canon Law*, II (4 ed., 1923), 130.

[86]Can. 578, n. 3.

temporary vows, should have a vote. This is not the general rule of the Code, but constitutions modelled on the *Normae* may remain in force.[87]

A religious who has exercised the office of cardinal or bishop and is now living in retirement in one of the houses of his institute lacks active voice.[88]

b. Those lacking active voice *by reason of particular law.*

A law of the Council of Trent was so interpreted as to exclude the lay brothers from voting in clerical institutes. Though this law is no longer in force, in many clerical institutes the lay brothers do not vote.[89] In many monasteries of nuns only the so-called choir nuns vote, although in this matter the Council of Trent did not forbid the lay sisters to vote, but directed that the provisions of the constitutions be observed.[90]

In the general and provincial chapters of religious institutes, all members of the institute lack active voice save those who are included in the exclusive list contained in the constitutions. The *Normae* of 1901 may be cited as being typical of the constitutions of many religious institutes.

In the *General Chapter* of an institute divided into provinces the following and these alone enjoy active voice: the Superioress General, her counsellors, the Secretary General, the Econome General, the Ex-Superioresses General, all Superioresses Provincial, two delegates from each province to be elected in the provincial chapter.[91]

In the *Provincial Chapter* the following enjoy active voice: the Superioress Provincial, her counsellors, all superioresses of houses in which twelve religious dwell, one delegate from each house of twelve religious.[92]

---

[87]Cf. *Normae* of 1901, n. 217.

[88]Can. 629, § 2.

[89]Cf. Conc. Trident. sess. XXII, *de ref.*, c. 4, Wernz, *Ius Decretalium*, II, n. 355.

[90]Sess. XXV *de regularibus*, c. 2; Piat, *Praelectiones*, II, 12.

[91]*Normae* of 1901—Nn. 213; 214; 220.

[92]*Normae* of 1901, n. 221.

CHAPTER TEN

The Act of Election

After the qualifications of the voters have been set forth by the Code, canons 169-174 proceed to describe the manner in which an assembly of properly qualified voters exercise their freedom of choice. The discussion of the act of election falls into two main divisions: 1) a consideration of proximate preparations and preliminaries which surround the act of election; 2) an examination of the two main methods of electing, namely, scrutiny and compromise.

ARTICLE I. *Proximate Preparations.*

A. *Prayer:*

Following the prescription of the Council of Trent[1] the constitutions and particular customs usually ordain various prayers and religious exercises as a preparation for the election. Public and private prayer to the Holy Ghost is ordered for a number of days preceding the chapter. On the day of the election the Votive Mass of the Holy Ghost is celebrated by the president of the chapter, at which Mass the voters (if they are not priests) receive Holy Communion. None of these exercises are required by the Code, but their omission may constitute a grave fault because of scandal.[2]

Often a sermon is preached to the voters reminding them of their duties in the election and stressing particularly their obligation of choosing the most worthy candi-

[1]Sess. XXIV, *de ref.*, c. 1.

[2]Cf. Piat, *Praelectiones*, II, 35. It is, of course, no grave fault if one or the other voter fails to go to Communion.

dates. The sermon is not always given, but in nearly every case particular law and custom will prescribe the reading of those sections of the constitutions and statutes which govern elections. Formerly it was necessary to read sections of the decree *"Nullus Omnino"* of Clement VIII.[3] Instead of this decree, which has been rendered obsolete by the Code, the pertinent passages of canons 506 and 507 should be read, if they are not already embodied in the constitutions.

B. *Officers of the Chapter:*

a. *The President:* A presiding officer is not strictly essential for the validity of the election, but it is certainly to the advantage of the voters and is required by the Code.[4] Often the president is designated by law. When there is no person who is *ex officio* the president of the group, then the presidency falls to him who enjoys precedence according to canon 106. The local ordinary or his delegate must preside at the election of the superioress in all monasteries subject to his jurisdiction. If the monastery is subject to a regular superior, the local ordinary may assist if he so wishes. If he assists, the local ordinary presides, but he is not obliged to assist at the election and, consequently, he may leave the entire matter to the regular superior on whom the obligation of presiding primarily rests.[5]

Canon 506, § 2, requires a word of explanation. It is concerned with the presidency of the election in a monastery of nuns. Two cases are contemplated by the canons: A) when the monastery of nuns is directly subject to the local ordinary; B) when the nuns are subject to a regular superior. The first case occasions little difficulty. The sec-

---

[3]Especially § 22, July 25, 1599—*Bullarium Romanum,* X, 665.

[4]Can. 171, § 1; for the statement that his presence is not essential for validity, cf. Coronata, *Institutiones,* I, 263; Ferraris, *Bibliotheca,* v. "Electio", IV, 22.

[5]Cf. can. 506, § 2.

ond case both before[6] and after the Code[7] has required authentic declaration in order to define the rights of the local ordinary and the regular superior.

A) When the monastery is subject to the local ordinary's direct jurisdiction.

In this case the local ordinary presides, enjoying a true presidency of effective jurisdiction and not merely an honorary chairmanship. He has power to direct and govern the act of election.[8] He has authority to settle practical questions of law that may arise, impose penances if necessary and, in general, exercise all discretionary powers.[9] He may not enter the cloister, but he collects the votes at the grating. The local ordinary need not exercise this office personally but may delegate it to another. The Code makes express mention of the local ordinary's delegate. In supervising the election the president is assisted by two priests who act as tellers. The Code does not say who appoints these tellers but since it is the office of the local ordinary to receive the votes,[10] it likewise should be his office to choose those who are to assist him in so doing.[11] The local ordinary is free to choose any two priests save the ordinary confessors of the nuns.[12]

B) When the monastery is exempt from the local ordinary's direct jurisdiction.

---

[6]Cf., e. g., Clement XII, const. *Admonet Nos*, 11 Aug. 1735, § 1, 3—*Fontes*, n. 297; Clement XIII, const. *Inter Multiplices*, 11 Dec. 1758, § 5-7—*Fontes*, n. 449; S. C. Ep. et Reg., *Luceorien*, 29 Apr., 1729, ad 1—*Fontes*, n. 1844; S. C. C. *Tiburtina*, 26 Apr. 1727, ad 1-3—*Fontes*, n. 3325; *Pharaonen.*, 19 Sept., 14 Nov., 1733 ad 1—*Fontes*, n. 3408.

[7]*Pont. Com. Interp.*, Nov. 24, 1920—*AAS*, XII (1920), 575; July 30, 1934—*AAS*, XXVI (1934), 494.

[8]Cf. *Pont. Com. Interp.*, Nov. 24, 1920—*AAS*, XII (1920), 575.

[9]Cf. Larraona, "Commentarium Codicis", VIII (1927), 22-23.

[10]Cf. Conc. Trident., sess. XXV, de *regularibus*, c. 7.

[11]Cf. Schäfer, *De Religiosis*, p. 223; Fanfani, *De Iure Religiosorum*, p. 114.

[12]Can. 506, § 3.

Some monasteries of nuns are exempt from the direct jurisdiction of the local ordinary and are placed under that of a regular superior. This is especially the case with monasteries of a "Second Order", that is, monasteries of nuns which have the same Founder and follow the same Rule and spirit as an Order of men. The guidance and supervision of the monastery is given to a member of the "First Order." Thus, a monastery of Carmelite nuns may be placed under the authority of the provincial superior of the Carmelite friars, who is called the regular superior of the nuns.[13]

The regular superior has the right and duty to assist at the election of the superioress in a monastery subject to him, provided the ordinary of the place does not wish to preside. If the regular superior presides alone, then he enjoys the same rights and has the same duties just ascribed to the local ordinary. The regular superior appoints the two priests to act as tellers and he receives the votes of the nuns at the grating.

The following points, however, must be observed in governing the mutual rights of the regular superior and the local ordinary: a) if the ordinary wishes, *he may always preside* at the election in the monastery subject to a regular superior. Therefore, he must be seasonably notified of the day and hour of the election. But the local ordinary *need not* assist at the election, either personally or through a delegate, and consequently he can leave the entire matter to the regular superior. b) If he decides to assist, he may do so either personally or by delegate. c) If he assists personally, then he presides with full power of effective jurisdiction.[14] The response of the Pontifical Commission just cited in the margin apparently settles a disputed point as to who appoints the tellers when both the local ordinary and the regular superior are present. Before the Code, the regular superior appointed the two tellers even when the local or-

---

[13]Cf. can. 500, § 2.

[14]*Pont. Com. Interp.*, July 30, 1934—*AAS*, XXVI (1934), 494.

dinary presided.[15] Certain authors maintained that the regular superior could continue to do so even after the Code.[16] But their reasons seem to be devoid of force after the response of the Pontifical Commission for Interpreting the Code, July 30, 1934.[17] Laraona, [18] for instance, says that the regular superior appoints the tellers because he is the true jurisdictional superior of the election. The Pontifical Commission, however, says that the local ordinary is the jurisdictional president of the chapter. It would seem to derogate from the effective presidency of the local ordinary, if the regular superior could appoint the two priests who act as tellers at the election.[19] d) If the local ordinary assists through a delegate, then the delegate presides with full powers of jurisdiction.[20]

In all other institutes of women, whether these be of pontifical or diocesan right, the ordinary of the place where the election is held presides either personally or through a delegate at the election of the superioress general. The Code does not give the local ordinary the right to preside at the elections of the other superiors in these institutes. Custom or the constitutions may give him the right to preside at the elections of the general counsellors and secretary, which ordinarily follow the election of the superioress general.[21]

b. *The Secretary:* The secretary of the chapter holds office either by law or custom. In clerical exempt institutes the major superiors may appoint notaries[22] and if there is

---

15Cf. the preamble to the responses of S. C. C. *Tiburtina*, 26 Apr., 1727—*Fontes*, n. 3325; Bachofen, *Compendium*, p. 212.

16Larraona, "Commentarium Codicis", *CpR* VIII (1927), 26-27; Coronata, *Institutiones*, I (ed. 1928), 640.

17*AAS*, XXVI (1934), 494.

18"Commentarium Codicis," *CpR* VIII (1927), 26-27.

19Cf. Coronata, *Institutiones*, I (2 ed., 1939), 660.

20*Pont. Com. Interp.*, Nov. 24, 1920—*AAS*, XII (1920), 575; July 30, 1934—*AAS*, XXVI (1934), 494; cf. can. 106, n. 1; Maroto, "Annotationes", *CpR*, II (1921), 35.

21Cf. Schäfer, *De Religiosis*, p. 222; see also p. 224; Vermeersch-Creusen, *Epitome*, I, 323.

22Canon 503.

a provincial notary or secretary he may well act as secretary of the provincial chapter. In the election of the diocesan administrator the regular secretary of the board of consultors may fill this office.[23]

c. *Other Officials:* For the smooth conduct of the chapter it is customary to appoint one or more masters of ceremonies, a hebdomadary to preside at the Divine Office and other services, as well as other minor officials.[24]

C. *Presentation of Credentials:*

The presiding officer should interview those present and satisfy himself that each one has a right to participate. Superiors who vote in virtue of their office are usually sufficiently identified; delegates must present the document which testifies to their valid election.[25] If a doubt arises as to the qualifications of a voter, authors usually resolve the doubt on the basis of the principle, *Melior est condicio possidentis.* In other words, if it cannot be determined whether the voter has ever possessed the right to vote, if, for instance, it is doubtful whether he has the requisite age or number of years in religion, then he is to be excluded. But if it cannot be determined whether the voter has been deprived of a right to vote which he once certainly possessed, then he is to be admitted.[26]

D. *Official Opening of the Chapter:*

It is customary for the president to open the chapter in a formal manner and to declare in the name of all that the chapter does not wish either to admit anyone who has no right to be present, or to exclude anyone who has a right to vote.

---

[23]Jaeger, *The Administration of Vacant Dioceses*, p. 124.

[24]Cf. Pius X, Const., *Vacante Sede*, Dec. 25, 1904 n. 43—*C. I. C.* Docum. I; *Rituale Romano-Seraphicum*, Tit. IV, cap. II, n. 2.

[25]For the list of voters who usually constitute a general or provincial chapter, see supra p. 132.

[26]Passerini, *De Electione Canonica*, XIV, nn. 34-50; Maroto, *Institutiones*, I, 754; Coronata, *Institutiones*, I, 264.

E. *The Oath:*

Canon 506, § 1, directs that all men religious before proceeding to vote swear to elect the more worthy candidate. Women religious, lest they be troubled by scruples, are not obliged to take this oath. The oath may be taken according to a formula like the following:

> Ego, N. N., iuro et promitto Deo omnipotenti, beatae Mariae Virgini, [S. Patrono religionis], et omnibus Sanctis, me in hac electione, iis daturum meum votum, quos in conscientia mea meliores et aptiores iudicavero. Ita me Deus adiuvet.[27]

To discuss the specific requirements for various offices is beyond the scope of this dissertation, but it may be noted here that the oath binds the voter to elect the person who is most capable, *all things considered.* It is true that one is bound before God to elect the best person obtainable and one may not be satisfied with electing a merely worthy person if a better is to be had. Nevertheless, the good qualities must be considered in relation to time, place, and other circumstances. The common good of the institute is the supreme consideration. It may happen that at a given time a province or institute requires greater expansion of activities, or a restriction of activities, or the assumption of a new type of work. The man best fitted to meet the situation is the man who is to be chosen. Perhaps the more observant religious will not make the best administrator and at times the more learned man will lack the executive ability needed at the moment; therefore, one cannot simply state that the man most highly endowed with learning and sanctity is to be elected. The person who is best fitted to cope with the problems confronting the institute and who is at the same time best qualified to guide and sanctify his

---

[27] Cf. *Rituale Romano-Seraphicum,* Tit. IV, cap. I, n. 14.

subjects is the man for whom the voter swears to cast his ballot.

The common good of the institute and the preservation of peace and harmony may require that general superiors, for instance, be chosen in turn from various nationalities or language groups. In this case the voter is legitimately restricted in his choice to the best qualified candidate of that particular language.[28]

When the results of the first or second ballot prove to the voter that the person whom he deems best qualified has no chance of being elected, the voter is not bound to continue to vote for his candidate. The balloting clearly indicates that his choice is ruled out in the present circumstances. Accordingly he should shift his vote to another. It is never permitted to vote for an unworthy candidate, but it is obligatory to vote for a less worthy candidate in order to prevent the election of one who is unworthy.

F. *Preliminary Discussion:*

The voters are bound to inform themselves regarding the character and qualifications of the various candidates for office. Ordinarily this obligation will be fulfilled by means of preliminary discussions.[29] These discussions may be either public or private, that is, they may be conducted as part of the public business of the chapter, or they may consist of private consultations between individual voters. Public discussion is not obligatory, but neither is it in any way forbidden by the Code. A discussion conducted under competent chairmanship with due observance of truth and charity may serve to prevent all suspicion of intrigue. The experience of each group of voters will determine whether such discussion will be for good or ill and how it is to be conducted. Fanfani[30] thinks that a public discussion will rarely be expedient. Augustine[31] notes that at the abbey

---

[28]Passerini, *De Electione Canonica,* XXX, 150.

[29]Piat, *Praelectiones,* II, 36; Schäfer, *De Religiosis,* p. 219; Maroto *Institutiones,* I, 755.

[30]*De Iure Religiosorum,* p. 118.

[31]*A Commentary on Canon Law,* II, 127, not. 52.

of Einsiedeln in Switzerland a *"Murr-kapitel"* is held in which everyone is allowed to criticize what displeased him in the preceding regime.

As to private discussion, canon 507, § 2, says that all religious voters must beware of direct or indirect procuring of votes for themselves or for others. The question of the illicit procuring of votes, or the *mala subornatio* as it is called, is discussed more fully in the chapter on "Invalid Elections." The historical background of canon 507, § 2, shows that the law is directed primarily against the vice of ambition and forbids the procuring of votes for oneself, or for another at this other's request, or as a result of a simoniacal or ambitious agreement. It is lawful even for religious to endeavor by a prudent employment of good reasons and honest motives to induce others not to elect an unworthy candidate or to persuade others to elect a more worthy candidate. Threats, fraud and falsehood, mutual agreements and pacts, undue interposition of the authority of superiors, over-urgent pleading, all these constitute the illicit procuring of votes; but persuasion that is good and upright in its intention, object, and circumstances, is not forbidden. If charity, justice, and individual liberty are jealously safeguarded, anything like an organized campaign will be quite impossible.

G. *Some additional preliminaries:*

a. *The General Absolution:* This is usually imparted before the election of regulars. Many of the disabilities of the old law have now been removed and therefore this absolution, which was formerly useful for restoring voting qualifications, has now become little more than a ceremony which can be omitted without occasioning any result of invalidity or unlawfulness in the election.

b. *Statements regarding the discharge of Mass obligations:* Formerly no superior could validly vote in the election of major superiors in institutes of regulars, unless he could and did testify that all Mass obligations had been satisfied or could be satisfied in a very short time.[32] This formality may still exist in some institutes, but in virtue of common law it has no effect on elections at the present time.

ARTICLE II. *The Form of Election.*

Since the IV General Council of the Lateran (1215) three forms or methods of election have been recognized. They are: acclamation, scrutiny, and compromise.[33] An election takes place by acclamation when the electors spontaneously greet the name of the candidate with enthusiasm and it is evident to all that a ballot is useless, the result being known in advance. Formerly this method was devoid of effect if there was even one dissenting voice. Most canonists agree that acclamation has been abolished by the Code.[34]

Leaving aside this extraordinary form which was always something of an exception, there are now two possible methods of holding an election: scrutiny[35] and compromise.[36]

An election takes place by *compromise* when all the electors confide the election to one or several specified persons, either members of the electoral college or strangers, and ratify in advance the choice made by such accredited electors. These duly authorized deputy-electors are called *compromissarii.* Formerly this exceptional method was resorted to, either to terminate long and fruitless sessions, or when there was a lack of information concerning the candidates. The compromise must be agreed to by all the electors without exception. It may be absolute, i. e., leaving

---

[32] For the old law, see Ferraris, *Bibliotheca,* v. "Electio", IV, 84-85; Piat, *Praelectiones,* II, 17.

[33] C. 42, X, *de electione et electi potestate,* I, 6.

[34] Cf. Cappello, *Summa Iuris Canonici,* I, 347; Chelodi, *Ius de Personis,* p. 238; Coronata, *Institutiones,* I, 262; Maroto, *Institutiones,* I, 752; Fanfani, *De Iure Religiosorum,* p. 104.

[35] Can. 171.

[36] Can. 172-173.

the *compromissarii* quite free, or conditional, i. e., accompanied with certain reservations concerning the manner of election, the persons to be elected, the time-limit within which the election should be held and so on.[37]

Scrutiny is the normal form of election. Two or more tellers are appointed who receive the votes from each of the electors. The tellers count the votes and tabulate the result. Usually the person who receives the absolute majority of the valid votes cast is declared elected. Much more, of course, must be said concerning all of the points just mentioned. Canon 171, § 4, (which directs that the votes be burned) shows that the legislator contemplates a written vote as the normal procedure. This, however, does not seem to be essential. Before the Code many authors[38] held that the secrecy required by the Council of Trent did not demand the use of a written vote and there seems no reason for demanding more today.

The forms of scrutiny and compromise are of equal value in the eyes of the general law. However, it is not lawful for a subordinate group of voters to alter the electoral customs which have been established by higher authority and which are equivalent to particular laws. Therefore, if compromise were the customary form of election in a given religious institute, a provincial chapter would not be at liberty to adopt the method of scrutiny. This change would have to be made by the general chapter of the institute.[39]

Before the two forms of election can be discussed in detail, it is necessary to clarify a number of terms which will be employed in this and the following chapters. Unless the contrary is evident, an "election" *(electio)* means the canonical calling of a qualified person to a vacant ecclesiastical office or benefice by an assembly of lawful voters. Therefore, the term "election", when taken alone, does not refer

---

[37]Cf. A. Boudinhon, *Cath. Encycl.*, art. "Election", V, 376.

[38]Thus, Reiffenstuel, Lib. I, tit. 6, n. 124 and 331; Piat, *Praelectiones*, II, 8, not. 5, and others there cited.

[39]Cf. Goyeneche, "Consultationes", *CpR*, IV (1923), 49.

to an electoral meeting or chapter *(capitulum)* at which several canonical elections may take place. For example, in a religious institute a chapter may be held for the election of a superior general and four counsellors. Something may occur in the voting for the superior general which "renders the entire election invalid." This statement means that the superior general is invalidly elected. It does not mean that all the other acts of the chapter are invalid. The subsequent elections of the four counsellors may be perfectly valid.

A "vote" *(suffragium)* is the individual's designation of a determined candidate. This may be either written or oral. Where the material features of the written vote are stressed in the discussion, the term "ticket" *(scheda* or *schedula)* will be used. The term "ballot" *(scrutinium* as in canon 101, § 1, n. 1) refers to the whole number of votes cast at any one time. Thus, "C was elected on the first ballot."

A. *The Form of Scrutiny*

Canon 171

§ 1. Ante electionem per secreta suffragia deputentur, nisi iam propriis statutis deputati sint, e gremio collegii duo saltem scrutatores, qui una cum praeside, si et ipse e gremio collegii sit, iusiurandum interponant de munere fideliter implendo ac de secreto servando circa acta in comitiis, etiam expleta electione.

§ 2. Scrutatores curent ut suffragia secreto, diligenter, singillatim et servato praecedentiae ordine ab unoquoque electore ferantur; collectisque ad ultimum suffragiis, coram praeside electionis, secundum formam propriis constitutionibus vel legitimis consuetudinibus statutam, inspiciant an suffragiorum numerus respondeat numero electorum, suffragia ipsa scrutentur palamque faciat quot quisque retulerit.

§ 3. Si numerus suffragiorum superet numerum eligentium, nihil est actum.

§ 4. Suffragia statim, peracto unoquoque scrutinio, vel post sessionem, si in eadem sessione habeantur plura scrutinia, comburantur.

§ 5. Omnia electionis acta ab eo, qui actuarii munere fungitur, accurate describantur, et saltem ab eodem actuario, praeside ac scrutatoribus subscripta, in collegii tabulario diligenter asserventur.

The various steps to be followed in holding an election according to the form of scrutiny are carefully enumerated in canon 171. Many of these formalities are not essential to validity, since the Code has broken away from the rigid formalism which once characterized the method of scrutiny.[40]

a. *The appointment of tellers.*

The intervention of tellers *(scrutatores)*, who receive and examine the votes of the chapter, is essential to the form of scrutiny. These are either permanently designated by law or they receive their special appointment by secret vote of the chapter. If particular law says, for instance, that "the two youngest," or "the two seniors," act as tellers, this is sufficient designation. If there is no such provision in the constitutions or statutes of the electoral body, then the majority of canonists hold that the two tellers must be appointed by the secret votes of all.[41] Coronata,[42] however, adopts a different reading of canon 171, § 1. He

[40]Cf. Ferraris, *Bibliotheca*, v. "Electio", I, 23.

[41]Ayrinhac, *General Legislation*, p. 337; Augustine, *Commentary on Canon Law*, II, 136; Chelodi, *Ius de Personis*, p. 238; Maroto, *Institutiones*, I, 756; Cappello, *Summa Iuris Canonici*, I, 352; Jaeger, *Administration of Vacant Dioceses*, p. 121; Schäfer, *De Religiosis*, p. 226; Fanfani, *De Iure Religiosorum*, p. 114; the opinion of Wernz-Vidal is doubtful, since it is simply stated that the tellers are to be designated "per actum capitularem"—*Ius Canonicum*, II, 271.

[42]*Institutiones*, I, 265, not. 1.

says that the phrase *per secreta suffragia* is to be joined not to the following word *deputentur,* but to the preceding word *electionem,* so that the meaning is: In every election by secret vote two tellers must be appointed. Nothing is said concerning the manner in which they are to be appointed. There is something to commend this view.

The phrases *electio per scrutinium* and *electio per compromissum* were common modes of expression before the Code.[43] Likewise the phrases "to elect by secret vote," to "hold elections by secret vote" were employed.[44]

Coronata's reading of this phrase, then, is not unusual, but is quite in conformity with canonical usage. The interpretation, however, seems to do some violence to the entire context of the canon. There seems to be antithesis expressed between the tellers who are appointed by secret vote *(per secreta suffragia deputentur)* and tellers already appointed by law *(propriis statutis deputati).* It is certain that *deputati* is modified by the preceding words *propriis statutis,* and structural balance seems to require that *deputentur* also be modified by the preceding words *per secreta suffragia.*

No tellers are required for this secret election of tellers, for otherwise the process would be prolonged indefinitely. Fanfani suggests that the president propose the names of two tellers and then ask the assembly to manifest its consent by secret vote.[45]

"At least" two tellers must be appointed. The old law required three.[46] It is not forbidden to employ three, or even more, at the present time. Additional tellers may be appointed to obtain the votes of the sick.[47]

---

[43]Cf. Reiffenstuel, Lib. I, tit. 6, n. 68 and 108; Piat, *Praelectiones,* II, 8; c. 4, *de sententia et re iudicata,* II, 14, in VI°.

[44]Conc. Trid., sess. XXV, *de regularibus,* c. 6; Reiffenstuel, Lib. I, tit. 6, n. 343.

[45]*De Iure Religiosorum,* p. 114.

[46]C. 42, X, *de electione et electi potestate,* I, 6.

[47]Cf. Pius X, const. *Vacante Sede,* Dec. 25, 1904, n. 62—*C. I. C.,* Docum. I.

The tellers must be chosen from the body of the voters, except in the case of the election of an abbess in a monastery of nuns, in which election two priests are appointed. This question has already been discussed in article I, B, of the present chapter.[48] Any two priests, except the ordinary confessors of the nuns,[49] may be chosen for this office.

Probably the reason why two priests act as tellers in the elections of nuns is this: in every election the president and the tellers constitute a tribunal supervising the Balloting. Since the bishop is forbidden to enter the cloister to conduct the election, it is expedient that the other members of his tribunal be with him, outside the cloister. In all other elections of women religious this reason does not obtain and, therefore, the tellers are to be chosen from the body of the chapter.

b. *The Oath of the Tellers and of the President.*

The ordinary of the place or his delegate, the regular superior, and whoever else may preside at an election without being a member of the chapter, need not take an oath to perform his duty faithfully.[50] The two priests who act as tellers in the election of the abbess in a monastery of nuns probably are not obliged to take the oath, because they are not the tellers chosen from the body of the chapter on whom the obligation of canon 171, § 1, falls.

In all other instances, where president and tellers are chosen from the body of the chapter, all three must take an oath: a) to perform their duty faithfully; b) to keep secret whatever is done in the election, and that even after the completion of the election. This oath of secrecy does not forbid the tellers to publish the results of the balloting, nor

---

[48]Cf. Goyeneche, "Interventio Ordinarii in electionibus", *CpR*, XI (1930), 399; Fanfani, *De Iure Religiosorum*, p. 114; Schäfer, *De Religiosis*, p. 223.

[49]Can. 506, § 3.

[50]Canon 171, § 1.

oblige them to be silent about anything else which it is permissible for other voters to reveal. They are bound to observe secrecy with regard to knowledge which they acquire in the discharge of their office, for instance, the knowledge gained from an acquaintance with the handwriting of various voters.

c. *Distribution of Blank Tickets.*

If the blank tickets have not been distributed, the tellers will do so at this point. The form of ticket used in the election of the Roman Pontiff[51] may well be imitated in other elections.[52] This form can be worked out in various ways, but the essential feature of this type of ticket consists in its three folds.

The voter first writes *his own name* on the ticket and then seals this section within the first fold; he next marks down a *conventional sign* such as *"Gloria in Excelsis Deo,"* or a number chosen at random, or a Greek cross, etc., whereupon he folds and seals his ticket a second time; lastly he writes out *his vote* and folds his ticket the third and last time.

Ordinarily the tellers and president will open the last fold only. This will reveal the name of the person for whom the vote is cast and no further inquiry is necessary. If, however, someone is elected by a bare majority of one vote, the tellers can ask the one elected to manifest the conventional sign marked on his ticket. They will then search the votes for the sign, *"Gloria in Excelsis Deo,"* for instance, and discover whether or not the voter cast his vote for himself.[53] It is probably lack of acquaintance with this form

---

[51]Pius X, const., *Vacante Sede* Dec. 25, 1904, n. 61-65—*C. I. C.*, Docum. I.

[52]See also *Rituale Romano-Seraphicum*, Tit. IV, cap. III, Append., *Exemplum schedae.*

[53]This investigation is strictly required in the papal election; Cf. Pius X, const. *Vacante Sede*, Dec. 25, 1904, n. 75—*C. I. C.*, Docum I; particular statutes may require it in the elections of religious and others.

of ticket which has led some writers to wonder how it is possible to prove, in the case of a majority of one vote, whether or not the decisive vote was cast by a disqualified voter.[54]

d. *The Position of the President and Tellers.*

The president and tellers should be stationed at a table in a conspicuous place where they can be seen but not heard. In order to collect the written votes the tellers may come down to the places of the voters. It is possible (as will be explained further on) to vote orally; in this case the voter should go up to the table of the tellers.

e. *Collecting the votes.*

Canon 171, § 2, enumerates five words or phrases describing the manner in which the tellers are to discharge their task of gathering the votes. This is to be done:

A) *secretly: "secreto"* here in canon 171, § 2, derives from the IV Council of the Lateran,[55] whereas *secretum* in canon 169, § 1, n. 2, derives from the Council of Trent.[56] The Council of Trent required that a vote be secret in such wise that the names of the voters would never be revealed. No one should know for whom the others voted. This secrecy was not required by the IV Lateran Council; in fact, the required comparison of votes made it necessary for the tellers to write down the name of the voter opposite his vote and it was generally quite evident for whom each one had voted.[57] The *"secrete"* of the IV Lateran Council (from which *secreto* derives) meant that the voter should be alone with the three tellers in a corner of the chapter room while he was manifesting his vote. The decretal election, then,

---

[54]Cf. Jaeger, *Administration of Vacant Dioceses*, p. 120, not. 47.

[55]C. 42, X, *de electione et electi potestate*, I, 6.

[56]Sess. XXV, *de regularibus*, c. 6.

[57]Cf., e. g., c. 50, X, *de electione et electi potestate*, I, 6.

was not strictly secret, nor was it written. The Council of Trent made the election secret for religious, but did not require a written vote.[58] The Code makes a secret vote obligatory on all canonical voters, but it does not go further than the Council of Trent by requiring a *written* vote (although canon 171, § 4, assumes that this is the normal thing). Even today a voter may communicate his vote orally to the tellers without violating the secrecy of the election, as long as the tellers never reveal for whom the individual voted. The Council of Trent expressly permitted nuns to vote orally and this right is nowhere denied in the Code.[59] The tellers, then, must obtain the votes "secretly" either: a) by being careful that the tickets are sealed and that no one sees for whom another voter votes, or b) by receiving an oral vote in such a place and in such a manner that the others cannot hear the vote, when it is communicated.

B) *diligently:* this word also derives from the IV Council of the Lateran and perhaps meant that the tellers should exhort the voter to elect one whom he deemed in conscience to be qualified.[60] Today it means that the action of the tellers should be performed "carefully," that is, in such wise that there is no cause for comment or complaint.

C) *individually:* During the collecting of the votes the tellers should take care to obviate the invalidity which results if more votes are cast than there are voters present.[61] They should see to it that the votes are cast singly and that each voter casts but one vote.

D) *observing the order of precedence:* this is certainly not essential, but it is proper that they gather first the vote of the president and then their own votes.

---

[58]Bachofen, *Compendium,* p. 196; Reiffenstuel, Lib. I, tit. 6, nn. 124, 331; Piat, *Praelectiones,* II, 8, not. 5.

[59]Conc. Trid., sess. XXV, *de regularibus,* c. 7; cf. Maroto, *Institutiones,* I, 758; Wernz-Vidal, *Ius Canonicum,* II, 272; Coronata, *Institutiones,* I, 266.

[60]Cf. Bachofen, *Compendium,* p. 197.

[61]Can. 171, § 3.

E) *obtaining the vote of each one:* in order to prevent fraudulent substitution of votes, each voter should deposit his own vote in the ballot urn. The votes should not be carelessly passed from one to the other and then handed in bulk to the tellers.

f. *Counting the votes.*

The tellers are to count the votes in the presence of the president in the manner determined by the constitutions and legitimate customs. The constitution of Pius X, *Vacante Sede,* Dec. 25, 1904, directs that the individual votes be mixed by shaking the chalice into which the Cardinals have deposited them, whereupon the junior teller counts these votes by conspicuously extracting each vote singly from the first chalice and depositing it in a second empty chalice.[62]

If the number of votes is greater than the number of voters there is no election-result. The entire ballot is simply not counted. If, for instance, a chapter is obliged to finish the election within three ballots and this excess of votes occurs in the third ballot, the voters are legally entitled to vote once more.[63]

The Code does not discuss the case where the number of votes is less than the number of voters. This is simply an indication that some voters have renounced their right to vote, and need not hinder the proceedings in any way. If the number of votes is found to correspond to the number of voters, the tellers proceed to the next step.

g. *Reading and Announcing the Votes.*

The reading and announcing of the votes are actions that are required for the validity of the form of scrutiny, although no particular method of doing these things is es-

[62]Nn. 70-71—*C. I. C.,* Docum. I.

[63]Can. 171 § 3.

sential. Probably the most satisfactory method is had in the following procedure. The president opens the individual votes before he hands them to the tellers. The first teller will read them one by one and mark down for whom the vote is cast. As he proceeds with this he will pass the individual votes to the second teller who will duplicate the action of the first. The president and the tellers will then compare notes and finally announce the result to the assembly. The reading and announcing need not be performed as distinct acts. The second teller, for instance, may read the vote aloud when he receives it from the first teller so that all may hear. Something similar to this is done in the papal election. The third teller receives the vote from the second and reads it aloud. All the assembled cardinals write down the vote on sheets of paper that have been specially prepared for them.[64] The custom of not announcing how many votes each candidate received should be suppressed as contrary to canon 171, § 2. Only very special circumstances permit the ordinary to tolerate centenary and immemorial customs which are contrary to the Code.[65]

h. *Determining the Election-Result.*

Canon 174.

Is electus habeatur et a collegii praeside proclametur, qui requisitum suffragiorum numerum retulerit, ad normam can. 101, § 1, n. 1.

Canon 101, § 1, n. 1.

Circa actus personarum moralium collegialium: 1°. Nisi aliud expresse iure communi aut particulari statutum fuerit, id vim iuris habet, quod,

---

[64]Pius X, const. *Vacante Sede,* Dec. 25, 1904, n. 72—*C. I. C.,* Docum. I.

[65]Can. 5; Goyeneche, "Consultationes", *CpR,* XI (1930), 353-355.

demptis suffragiis nullis, placuerit parti absolute maiori eorum qui suffragium ferunt, aut, post duo inefficacia scrutinia, parti relative maiori in tertio scrutinio; quod si suffragia aequalia fuerint, post tertium scrutinium praeses suo voto paritatem dirimat aut, si agatur de electionibus et praeses suo voto paritatem dirimere nolit, electus hebeatur senior ordine vel prima professione vel aetate.

From the reading and publication of the votes it will be evident to the chapter whether or not an election has taken place. Canon 174 says that this is determined according to canon 101, § 1, n. 1. A detailed discussion of this canon is beyond the scope of this dissertation but it will suffice to note here that in the first and second ballots, an absolute majority of votes is required, e. g., 8 out of 15, for a juridically valid election.

An *absolute majority* means more than half the votes. *Invalid votes* must be deducted. If, for instance, 2 out of 15 votes are invalid, these votes must be subtracted from the general total and then anyone receiving 7 out of 13 votes is elected. *Blank Tickets* are invalid votes and consequently must be deducted from the total.[66]

When no absolute majority has been obtained either in the first or second Ballot the *relative majority* will suffice in the third; thus, if out of 15 votes, 4 go to one candidate, 5 to another, and 6 to a third one, the 6 votes decide the election. Should it happen that there is no relative majority on the third ballot, if, for instance, 3 votes go to one candidate, 6 to another and 6 to a third, the president may decide by giving his vote to one of the candidates who have 6 votes apiece. But if the president does not wish to do so, then he is elected who is senior by ordination, profession, or age. These standards for determining seniority

---

[66]Goyeneche, "Schedulae Albae", *CpR*, XV (1934), 24-30; Chelodi, *Ius de Personis*, p. 99, not. 3; Ojetti, *Commentarium de Personis*, II, 134.

must be applied exactly in the order given in the Code. Thus, if the two candidates with six votes apiece are secular priests, then he is elected who is ordained the longer; if they were both ordained on the same day, he who is senior in physical age. If the two candidates are religious priests, the standard of years in the priesthood is applied first as above, then the years of profession, and finally the physical age. Canon 101 allows particular laws and customs to modify these rules. Thus, in the Capuchin Order the standard of years in the priesthood is not applied; a tie is decided solely on the basis of years of religious profession and years of physical age. "But if. . . the votes are equal, he shall be declared elected who is senior by his first profession; and if the candidates made their profession on the same day, he who is senior by age."[67]

Some authors[68] think that the local ordinary when presiding at the election of nuns can decide a tie on the third ballot by casting a vote. Canon 101, however, seems to presuppose that the president is a member of the chapter with the right to vote even outside of the cases wherein there is a tie. The canon speaks of the president breaking the tie with "his vote", but the local ordinary does not possess a vote in the election of nuns.[69] Against this argument, Michiels[70] declares that *suo voto* in canon 101 does not mean "his vote" but "his decision." Michiels finds that the Code, when speaking of the vote possessed by a member of the chapter, consistently uses the word, *suffragium;* therefore, by introducing a new term, *votum,* the legislator indicates that the president may give the final decision even if he is not a voting member of the chapter. The matter remains doubtful and since the local ordinary, before the Code, was

---

[67]*Constitutiones O. M. Cap.*, art. 135.

[68]Larraona, "Commentarium Codicis", *CpR*, VIII (1927), 22; Vermeersch-Creusen, *Epitome*, I, 323; Coronata, *Institutiones*, I, 640.

[69]Cf. Chelodi, *Ius de Personis*, p. 422, not. 4.

[70]*Principia Generalia de Personis*, p. 390.

forbidden to cast the decisive vote in the event of a tie,[71] it would seem that canon 101 should be interpreted in the light of the former law.[72] Therefore, a president may break a tie on the third ballot if he so wishes, provided he is a voting member of the chapter.

The *Normae* of 1901 regulating the election of superiors general[73] required an absolute majority even on the third ballot. If the third ballot was without an election-result, then the choice was left to the Sacred Congregation in all cases wherein the electoral body had been assembled in Europe. Outside of Europe a fourth ballot could be taken. In this ballot, however, only those two religious were eligible candidates who in the third ballot received the greater number of votes. If, in the fourth ballot, both received an equal number of votes, the older by profession was elected the general.[74]

Several religious constitutions are similar to the *Normae* in permitting a fourth ballot in the election of the superior general (and superior provincial), in which ballot those two alone are eligible who in the third ballot received the greater number of votes.[75]

Unless more than three ballots are expressly permitted, it is strictly required that an election be completed on the third ballot, no matter how scattered the votes or how small the relative majority may be. A curious case may arise when in an electoral proceeding a postulation concurs with an election as understood in its proper canonical sense, that is, when the votes are divided between a person who is ineligible in view of some impediment which however yields to the ready possibility of a dispensation and one or more

---

[71] Cf. Ferraris, *Bibliotheca*, v. "Abbatissa", n. 29-30, and the decisions of the Sacred Congregations there cited.

[72] Can. 6, n. 4.

[73] N. 232.

[74] N. 233-234.

[75] Cf., e. g., *Constitutiones O. F. M.*, n. 420; *Constitutiones O. M. Cap.*, art. 135.

persons who are canonically eligible for the office. Canon 180, § 1, requires that the ineligible candidate who is being postulated receive two thirds of the votes in this instance. Therefore P (the person postulated) must receive ten out of fifteen votes. If, on the third ballot, P receives only nine votes and E, the eligible candidate, receives six, who must be declared elected? The Pontifical Commission for Interpreting the Code[76] has answered that E, the eligible candidate, must be declared elected to the exclusion of the one postulated. Canon 101 hinders further balloting and thus P is ruled out by canon 180, § 1, because he has not obtained two thirds of the votes.

The same must be said if there is more than one eligible candidate concurring with the one postulated. If P receives nine, E receives four, and F (another eligible candidate) receives two votes, E is elected by a relative majority. Suppose, in the case just given, that E was also ineligible. In this instance F would be declared elected with only two out of fifteen votes. Suppose that in the third ballot P received nine votes and C and D (two eligible candidates) received three votes apiece. In this case the president could—if he so wished—break the tie between C and D, or he could allow the election to be decided on the basis of seniority, always to the exclusion of P, the candidate who was merely postulated.[77]

The general law of the Code demands an absolute majority for the election of bishops, of abbots and prelates *nullius* and of vicars capitular. Therefore, since none of these can be elected by a relative majority, the chapter is bound to continue balloting until an absolute majority is obtained.[78]

---

[76]July 1, 1922—*AAS*, XIV (1922), 406.

[77]Cf. [Vermeersch?], "Responsa 1 iulii 1922—Annotationes" *Periodica*, XI (1922), 129.

[78]Cans. 321; 329, § 3; 433, § 2; cf. Jaeger, *Administration of Vacant Dioceses*, p. 128; Cocchi, *Commentarium*, II, 341.

i. *Proclaiming the Election-Result.*

Canon 174 directs that after the chapter has completed an election, the president is formally to proclaim and declare that the person has been elected. This proclamation is now a mere relic of the *electio solemnis sive communis,* which was formerly an essential part of every canonical election. At present the omission of this formality would have no effect on the validity of the election.[79]

Certainly the president of the chapter will be excused from proclaiming the election if he himself has been elected. In other cases also it seems probable that a custom whereby the first teller or some other voter proclaims the election may be retained.[80]

The votes should be burned after each ballot or after each session if more than one ballot takes place in a session.[81]

After the election-result has been announced to the voters, it is usual that it be solemnly announced also to the non-voters who have an interest in the outcome of the election, just as the election of the Roman Pontiff is proclaimed to the populace assembled in St. Peter's Square.[82] Following this proclamation, reverence is paid to the newly elected official and the *Te Deum* or other prayers of thanksgiving are recited.

The acts of the election should be drawn up by the secretary. These acts should ordinarily contain mention of the authority whereby the election was held and should note when and in what manner the summons to the voters was issued. The document should list all voters present togeth-

---

[79]Goyeneche, "Consultationes", *CpR,* XVIII (1937), 20; cf. c. 55, X, *de electione et electi potestate,* I, 6; c. 21, *de electione et electi potestate,* I, 6, in VI.°

[80]Cf. Wernz-Vidal, *Ius Canonicum,* II, 273; Schäfer, *De Religiosis,* p. 221; see also Schmalzgrueber, Lib. I, tit. 6, n. 49.

[81]Can. 171, § 4.

[82]Pius X, const. *Vacante Sede,* Dec. 25, 1904, n. 89—*C. I. C.,* Docum. I.

er with their title to vote; the day and hour of each session; and the number of voters present at the respective session; the result of each ballot with mention of how many votes each candidate received; finally the result of the election and the acceptance of the office by the one chosen. The acts should be signed by all the voters, or at least by the president, the tellers and the secretary. The document should be filed in the archives of the chapter.[83]

B. *The Validity of Votes.*

The question of invalid elections and invalid votes will be considered under the chapter on "Invalid Elections." Here it will suffice to state positively what are the requirements for a valid vote and what is the principle for determining invalidity.

Canon 169

§ 1. Suffragium est nullum, nisi fuerit:

1°. Liberum; et ideo invalidum est suffragium, si elector metu gravi aut dolo, directe vel indirecte, adactus fuerit ad eligendam certam personam aut plures disiunctive;

2°. Secretum, certum, absolutum, determinatum.

§ 2. Conditiones ante electionem suffragio appositae tamquam non adiectae censentur.

a. Every vote must be *free,* since election is a choice and consequently implies the absence of constraint. However, not any sort of constraint renders a vote invalid, but only such as forces a person to vote for just this particular individual; or for one out of a restricted list of persons. In

[83]Can. 171, § 5.

accordance with this canon, one is not free if he is forced to vote for A. One is not free if he is forced to vote for either A or B and for no one else. Force which is directed to these ends, whether that force be induced by fear or deceit, whether it be effected directly or indirectly, invalidates the vote and if the vote is decisive, the force in turn invalidates the election. If one is *prevented* by force, fear, or deceit from voting for D, his vote may be invalid because he may be indirectly forced to vote for either A or B and for no one else, because there are no other eligible candidates. But if there are many other eligible candidates the inability to vote for D will not render his vote for A or B invalid. More will be said concerning freedom in the chapter on "Invalid Elections."

b. A vote must be *secret.* The *secretum* in this canon, as was noted above, derives from the Council of Trent.[84] The secrecy specified by the law demands that during the voting no one know for whom the elector casts his vote and that after the voting this will continue to be a secret, unless the voter himself chooses to reveal it. There are many violations of secrecy which are blameworthy; but the only violation of secrecy which invalidates the vote occurs when one manifests one's vote in the very act of the voting and that to the greater part of the chapter.[85] To show one's vote to one or the other voter even in the very act of voting is not a "manifestation" in a legal sense. The Code does not define "*secretum,*" but there seems to be no reason to give the term a stricter meaning than the word "*occultum*" is given in canon 2197, n. 4.[86] At times it may be imprudent to reveal one's vote even after the election or already to manifest one's intention before the election, but this conduct does not affect the validity of the vote.

---

[84] Sess. XXV, *de regularibus,* c. 6.

[85] Passerini, *De Electione Canonica,* XVII, 35; Schäfer, *De Religiosis,* p. 219-220.

[86] Cf. Ferraris, *Bibliotheca,* v. "Electio", IV, n. 31-32; Coronata, *Institutiones,* I, 267; Wernz-Vidal, *Ius Canonicum,* II, 270.

In some religious institutes[87] it is customary for the president of the chapter to ask each voter privately for whom he intends to vote and to make inquiries concerning the fitness of various candidates. This is called the *praescrutinium*. To conduct such an unofficial scrutiny or to hold a "straw vote" might be objectionable where such procedure is contrary to custom, but it would not violate secrecy to the extent of rendering the vote invalid.[88]

c. A Vote Must be *Certain, Absolute, and Determined.*

A vote must be so *certain* and unmistakable that the tellers can identify the person for whom the vote is cast. If, for instance, there are two Fathers John in the chapter, and a voter simply writes down "Father John" without further identifying the man, the vote is null, because his choice is uncertain. The tellers cannot simply conclude that the voters intended to vote for Fr. John Capistran who will probably be elected, rather than for Fr. John Berchmans whose chances for election merit little, if any, solid consideration.

A vote must be *absolute* and unconditional. Conditions are of two kinds, intrinsic and extrinsic. The intrinsic conditions merely express something that is implied in every canonical vote and hence are valid. Thus one may say: I vote for Fr. John provided he asks for confirmation within eight days, or, provided he accepts the election etc. These are intrinsic conditions; they are not invalid but they are usually quite meaningless.

The extrinsic condition makes the value of the vote depend on something extraneous to the vote itself. To say: "I vote for Fr. James, if he is a Doctor of Theology," places an extrinsic condition and renders the vote invalid. Note that these conditions are different from those mentioned in canon 169 § 2. The conditions implicitly adverted to in

---

[87]Cf., e. g., *Constitutiones O. F. M.*, n. 456.

[88]Goyeneche, "Consultationes", *CpR*, XVII (1936), 148-150.

paragraph one are such as are attached to the vote and are made in the very act of voting. The conditions considered in the second paragraph are such as are made before the election. The conditions stipulated in the act of the voting render the vote invalid. The conditions agreed to before the election do not nullify either the vote or the election, but are simply declared to be without value in themselves.

A vote must be *determined*. The I General Council of Lyons (1274) reprobated in its third canon all conditional, alternative, and uncertain votes.[89] The Code state the rule positively and thus "determined" is employed as the opposite of "alternative." Hence one cannot say: "I vote for Fr. James, provided he has at least 8 votes; otherwise, I vote for Fr. Thomas."

Canon 169, § 2, is directed against the abuse of electoral capitulations.[90] The capitulations often amounted to a full program of government which a bishop or religious superior was bound to carry out. When elections were held, all bound themselves by oath to uphold the capitulations if they were elected and on this condition the election was held. Such conditions are now entirely reprobated and, if made, their content is to be completely disregarded.

Biederlack-Führich raises the doubt as to whether an elected superior is bound to abide by capitulations which he has affirmed under oath.[91] Fanfani[92] answers that if these capitulations restrict his power he is not bound to observe them, but if they are for the good of the community, for instance, the case of a promise to be regular in attending the Divine Office, then he is bound to keep his oath. But in the light of the sources this answer seems to attach a value to such a capitulation which canon 169, § 2, expressly denies to it. Even agreements which are useful for monasteries and chapters, and not contrary to natural law, have been for-

---

[89]C. 2, *de electione et electi potestate*, I, 6, in VI.°

[90]See supra, p. 75.

[91]*De Religiosis*, ed. 1919, III, art. 1, (cited by Fanfani, *De Iure Religiosorum*, p. 108).

[92]*De Iure Religiosorum*, p. 108.

bidden in times past by the sacred canons and Apostolic constitutions.[93] On the other hand, no oath of any kind can give an added strength to an agreement which is illicit in its purpose and invalid in its form.[94] Even though a superior may be bound by some other claim to do the things which he promised before his election, no new obligation arises from this valueless electoral condition.

d. *Voting for Oneself is Invalid.*

Canon 170.

Suffragium sibimetipsi nemo valide dare potest.

To vote for oneself is an act of ambition which the law punishes by invalidating the vote. If an election to office takes place by a majority of more than one vote, it may perhaps never be discovered that an individual voted for himself. The offense is a serious moral transgression,[95] but the matter will have no juridical effect in the external forum. If, however, a person is elected by a margin of one vote and that vote is his own, the entire election is invalid. How can a chapter protect itself against this invalidity? Some constitutions, for example the Constitutions of the Dominican order, prescribe that if any of the voters is elected superior, a bare majority of votes does not suffice, but there must be at least one vote more than the bare majority. Thus, if anyone has voted for himself, his vote is indeed invalid, but, as he still retains a majority of the votes, his election would not be invalid.[96]

---

[93]Cf. Benedict XIV, const. "*Pastoralis*", June 15, 1754, § 4—*Fontes*, n. 430.

[94]Cf. c. 1, *de iureiurando*, II, 11, in VI°; canon 1318, § 1.

[95]Prümmer, "An Invalid Election and its Consequences", *Homiletic and Pastoral Review*, XXX (1929), 73.

[96]Prümmer, *ibid.*, p. 75; cf. Fanfani, *De Iure Religiosorum*, p. 108.

If the candidate elected in the papal election has a bare two-thirds majority, his ballot must be opened (in the manner described above) in order to make sure that he has not voted for himself. Religious institutes have similar prescriptions.[97]

If an institute has no way of preventing self-election, the individual so elected is morally bound to resign as soon as possible, although he is not obliged to defame himself. If he holds office in a clerical exempt religious institute he is exercising a strictly ecclesiastical office[98] and thereby his acts achieve validity in virtue of canon 209. His position, however, never becomes regularized.[99]

C. *The Form of Compromise*

Canon 172

§ 1. Electio nisi aliud iure caveatur, fieri etiam potest per compromissum, si nempe electores, unanimi et scripto consensu, in unum vel plures idoneos sive de gremio sive extraneos ius eligendi pro ea vice transferant, qui nomine omnium ex recepta facultate eligant.

§ 2. Si agatur de clericali collegio, compromissarii debent esse sacerdotes, secus electio est invalida.

§ 3. Compromissarii debent pro validitate electionis conditiones compromisso appositas, quae non sint contra ius commune, observare; si nullae conditiones additae fuerint, servandum ipsis est ius commune circa electiones; conditiones autem contra ius pro non appositis habeantur.

---

[97]Cf. *Ordinances of the General Chapters O. F. M. Cap.*, n. 168, § 2.

[98]Canons 501 § 1; 145, § 1.

[99]Cf. Prümmer, "An Invalid Election", Hom. and Past. Rev., XXX (1929), 74.

§ 4. Si ab electoribus in unam tantum compromissum fuerit personam, haec nequit seipsam eligere; si plures designati fuerint compromissarii, nemo ex iis proprio consensu potest accedere reliquis ipsum eligentibus ut electionem sui compleat.

Canon 173

Cessat compromissum et ius eligendi redit ad compromittentes:

1°. Revocatione a collegio facta, re integra;

2°. Non secuta aut non servata aliqua conditione compromisso apposita;

3°. Electione absoluta, si fuerit nulla.

a. *Definition of Compromise.*

An election takes place by compromise when the voters unanimously transfer their right of election to one or several persons, either members of the electoral college or strangers, who for this single instance elect in the name of all.[100]

b. *The Use of Compromise.*

The form of compromise may be employed by all voters who are not expressly forbidden by law to use this form. Before the Code it was generally held that religious were forbidden to use the form of compromise.[101] Now the general rule is that religious may proceed by way of compromise in their elections, unless their constitutions expressly forbid this. If the constitutions merely outline election in accordance with the canons of the Code without explicit

---

[100]Cf. can. 171, § 1.

[101]See *supra* p. 70.

reference to compromise, it would seem that compromise could be used. However, custom as set down in rituals and ceremonials has, in many cases, established a definite form of election which no authority inferior to the supreme legislative body in the institute is at liberty to change. Canon 507, § 1, implicitly orders the members of the institute to follow this established form without variation.

In order to use the form of compromise in a given election, all those who are entitled to vote in that election must give their unanimous and written consent. Fanfani requires that the voters first assemble as if for an election by scrutiny and only then may they unanimously agree to compromise.[102] Others [103] say that the voters may agree to a compromise and express their written consent by letter without the necessity of convocation. It would seem, however, that canons 162-163 apply to the form of compromise as well as to the form of scrutiny. Therefore, all must be summoned and the right to proceed by way of compromise belongs to those who are present on the day fixed in the summons. Canon 105, n. 2, also furnishes an analogy for requiring the presence of the assembled voters before instituting a compromise. This canon says that when a superior requires the advice or consent, not of one or the other person, but of several together, these persons must be legitimately called together.

Unanimous consent is required both for the resolution to proceed by way of compromise and for the selection of certain persons to carry out the compromise. Coronata[104] says that it is not necessary that the voters be unanimous concerning the persons of the *compromissarii;* it is enough if they are unanimous about proceeding by way of compromise. But this does not seem to be correct. The essen-

---

[102]*De Iure Religiosorum,* p. 105.

[103]Jaeger, *Administration of Vacant Dioceses,* p. 125-126; Coronata, *Institutiones,* I, 276; Maroto, *Institutiones,* I, 764.

[104]*Institutiones,* I, 277.

tial characteristic of compromise is the trust reposed in the *compromissarii* by those who commit their right to them. If the wording of canon 172, § 1, is not entirely clear, all doubt is dispelled by referring to the Constitution *Vacante Sede* of Pius X, December 25, 1904, where in number 55 it is clearly shown that *all* the cardinals must choose to proceed by way of compromise and all must unanimously choose the *compromissarii.* There may of course be previous discussion as to which persons will be chosen, but all must finally agree to entrust their right to the *compromissarii* selected. Maroto[105] says that it is not necessary that all unanimously agree on the circumstances and conditions attached to a compromise. It will be enough, he says, if the majority agree to these. The Code is not very detailed in considering this point, but in accordance with canon 20 reference to the Constitution, *Vacante Sede,* number 55, helps to explain canon 172, § 1. Hence, in the document containing the compromise all circumstances must be explicitly mentioned and to all these things the entire assembly of voters must agree. There can be previous discussion and voting on what conditions are to be attached to the compromise but anything that is finally placed upon the written document must be subscribed to by all, *nemine discrepante*

c. *The Compromissarii.*

The *compromissarii* may be: a) one or several; b) members of the chapter or outsiders. If the chapter is composed of clerics, it is necessary that the *compromissarii* be priests.

The persons chosen must be fit. Since compromise is a form of election the standards of fitness will be determined by applying the canons of this article, especially canon 167. It is advisable to choose an odd number of *compromissarii* in order to avoid a deadlock.

---

[105] *Institutiones,* I, 764.

d. *The action of the compromissarii.*

If no considerations are placed upon the action of the *compromissarii,* then they are bound to observe the common law on all points that do not specifically refer to another form of election, viz., scrutiny. They are not, therefore, obliged to appoint tellers. The voters may attach to their compromise any conditions that are not contrary to the common law. They may require, for instance, that the *compromissarii* consult certain persons, such as the metropolitan or the suffragan bishops. The conditions may also be suspensive as appears from canon 173, n. 2.[106] This means that they may, for instance, designate certain persons to choose the candidate "provided we do not arrive at an absolute majority before noon." If this condition is not realized, the *compromissarii* have no power.

The *compromissarii* may choose one of their own number but he may not vote for himself, nor agree to the choice of the others so as to make it unanimous. This is a further application of canon 170. Before the Code it was possible for a *compromissarius* to "accede" to the choice of the others if they selected him as their candidate. This is now forbidden.

e. *The Cessation of Compromise.*

The ordinary way in which a compromise ceases is through the valid and completed exercise of the power. As soon as the *compromissarii* have chosen a suitable person for the vacant office, their power ceases, and if they are to act again, they must receive a new mandate from the voters.

In canon 173 the Code enumerates three other ways in which a compromise may cease.

A) *by recall:* The chapter may revoke their consent to a compromise provided the *compromissarii* have not yet

---

[106] "Non secuta. . . aliqua conditione. . . "

begun to act. They are considered to have begun their deliberations the moment they begin to treat formally of the person to be elected. At least the majority of the chapter must desire the revocation of the compromise.[107]

B) *by non-fulfillment of condition:* whether through the fault of the *compromissarii* or not, if they fail to observe a condition, the compromise ceases. If, for instance, the condition was placed that the *compromissarii* select a member of the chapter, the compromise is nullified and the choice is invalid, if the *compromissarii* chose an outsider.

C) *by an invalid election:* If the *compromissarii* choose an unworthy person or render their choice null in some other way, then, no matter what the cause of this nullity, the compromise ends unless the voters renew it.

In all these cases the right of election does not under the present law devolve on the superior, but returns to the original electors, unless the time-limit has expired or unless the electors have approved the irregularities which rendered the election null. Canon 178 lists two cases in which the electors are deprived of their right and the appointment devolves on the superior: a) if the time-limit has expired; b) if the electors are deprived of their right as a punishment. If the *compromissarii* have incurred deprivation of active voice because of some irregularity in connection with the election (e. g., the election of an unworthy candidate), the voters do not lose their right to vote unless they have shared in the guilt in accordance with canon 2209, § 1-3.

D. *Limited Compromise.*

There is a special form of conditioned compromise known as "limited compromise" which was used by many religious in their elections before the Code.[108] In limited

---

[107]Fanfani, *De Iure Religiosorum*, p. 106; Coronata, *Institutiones*, I, 279.

[108]Piat, *Praelectiones*, II, 9.

compromise, as described by canonical writers,[109] the electors transfer to the *compromissarii* the power of electing on condition that they secretly investigate the votes of the chapter and then nominate and elect him whom they find to be the choice of the majority. The secret investigation of the votes of the chapter is carried out exactly according to the form of scrutiny but after the votes have been collected, counted, and read, one of the tellers acting in the role of *compromissarius* proclaims the election according to a form like the following:

> I, N. N. *compromissarius,* in my own name and in the name of my associate *compromissarii,* in virtue of the limited compromise granted to us, elect and declare elected the Reverend Father N. N., to whose election the majority of you have consented.[110]

Reiffenstuel[111] says that this form was followed because it was simpler, quicker, and subject to less invalidating formalities than simple scrutiny. The meaning of his words is clear from a glance at the legal development of the decretal *"Quia propter"* with reference to the form of scrutiny. Writing in 1254, Laurence of Somercote, declared that the form of scrutiny was subject to "infinite dangers." The reason for being on guard against these legal pitfalls was that the decretal *"Quia propter,"* after giving a rather detailed description of the form of scrutiny, added: "Aliter electio facta non valeat. . . ."[112] Hence, the canonists found that most of the procedure was necessary for validity. Laurence of Somercote enumerated six *substantialia* so necessary for an election that if any of them be passed

---

109Reiffenstuel, Lib. I, tit. 6, n. 72; Passerini, *De Electione Canonica*, XXII, 5; Piat, *Praelectiones*, II, 9; Maroto, *Institutiones*, I, 763.

110Cf. *Rituale Romano-Seraphicum,* Tit. IV, cap. I, n. 29; Reiffenstuel, Lib. I, tit. 6, n. 78.

111*Loc. cit.*

112C. 42, X, *de electione et electi potestate,* I, 6.

over, the election is rendered null by law.[113] By an ingenious process of subdivision later canonists multiplied these *substantialia* to eighteen.[114] It is not surprising, therefore, that canonists sought for a less "dangerous" method of election.

The canonists who worked out the form of limited compromise seem to have reasoned as follows: In the form of (absolute) compromise it is necessary only to commit the election to fit persons and their choice becomes unquestionably valid. The disadvantage in this is that the voters give up their own power of selection. If the advantage of scrutiny (the free choice of the majority) can be combined with the advantage of compromise (certainty of validity) the result will be ideal. True it is, that the decretal *"Quia propter"* outlaws any forms other than the three which it lists: acclamation, compromise, scrutiny, but is there anything illegal in combining two forms to produce a mixed form? They thought not. They followed the form of scrutiny in all things save that the office of teller and the charge of proclaiming the election was vested in *compromissarii.*

This form of election was subject to attack during the XIII century, but was declared valid by Boniface VIII.[115] Its use by religious was questioned after the Council of Trent, but canonists agreed that it might still be used.[116]

The use of this form after the Code may be defended on the basis of canon 172, § 3.[117] Since conditions may be attached to any compromise, it is valid and licit to draw up a compromise according to which the *compromissarii* shall be bound to proceed according to the form of scrutiny. If this explanation is followed, it would seem that the *com-*

---

[113]*Lincoln Cathedral Statutes*, II, cxxxvi; see *supra* p. 57.

[114]Cf. Ferraris, *Bibliotheca*, v. "Electio", I, 23.

[115]C. 29, *de electione et electi potestate*, I, 6, in VI°.

[116]Passerini, *De Electione Canonica*, I, 61; Reiffenstuel, Lib. I, tit. 6, n. 78; Piat, *Praelectiones*, II, 9.

[117]Cf. Goyeneche, "Consultationes", *CpR*, IV (1923), 47-51; Maroto, *Institutiones*, I, 763-764; Coronata, *Institutiones*, I, 280-281.

promissarii must be chosen unanimously, for that is the only form of compromise contained in the Code. Historically the *compromissarii* in limited compromise did not have to be chosen unanimously, but a majority vote was sufficient, since they were practically the same as tellers.[118]

Perhaps the better explanation of limited compromise at the present day is that the form is little more than a matter of ceremonial which derives from a time when limited compromise had juridical significance. Scrutiny is no longer subject to "infinite dangers" as it was in the XIII century; therefore, the necessity of resorting to a legal device to prevent invalidity no longer exists. Even when Reiffenstuel wrote at the end of the XVII century he was at pains to prove that limited compromise was slightly different from scrutiny.[119] Today the differences have all but completely vanished. The entire process of "limited compromise" is exactly like the form of scrutiny; the proclamation made by the teller in announcing the election in which he terms himself a *compromissarius* is today nothing more than a relic of canonical history.

---

[118]Passerini, *De Electione Canonica,* XXII, 20.
[119]Lib. I, tit. 6, n. 77.

CHAPTER ELEVEN

THE CONCLUSION OF THE ELECTION

Under the heading, "conclusion of the election," one might include many of the things which have been mentioned in the foregoing chapter, such as the proclamation of the election, the drawing up of the acts of the election, etc. As the term is used here, however, it refers to those acts which complete the choice of the voters by changing their simple "call" into a true ecclesiastical appointment. These acts are enumerated in canons 175-177. They include the notification of and acceptance by the candidate, the petition for confirmation, and the actual confirmation on the part of the superior. With reference to full-fledged canonical appointment the choice of the voters is something merely potential until it is rendered actual by the consent of the one elected and his eventual confirmation in office by the ecclesiastical authority. This actualization is the final stage in the process. It may be designated the conclusion of the election.

ARTICLE I. *Notifying the Person Elected*

A. *Notification in General*

Canon 175

Electio illico intimanda est electo, qui debet saltem intra octiduum utile a recepta intimatione

manifestare utrum electioni consentiat, an eidem renuntiet; secus omne ius ex electione quaesitum amittit.

After an election has taken place the one chosen must be notified immediately and within eight days he must decide whether or not to accept the office. If he does not manifest his consent within the time given he automatically loses all right to the office. That the voters notify the one elected without undue delay has been the law since the II Council of Lyons (1274).[1] Formerly canonists held that there was no undue delay if notice was given within eight days.[2] At first sight it might seem that this opinion could still be followed, since the law is substantially unchanged.[3] However, the legislator has shortened the time for acceptance from one month to eight days; and the time within which the one elected must seek confirmation has suffered a similar curtailment. The apparent intention of the legislator has been to accelerate the process of election.[4] Therefore in the light of its context[5] *"illico"* probably means a shorter period of time than the eight days allowed by authors before the code. The law is certainly fulfilled if notice is given within three days.

If the one elected is present at the voting, no formal notification need be given him. The obligation of sending the notification to an absent person rests with the entire electoral body, but in practice the president of the chapter will see that the duty is fulfilled by directing the secretary to send the notice.

Where constitutions forbid religious to refuse an election, their consent is not required and therefore they need

[1]C. 6, *de electione et electi potestate*, I, 6, in VI°. The wording of this canon is *"quam citius"*. There is scarcely more than a verbal difference between this phrase and the *"illico"* of canon 175.

[2]Reiffenstuel, Lib. I, tit. 6, n. 310-311.

[3]Canon 6, n. 2.

[4]Cf. canons 175 and 177, § 1.

[5]Canon 18.

not be formally notified about their election. Their consent is contained in their general will to do all that the institute requires of them. Hence, it is not contrary to the Code to omit the notification and to send the acts of election immediately to the superior whose confirmation is required.[6]

Whether the one elected is present or not in the chapter he is given eight days from the receipt of notification within which to consider whether to accept or refuse the election. The eight days are a period of time which does not elapse whenever the person is hindered from acting. The day on which notice is received is not counted. Therefore, if A receives notice of his election on March 4th, he can postpone his acceptance until midnight of March 12th. If impediments intervene the time will be lengthened by as many days as he was impeded. If a religious is elected to an office which he cannot accept without permission of his superior,[7] the count of eight days does not begin until he receives notice that permission has been granted. It is sufficient that the one elected forward the manifestation of his consent within eight days. It is not required that his formal acceptance reach the chapter within that time.

If the one elected is not hindered in any way and still neglects to forward the manifestation of his consent within eight days, then the law deprives him of all right which he has acquired by being elected. This "acquired right" cannot be the *ius ad rem* spoken of in canon 176, § 2, for that is not obtained until acceptance is made of the election. The right spoken of in canon 175, which is given by the mere fact of being elected might be called a hypothetical *ius ad rem* or a potential claim which acceptance makes actual. It is a right to exclude all others from any claim to the office and a right which prevents the chapter from holding another election, or the superior from making an appointment, at any time within the eight days given to the newly elected person for consideration.

---

[6]De Meester, *Compendium,* II, 292.

[7]Canon 626.

B. *Refusing an election.*

Canon 176

§ 1, Si electus renuntiaverit, omne ius ex electione quaesitum amittit, etsi renuntiationis eum postea poeniteat; sed rursus eligi potest; collegium autem intra mensem a cognita renuntiatione ad novam electionem procedere debet.

Canon 176 declares that if the one who was elected refuses the election, he loses all right to the election even though he later repents of his refusal. The right spoken of here is the same hypothetical *ius ad rem* that is mentioned in canon 175. But who are free to give up this right and refuse an election? Canon 184 declares that anyone is free to resign an office unless specially forbidden to do so. Hence *a fortiori* one may renounce an imperfect right to an office. Even one who has been elected Sovereign Pontiff may refuse to accept, but though the individual has the right to refuse, still a canonical election is a solemn call of the Church and it is usually a better act of humility to accept rather than to decline the office.[8]

It is classic doctrine that the constitutions of religious may limit their right to renounce elections.[9] This is not contrary to the Code. The Code does not say that everyone must have the right to decline; it merely gives directions about the effect of a refusal, if one can and does decline. Some religious constitutions forbid all refusals of office; others advise against refusal; others, still, limit renunciations by making their effect depend on the will of the chapter.

If the constitutions say nothing positive about the obligation to accept elections, the common law prevails and those elected are given eight days to decide whether to ac-

[8]Cf. Pius X, Const. "*Vacante Sede,*" Dec. 25, 1904, n. 86—*C. I. C.*, Docum. I.

[9]Passerini, *De Electione Canonica,* XX, 19.

cept or refuse. Religious are not excepted from this general law. But, if the constitutions are silent, can any superior compel a religious to accept? Charles Augustine says that no superior can compel acceptance, because the freedom to refuse office has not been taken away by profession.[10] Vermeersch,[11] however, says that in an institute of pontifical right the Holy See can command acceptance, and in a diocesan congregation the local ordinary can command a religious to take office. Augustine probably has in mind the principle that a religious superior in demanding obedience cannot exceed what is expressly or impliedly contained in the rule. However, it is implicitly contained in every rule that all are bound to work for the common good of the institute. Therefore, if the higher superiors of the institute (certainly the Holy See for a pontifical institute and the local ordinary for a diocesan institute,) deem it necessary for the common good that a certain individual take office, this could be commanded under obedience. The assembly of voters alone can never impose the obligation of accepting their election, unless this power is given by the rules of the institute. The constitutions of the Claretians allow the chapter to impose the obligation of accepting in virtue of the vow of obedience, provided a majority of the voters decide not to accept the candidate's refusal of election.[12] If a Capuchin Provincial-elect withholds his consent he cannot be compelled to accept by the Definitors alone, but he may be obliged to do so by the Minister General or by the assembled Provincial Chapter.[13] The Constitutions of the Friars Minor positively forbid the refusal of one's election. In the case of the Friars Minor and in similar cases in other institutes one who is elected must immediately accept. If a release is desired, recourse must be had to the superior capable of dispensing from the constitutions, namely, to the

---

[10]*A Commentary on Canon Law,* II, 144-145.

[11]*Periodica,* "De Electione Capitulari", XI (1923), (153).

[12]Pars I, n. 61, cited by Goyeneche, "Consultationes", *CpR* XVIII (1937), 162.

[13]*Ordinationes O. M. Cap.,* n. 198.

local ordinary in a diocesan institute and to the General Superiors or the Holy See in an institute of pontifical right.[14]

If the one elected refuses and intimates his refusal to the assembly, he loses all right to the election even though later he repents of his refusal. To have its effect the refusal must be conveyed to the assembly of voters and not merely expressed to one or the other isolated individual. A prudent distinction will also be made between the initial reluctance of a man which might be expressed in terms of refusal, and a considered act of renunciation.

Even though a refusal nullifies the entire election which preceded it, the chapter is not prevented from reelecting the same individual. This liberty makes it possible for the chapter to take advantage of a worthy person's change of mind. Even after he has refused the election he may yield to the urgings of those who judge him to be best fitted for the office, whereupon the chapter is still free to elect him.

After a refusal the assembly must proceed to a new election within a month from the time they learn of the refusal. It would seem that the chapter may take a month's time before holding a new election every time their choice is rendered inefficacious by a refusal, provided this delay and postponement is not brought about fraudulently. The legislator makes rules for ordinary circumstances and does not contemplate a series of refusals.

The month that is given must be regarded as continuous time, since useful or practicable time as a creation of law may not be presumed but must be expressly granted by the law. There is every reason why the law wishes the time between a refusal and a new election to be as short as is convenient. There is, however, a practicable space of time between the date of the refusal and the time when the chapter learns of the refusal. The count of the month does not start until the one charged with convoking the voters to an election receives notice of the refusal. The same prin-

[14]Cf. Oesterle, "Vier Faelle aus dem Ordensleben", *ThPrQS*, LXXXVIII (1935), 354-55.

ciple applies here as that which was discussed in connection with canon 161. It is not necessary that all the voters or even a majority of them know of the refusal before the count of the month begins. Questions of knowledge do not depend on majorities. Before a fact is said to be known in a locality it is not necessary that the majority of the people know it. Coronata speaks of a "collegiate knowledge" of the refusal being necessary,[15] but neither here nor in canon 161 is the assembly made the subject of this knowledge. The fact of the vacancy or refusal being known is expressed in both canons, in the passive grammatical voice.

C. *Accepting an Election.*

Canon 176

§ 2. Acceptatione electionis electus, si confirmatione non egeat, plenum ius statim obtinet; secus, non acquirit nisi ius ad rem.

§ 3. Ante acceptam confirmationem ipsi praetextu electionis non licet sese immiscere administrationi officii sive in spiritualibus sive in temporalibus, et actus ab eo forte positi nulli sunt.

Canon 175 directs that the one elected should *manifest* his consent within eight days. It therefore seems more in conformity with the law and with the practice at papal elections[16] that the acceptance be express and not merely tacit. However, the acceptance of the one elected is sufficiently evident if he does not decline the election, but receives the homage of the voters, takes the prescribed oaths, petitions for confirmation and otherwise reveals his consent.

The acceptance of the election-result closes the process of the election as far as the assembly of voters is concerned,

---

[15] *Institutiones*, I, 284, n. 9.

[16] Pius X, const. *Vacante Sede*, Dec. 25, 1904, n. 87.

but it is not always the final stage in a complete canonical election. A completed election, like every other canonical appointment, involves two things: 1) designation of the person; 2) bestowal of the ecclesiastical office. The voters can designate the person, but lacking the power to confer jurisdiction higher than they themselves possess they cannot bestow office. The actual conferral of office must therefore take place in one of two ways: either a) the choice is *confirmed* by a higher superior, or b) the *law* itself attaches ratification to the mere acceptance of the one elected.

If the mere act of acceptance ratifies the election, then the one elected immediately upon his acceptance of his election enjoys the *ius in re* or full rights of office. If, however, confirmation is required, then the candidate has only a *ius ad rem* upon a similar acceptance of his election. This means that he has a claim to be confirmed and given title by the higher superior, but until this is done he lacks all rights of office. In fact, the office is still vacant.

If by an act of acceptance one has acquired full rights of office there is usually nothing further required for the exercise of his office. But in some cases further procedure is necessary. Thus, confirmation is not required for the election of a vicar capitular. He obtains full rights by acceptance, but before exercising jurisdiction he must make the prescribed profession of faith.[17] In most religious institutes the election of the superior general requires no confirmation. One who has been elected but who still requires confirmation has no true rights of office and consequently can perform no official acts. If he attempts to act in either the spiritual or the temporal affairs of his office the acts placed by him are null and without effect.

The canon, it is to be noted, forbids the one elected from meddling in the affairs of his office *on pretext of his election.* He may, therefore, continue to act in virtue of a previously acquired title. A vicar capitular who is elected bishop may continue to administer the diocese, not indeed as bishop-

---

[17]Canon 438.

elect but unquestionably as vicar capitular. However, if someone other than the bishop-elect was acting as vicar and then died before confirmation for the bishop-elect was received, it would be contrary to canon 434, § 1, to choose the bishop-elect as vicar capitular. Passerini taught that an administrator if elected to a vacant office must immediately resign his post and await confirmation.[18] This is certainly not required by the Code.[18a]

The constitutions of religious institutes variously regulate the conduct of an elected nominee between his election and confirmation. The constitutions of the Friars Minor declare that a provincial-elect has no authority whatever until confirmed, but he is normally confirmed immediately by the delegate of the Minister General who has presided at the chapter.[19] The constitutions of the Capuchins declare that a provincial-elect may exercise his office as the commissary or delegate of the Minister General until confirmation is received from the General.[20] The President of the Pontifical Commission for interpreting the Code declared that this arrangement was not contrary to canon 176, § 3,[21]

---

[18] *De Electione Canonica*, XXXIII, 4.

[18a] Cfr. canon 334, § 2.

[19] *Constitutiones*, n. 413.

[20] Art. 149.

[21] "Rev. mo Procuratori Generali Ord. Min. Capuccinorum,

Dubio a P. T. Rev. ma proposita, nempe: 'An Constitutionum Ord. Min. Capuccinorum dispositio, qua Ministris Provincialibus noviter electis officium exercere permittitur ante confirmationem, sit certo et absolute iure communi in Codice statuto contraria, ita ut abrogata haberi debeat.'

Infrascriptus Emus. Commissionis Praeses respondet:

Negative, quatenus Minister Provincialis agit tanquam Commissarius R. mi P. Ministri Generalis.

Quae dum P. T. Rev. mae significo, cuncta fausta a Deo adprecor.

Romae, 15 augusti 1918.

P. Card. GASPARRI,

Praeses Comm.

Aloisius Sincero, Sec."—*Analecta O. M. Cap*, XXXIV (1918), 153.

inasmuch as the provincial-elect acted as the commissary of the Minister General, and not (the implication of the decision seems to be) on pretext of the election.

ARTICLE II. *Confirmation of the Election.*

Canon 177

§ 1. Electus si electio confirmatione indigeat, saltem intra octiduum a die acceptatae electionis confirmationem a competente Superiore petere per se vel per alium debet; secus omni iure privatur, nisi probaverit se a petenda confirmatione iusto impedimento fuisse detentum.

§ 2. Superior, si electum repererit idoneum, et electio ad normam iuris fuerit peracta, nequit confirmationem denegare.

§ 3. Confirmatio in scriptis dari debet.

§ 4. Recepta confirmatione, electus obtinet plenum ius in officio, nisi aliud in iure caveatur.

If confirmation is required the one elected must present his petition to the confirming superior within eight days of his acceptance. This is usually done by forwarding the acts of the election to the superior in order that he may judge both the process of the election and the merits of the candidate. The person elected may make this petition personally, since he is merely prosecuting a right given him by the election. For doing so he cannot be accused of any ambition. The chapter, however, may also present the petition, offering it in his name and adding commendatory letters.

Formerly the one elected was given one month within which to request confirmation. This period of time has been reduced by the Code to eight days and this latter period of abbreviated time is per se to be reckoned as continuous time, but admits of some extension if the existence of an impediment can be proved. The meaning of the law is that the one elected should immediately take steps to secure confirmation. If his petition is not sent within eight days he has the burden of proving that he was justly impeded. After the lapse of eight days during which one could have applied for confirmation but did not do so all right to the office is lost.

A. *The Competent Superior.*

Normally the superior who confirms the election is the immediate higher superior. That is, the elections of local priors are confirmed by provincials; the provincials-elect are confirmed by the Superiors General. The confirming powers of metropolitans have long since disappeared and bishops-elect are always confirmed by the Roman Pontiff.

A distinction must be carefully made between the authority to declare and the authority to confirm an election. The local ordinary who presides at the election of the superioress general of an institute of pontifical right can declare the election, but he has no real authority over the outcome. Unless the constitutions provide otherwise, the election is completely ratified by the mere consent of the one elected. If the process has been legal the local ordinary can do no more than declare that the individual chosen has received sufficient votes and is elected. If he has grave doubts about the wisdom of the choice he must have recourse to the Holy See. Likewise, the presiding officer at the election of an abbess in a monastery of nuns[22] may announce the outcome of the election, but has no power to confirm or rescind the action of the chapter. But, at the election of the superioress general in a diocesan congregation the local ordinary presides with full power to confirm or rescind the election. This right applies only to the election

[22]Cf. canon 506, § 2: local ordinary, regular superior or the delegate of either.

of the highest superior of a diocesan congregation. If such an institute is divided into provinces the local ordinary has no right to confirm the elections of provincial superioresses, unless this right is given him by the constitutions.

The local ordinary referred to throughout this paragraph is not the ordinary of the principal house or motherhouse, but the ordinary of the place where the election is actually held.[23]

The power to confirm the act of an ecclesiastical election can be made the object of a power delegated to others. Therefore the delegate of a superior general at an election in a pontifical religious institute[24] as well as the delegate of the local ordinary at an election in a diocesan congregation[25] may exercise the power of confirming or rescinding the election.

B. *The Judgment in the Act of Confirmation.*

Canon 177, § 2 directs: If the superior finds that the person elected is qualified for the office and that the election has taken place according to law, he cannot refuse his confirmation. This general rule also governs the action of the local ordinary (or his delegate) in confirming or rescinding the election of the superioress general of a diocesan institute. The law on this point in canon 506, § 4, says that the local ordinary will confirm or abate the election of the superioress "as his conscience dictates," but in judging the election his prudence and discretion are limited solely to the person elected. She may not be the most qualified, nor may she be the *most worthy*, but if in conscience the ordinary judges her to be *really worthy* he cannot refuse his confirmation, provided always that the act of the election proceeded in accordance with the requirements of the law.

---

[23]*Pont. Comm. Interp.*, July 2, 1921,—*AAS* XIII (1921), 481.
[24]Cf. Constitutiones O. F. M., n. 413.
[25]Can. 506, § 4.

Therefore, all superiors with the power to confirm an election must act, not at their personal pleasure, but as their conscience dictates concerning the merits of the candidate before them. This means that they must confirm the election if its procedure was conducted according to law and if the one elected can be designated simply as worthy.

There is a difference between the obligation of the voters and the obligation of the confirming superior. The voters are always bound and, in institutes of men, must also swear to elect the most worthy person, but the confirming superior must approve of any candidate who is found simply to be worthy. The voters must seek out good qualities in a comparative and superlative degree, the confirming superior must be satisfied to find good qualities in a positive degree. The reason for this flows from the nature of an election. It is a process in which the law allows a group other than the superior to select an office-holder. If the superior's judgment concerning the more worthy person were always permitted to over-rule the corporate judgment of the voters, the very purpose and inherent idea of election would be frustrated. Moreover, by law, and therefore by the will of the Church, a duly conducted election gives to a worthy person upon his act of accepting the election a strict claim in justice *(ius ad rem)* which no superior is permitted to disregard.

The superiors in the Dominican Order seem to have a wider power of annulling elections than that given by the common law. They may reject the one elected whenever this is deemed "expedient for the general good of the Order." This phrase may be equivalent to the *"pro conscientiae officio"* of the common law, but it seems to allow a wider discretion to the confirming superior and was therefore specifically permitted to remain in force after the Code by a rescript of Pope Benedict XV.[26]

---

[26]Feb. 11, 1920—*Analecta O. P.*, XIV (1920), 3 (cited by Fanfani, *De Iure Religiosorum*, p. 124.)

Since the one elected, once he has notified the acceptance of his election, has a strict claim in justice, it follows also that the confirmation should not be long delayed. No set time is fixed by the Code within which confirmation must be given, but if the delay is protracted the candidate may have recourse to the next higher superior, who will either see that confirmation is given or give the confirmation himself.[27]

The act of confirmation should always be drawn up in writing, though this form is not necessary for validity. Wernz[28] distinguishes between a confirmation *in forma specifica,* which corrects and supplies for any defects which may have taken place in the election or which may be present in the candidate, and a confirmation *in forma communi,* which merely ratifies the election without adding any new value thereto. An approval which would supply for all defects implies a series of hypothetical dispensations from the common law which only the Holy See could give.

When confirmation has been received the one elected obtains full rights of office unless the law prescribes otherwise. This means that he acquires the exercise of jurisdiction without the necessity of taking corporal possession of his office,[29] unless the law prescribes this as it does for bishops and pastors,[30] or unless the law prescribes some other formalities.

---

[27]De Meester, *Compendium,* II, 293.
[28]*Ius Decretalium,* II, n. 385.
[29]Barbosa, Lib. I, tit. 6, c. 15.
[30]Canons 334, 461.

CHAPTER TWELVE

Invalid Elections And Other Electoral Defects

Mention of the outstanding delinquencies which may be committed in connection with the holding of ecclesiastical elections together with the respective penalties automatically attached or canonically attachable to them is contained in canons 2390-2394. The principal topics there treated furnish headings under which other defects not amounting to canonical delinquencies may be conveniently grouped.

ARTICLE I. *Violation of Liberty*

Canon 2390, § 1

Libertatem electionum ecclesiasticarum quovis modo per se vel per alios impedientes, vel electores aut electum, peracta canonica electione, propter eam quoquo modo gravantes, pro modo culpae puniantur.

The manner in which liberty can be violated is indicated in canon 169, § 1, n. 1, which states that a vote is invalid if a voter is directly or indirectly coerced by grave fear or fraud to vote for a certain individual or to choose one out of a restricted list of individuals.

A. *Violence:* Irresistible physical violence destroys the very notion of free choice and therefore a vote, like any other juridical act performed under violence, is entirely invalid.[1]

B. *Grave Fear:* This kind of fear can be termed a moral violence. According to the natural law acts performed out of grave fear are voluntary, even though the party would not have performed them if he were not afraid. The positive law of the Church declares that acts performed under the influence of grave fear are valid but voidable, unless the law declares otherwise.[2]

Canon 169, § 1, n. 1, is one of the instances where the positive law states that an act performed out of such fear is null and void. In order that a vote be invalid:

The fear must be grave: Slight fear does not affect the validity of the election, nor does so called reverential fear.[3] The fear must be such as to terrify a strong man, though the application of this standard will admit of a certain amount of relativity. The evil feared must be something of serious import; the fear must arise not from purely internal and subjective causes, but from an extrinsic cause, and the evil must certainly or at least probably threaten at the time of the election. Canon 169 does not say that the fear must be caused unjustly. Before the Code some taught that a superior might justly threaten an elector with a grave evil in order to have him vote for a worthy candidate.[4] The law, however, provides other means for securing a good election and hence it may be said that all employment of fear in connection with an election is unjust and unlawful, regardless of the good purpose it may be deemed to serve.

The fear must directly or indirectly aim at extorting a vote. The Code does not say, as it does in canon 1087, § 1, *a quo ut quis se liberet eligere cogatur,* but apparently the

---

[1]Can. 103, § 1.

[2]Can. 103, § 2.

[3]Piat, *Praelectiones*, II, 56; Passerini, *De Electione Canonica*, IV, 27.

[4]Cf., e. g., Passerini, *De Electione Canonica*, IV, 3.

same result is achieved by the use of the term *indirecte.* In other words, with regard to marriage, it is quite agreed that fear invalidates the act, if the marriage is chosen as a necessary means of avoiding the fear, even though the extrinsic cause of the fear did not aim at forcing matrimony.[5] But, with regard to voting the canon says one must be induced by fear *ad eligendam* and, at first sight, it might appear that the one causing the fear must aim at extorting a vote. The use of *indirecte,* however, invalidates the vote of one who thinks that voting for a certain person is a necessary means for overcoming a grave fear, even though the one causing the fear did not intend to extort a vote.

This is not the exclusive effect of the term *indirecte.* A vote is also invalid if the grave evil is threatened, not to the person of the voter, but to his relatives or close friends, who will suffer unless a vote is given to a certain individual.[6]

One must be forced to vote *for a determined individual or for one out of a restricted list.* It is clear that if one is forced to vote for a determined individual the liberty of election is taken away, but before the Code it was disputed whether the liberty of election was destroyed if one were forced to vote for one of several determined individuals. Practically all canonists admitted that this was illicit and furnished grounds for at least voiding the election,[7] but some maintained that the election in itself was not invalid.[8] The Code has settled this dispute in favor of those who maintained the invalidity of the election.

It is to be noted that invalidity does not arise if one is forced by law to vote for one of several individuals who are

---

[5]Cf. Cappello, *De Sacramentis,* III, 690.

[6]Cf. Chelodi, *Ius de Personis,* p. 239, note 2; Cappello, *Summa,* I, 352-353.

[7]A decision of the Sacred Congregation of the council, May 27, 1627, (*Fontes,* n. 2441), declared that it was unlawful *(non licere)* for a regular superior to propose two or three names from which one was to be elected.

[8]Cf. Schmalzgrueber, Lib. I, tit. 6, n. 66.

determined by qualities defined in law, e. g., if one is bound to vote for a doctor of theology or of Canon Law, or for a member of the chapter. Circumstances may bring it about that one is limited to a choice between one or two individuals. But this does not affect the validity of the election.[9]

At times grave fear may invalidate the vote if one is *prevented* by threats from voting for a certain individual. Ordinarily, this fear would leave a man free to choose between the other eligible persons, but in some cases the exclusion of one candidate would restrict the choice sufficiently to render the vote invalid. In other words, by excluding one or more candidates, one *indirectly* forces a voter to choose an individual from a restricted list.

C. *Fraud and Deceit.* These agencies produce the same effects as grave fear. The term used by the Code is *dolus* and includes all guile, deceit, or plotting employed to circumvent, ensnare, or deceive another. What has been said concerning fear applies in like manner to fraud. The deceit must tend either directly or indirectly to cause a person to give his vote to a certain individual or to one of several determined individuals and to no one else. The law contemplates, in the first place, an active and positive fraud which results in a vote being given to a certain individual. But it is possible for a vote to be rendered invalid if the fraud is exercised negatively. It may happen, for instance, that the list of truly eligible candidates is very small; if the voters are induced by fraud to withhold their votes from certain individuals they are *indirectly* coerced into giving their votes to one determined person or to one person out of a very limited group.

Both fear and fraud will invalidate a vote, but they do not invalidate an election, unless their effect touches more than half of the chapter, or unless the deciding vote or votes were cast under the influence of fraud or grave fear.

Canon 2390 prescribes that those who interfere with the freedom of ecclesiastical elections in any way what-

[9] Cf. Maroto, *Institutiones*, I, 782.

ever, either by themselves or through others, should be punished according to the gravity of their fault; the form of punishment is not determined by the Code. Those also are to be punished who, after the completion of the election, in any way molest the one elected or also the voters because of the result of the election.

D. *Subornation.* As used by canonists in Latin works, "subornation" is taken to mean any act by which one endeavors to persuade or induce others to do or to omit something either for a good or for an evil end.[10]

The canonists, therefore, distinguish between *subornatio bona* and *subornatio mala.* As applied to elections the terms mean the effort to procure votes either for a good or for an evil end. Before the code the principal law on the subject of procuring votes was the Constitution *"Nullus Omnino"* of Clement VIII, July 25, 1599, which stated in § 22:

> Caveant omnes a directa vel indirecta votorum seu suffragiorum procuratione tam pro seipsis quam pro aliis, tum in Capitulis locorum, tum in caeteris, praesertim generalibus Capitulis aut Congregationibus.[11]

Since this law is repeated almost verbatim in canon 507, § 2, the interpretation given to it by the classic authors is of the greatest value today.[12]

Some canonists considered that the constitution of Clement VIII forbade every type of subornation, whether good or evil, and also prohibited all preliminary discussions before elections. In argument they asserted that the Council of Trent had commanded that elections be secret, but he who persuaded another to cast his vote in favor of

---

[10]Cf. Passerini, *De Electione Canonica,* V, 44; Maroto, *Institutiones,* I, 44. In English usage "to suborn" means to incite or instigate to an evil act, especially a criminal act.

[11]*Bullarium Romanum,* X, 665.

[12]Cf. Can. 6, n. 2.

a certain person thereby revealed for whom he himself intended to vote. Furthermore, they said, the constitution of Clement VIII, spoke in general terms and therefore was to be understood in the most general manner; finally, disadvantages were sure to arise from any type of subornation.

Most of these arguments carry little weight. One who reveals his vote beforehand does not violate the secrecy of the election, as was explained earlier. Secondly, some form of honest discussion may often be required by natural law before a person can make a reasonable choice. And, surely, the positive law cannot eliminate what is necessary. Moreover, the purpose of the law was to check ambition and eliminate an evil; hence, the provisions of the law must be judged in the light of this purpose. As to the disadvantages arising from wholesome persuasion or honest discussion, these are accidental and the law rarely aims at abolishing exceptional and accidental inconveniences.[13] The procuring of votes must be judged according to: a) the intention which actuates the one who procures the votes; b) the means employed; c) the object, namely, the person whose election is desired. If all three elements are good, the persuasion is good. If any of them is evil, the person procuring the votes is guilty of *mala subornatio*.[14]

The one procuring the votes must intend to benefit the Church and not to seek his own advantage. The person whose election is desired must be the person best qualified for the office. Regularly it is considered ambitious and frequently also criminal to seek a vote for oneself.

In virtue of the constitution of Clement VIII (and therefore also in virtue of canon 507, § 2, which repeats it) the voters are not forbidden to discuss among themselves the qualities of the candidates and, with due regard for justice and charity, to take counsel concerning their defects and faults as well as their qualifications and capability. Furthermore, it is lawful for religious as well as for seculars

---

[13]Passerini, *De Electione Canonica*, V, 44-45.

[14]Cf. Piat, *Praelectiones*, II, 52.

to endeavor by a prudent employment of good reasons and honest motives to induce others not to elect an unworthy or a less worthy person, but to persuade them to elect a worthy rather than an unworthy candidate or a more worthy person rather than one less worthy.[15]

Authors since the Code speak less clearly on this subject than those who wrote before the Code. Schäfer, for instance, says that all subornation even for a good purpose is forbidden to religious by canon 507, § 2.[16] Coronata, likewise, admits nothing more than simple inquiry and truthful answers concerning the merits of the various candidates.[17] Others hesitantly allow positive advice and a measure of persuasion, provided one is asked to give such advice.[18]

Maroto follows the best opinion obtaining before the Code and states that it is lawful even to promote the election of one who is qualified, as long as the end, means, and circumstances are good.[19] Therefore, preliminary discussions both in public and in private, the proposal of better qualified candidates, the prudent corroboration of one's proposals with sound reasons and honest motives, all these acts are licit. Threats, fraud and falsehood, mutual agreements and pacts, undue interposition of the authority of superiors, over-urgent pleading, these constitute illicit procuring of votes. If pushed far enough they may violate the liberty of election and render a vote invalid. If charity, justice and

---

[15]Passerini, *De Electione Canonica,* V, 48-49; Rodericus, *Quaestiones Regulares,* II, q. 56, art. 1; De Peyrinis, *Subditus et Praelatus,* q. I, c. 31, § 2; Piat, *Praelectiones,* II, 52.

[16]*De Religiosis,* p. 219; in the next paragraph, however, he cites Prümmer *(Manuale Iuris Canonici,* p. 244, q. 185) as saying that an effort to procure votes for a better qualified candidate is not illicit, provided it be done with a right intention and by licit means, during the preliminary discussions.

[17]*Institutiones,* I, 638.

[18]Cf. Chelodi, *Ius de Personis,* p. 421; Fanfani, *De Iure Religiosorum,* p. 109.

[19]*Institutiones,* I, 784.

individual liberty are carefully safeguarded, anything like an organized "campaign" will be quite impossible.

E. *Exclusion of Lawful Voters:* Extreme violation of liberty in elections exists when an election is held without the knowledge of certain voters. If it is possible to summon a voter and the chapter or its president slights him when issuing the letters of convocation, the election is valid. But this one voter can have the election nullified even after confirmation, provided he seeks redress of his rights within three days after learning of the election.[20] If more than a third of the lawful voters are excluded in this way, the entire election is invalid.[21] The Code says nothing about the rights of those voters who have indeed been summoned to the election, but who are unjustly expelled from the electoral assembly or are forcibly prevented from entering the chapter room. It would seem that an analogy exists between their rights and those of the voters who are not summoned. Hence, on the basis of canon 20, it may be said that if any single voter is unjustly expelled or is otherwise prevented from voting by the president or by a majority of the chapter, this voter may have the election nullified. If more than a third of the lawful voters are so treated, the entire election is automatically invalid.[22]

ARTICLE II. *Outside Interference*

Canon 2390, § 2

Quod si electioni a collegio clericorum vel religiosorum peragendae, laici vel saecularis potestas sese illegitime, contra libertatem canonicam, immiscere praesumpserint, electores qui hanc immixtionem sollicitaverint vel sponte admiserint,

[20]Can. 162, § 2.

[21]Can. 162, § 3.

[22]Cf. Maroto, *Institutiones*, I, 735.

> **ipso facto privati sunt pro ea vice iure eligendi; qui vero suae electioni taliter factae scienter consenserit, fit ad officium vel beneficium, de quo agitur, ipso facto inhabilis.**

A. *Lay Interference.* If secular persons or the civil power attend an ecclesiastical election on the pretext of lending protection, if they demand that their consent be asked before holding the election, if they exercise a power of veto, or if they actually cast a vote in the election, then the entire election is invalid, provided these acts have some effect[23] and eventuate in something more than just frustrated attempts.

If these acts are no more than attempts and do not influence any of the voters, they can be simply ignored; but if the actions of the lay person have an effect on even a small number of the voters, the election is invalid. The law favors ecclesiastical liberty and is to be given a broad interpretation.[24]

Once the lay interference has been removed, the chapter may proceed to a new election. If, however, any of the voters have asked for the secular interference or have willingly admitted it, canon 2390, § 2, declares that they are automatically deprived of the right to vote for that instance, and if the candidate has knowingly *(scienter)* consented to his election under these circumstances he is rendered ineligible to the particular office concerning which the interference was entertained.

If some of the voters have resisted the lay interference, these are not deprived of their vote and they alone may hold the new election. If the entire chapter has willingly admitted the intervention, the appointment devolves upon the next higher superior.[25] This will be the superior with

---

[23]Cf. can. 166 and see *supra* p. 121.

[24]Cf. Laymann, *Quaestiones de electione praelatorum*, q. 20 (cited by Pirhing, Lib. I, tit. 6, n. 18).

[25]Can. 178.

power to confirm the election or, if the election was one which required no confirmation, the superior who has power to remove the incumbent from office. The chapter or the single voters are deprived of active voice for this one instance only. Therefore, the next time the office becomes vacant all have the right to vote as usual.

B. *The Intervention of Outsiders.* Even clerics and religious who are not members of the chapter may not be admitted to a vote. If the chapter admits a person who lacks active voice, the entire election is invalid.[26]

C. *The Participation of Disqualified Voters.* A member of the chapter who has been deprived of his active voice may not participate in the election. Those so disqualified are listed in canon 167, § 1. If any of those mentioned are admitted to vote, the single vote is invalid, but the election itself is valid except in two instances: 1) if the invalid vote was decisive; 2) if an excommunicated person, after declaratory or condemnatory sentence has been passed, is knowingly admitted to vote.

If a voter has apostatized and joined a non-Catholic sect he loses his active voice.[27] If after being disqualified he is admitted to vote by a chapter composed of eleven members (the apostate included), the mere fact of his admission does not invalidate the election. If, however, A is elected by a vote of 6 to 5, and the apostate's vote was cast for A, then A's election is invalid. A similar result will follow if several disqualified persons are admitted. If, in the case given, three apostates had cast votes, one voting for A and two for B, then A is elected by a vote of 5 to 3. Canon 167, § 2, is simply an application of canon 101, § 1, n. 1, *demptis suffragiis nullis;* the invalid votes must be subtracted.

If an excommunicated person who has been censured through condemnatory or declaratory sentence is knowingly admitted to the chapter, the election is invalid. This result

[26]Can. 165, See *supra* p. 115-120.

[27]Can. 167, § 1, n. 4.

applies to the excommunicated person only. If one who has been suspended or interdicted is admitted to vote, even after sentence, the mere fact of his admission to vote does not render the election invalid.[28] The election is invalid only if the decisive vote is cast by the person under sentence of suspension or interdict.[29]

ARTICLE III. *The Election of an Unworthy Person*

Canon 2391, § 1

> **Collegium quod indignum scienter elegerit, ipso facto privatur pro ea vice iure ad novam electionem procedendi.**

An electoral college which knowingly chooses an unworthy person *(indignus)* commits a canonical offense. It is rather difficult to determine the precise meaning of *indignus* in this canon.[30] The concept is similar to the more definite expression, "*publice indigni*" of canon 855, § 1. An unworthy person is certainly not the same as an unqualified *(inidoneus)*.[31] A person who is unqualified labors under an impediment from which the Church can, and often does, dispense. Such a person cannot be elected but may be postulated.[32] Every unworthy person is also unqualified, but not every unqualified person is unworthy. A particular note of moral deficiency attaches to the term, "unworthy."

---

[28]Wernz-Vidal, therefore, seem to be incorrect in saying that the *admission* of one under censure or infamy of law, after sentence, invalidates the election.—*Ius Canonicum,* II, 274.

[29]Cf. can. 167, § 2.

[30]Mörsdorf (*Die Rechtssprache des Codex Iuris Canonici,* p. 35) cites the employment of the term, "*indignus*" in canon 2391, § 1, as an instance of the many "juristisch unbestimmte Ausdrücke" used in the Code.

[31]Cf. Coronata, *Institutiones,* IV, 640.

[32]Can. 179, § 1.

It includes not only those who are legally infamous or who are laboring under censure, but also notorious apostates, heretics and schismatics as well as public sinners and persons whose conduct is sinful and scandalous.[33]

If the chapter *knowingly* elects an unworthy person, the choice must be rejected by the confirming superior and the voters are made incapable of proceeding to a new election. The effect of the word, "knowingly," in the canon is to require that the voters act with full knowledge and deliberation before they incur the penalty; any lessening of imputability absolves them from the automatic deprivation of vote.[34] However, in normal cases it is presumed that the chapter made its choice with full deliberation and knowledge, because it is their duty to investigate the qualities of the person whom they elect. Unlike the penalty in § 2 of canon 2391, which affects the individual voters, this penalty affects the chapter. If the majority elect someone who is unworthy, all the voters (even those who are innocent) are deprived of the right to vote in this instance. The appointment of a worthy official devolves upon the next highest superior, but when the office becomes vacant once more, the voters may vote as usual.

Not only is every chapter bound to avoid making a bad choice, but all are bound (and chapters of men are bound under oath) to elect the best candidate available.[35] The penalty of this canon, however, is inflicted only when the choice is positively bad.

Is the election of an unworthy person void from the beginning? It seems that it is. The law says that the chapter is deprived of the right to proceed to "a new election." In making this disposition the legislator seems to suppose that the original choice of the unworthy person was null and void. Moreover, since a person who is laboring under an impediment which yields to dispensation cannot be elect-

---

[33]Cf. cans. 855, § 1; 1942, § 2; Mörsdorf, *op. cit.*, p. 35.

[34]Cf. can. 2229, § 2.

[35]Can. 506, § 1.

ed validly, but must be postulated, *a fortiori* an election is invalid if the person is affected by an impediment which will not yield to dispensation.[36]

ARTICLE IV. *Neglect of the Substantial Form of an Election*

Canon 2391, § 2.

Singuli vero electores qui substantialem electionis formam scienter non servaverint, possunt pro gravitate culpae ab Ordinario puniri.

This canon indicates that there is such a thing as the substantial form of an election, but it does not specifically state what that form is. The substantial form, in general, are those things which constitute the essence of a juridical act and those solemnities which the sacred canons require under pain of nullity.[37]

At the head of the article on elections, canon 160 directs that the norms of the canons to follow be observed in all elections, but such a general direction does not make the entire procedure necessary for validity. Only those laws are invalidating which expressly or equivalently state that the action is void or that the person is juridically devoid of the requisite capacity.[38] In other places when the Code desires to establish the substantial form of an act, as in matrimony, for instance, the things necessary for validity are carefully enumerated.[39] Therefore, it might seem that only those things constitute the substantial form of an election which are followed by an invalidating clause as, for instance,

---

[36]Cf. can. 179, § 1.

[37]Cf. can. 1680, § 1; Passerini, *De Electione Canonica,* IX, 44; Chelodi, *Ius Poenale,* p. 139.

[38]Can. 11.

[39]Cf. can. 1094 ss.

in canon 165: *secus electio est ipso facto nulla.* But, to adopt this interpretation would give a new meaning to the term "substantial form" as applied to elections. Moreover, distinct and special penalties are imposed for the violation of certain substantial conditions, for instance, for the abuse of secular power,[40] for the election of an unworthy person,[41] and for simony.[42] Hence, canon 2391, § 2, must apply to something else.

In the former law the form of an election meant the procedure described in the decretal *"Quia Propter."*[43] It meant the methods of scrutiny, compromise, and acclamation. There was no doubt that these forms were substantial, because the decretal said: "Aliter electio facta non valeat." Although the forms of scrutiny and compromise are listed in the new law, no invalidating clause is attached to these forms as such. But here in canon 2391, § 2, mention is made of the substantial form of an election. If the term is understood in the light of the former law, then the observance of the two forms listed in canons 171 and 172 is equivalently declared to be necessary for the validity of an election.[44]

It still remains rather difficult to establish which elements in these two forms must be observed for validity. Under the old law every step in the process was carefully indicated and canonists could accurately list the *substantialia.*[45] For determing what is essential in the present law, the criteria offered by Maroto are probably the best avail-

---

[40]Can. 2390.

[41]Can. 2391, § 1.

[42]Can. 2395.

[43]C. 42, X, *de electione et electi potestate,* I, 6. After establishing scrutiny, compromise, and acclamation in place of the *diversas electionum formas* practiced up till then, the decretal says "Qui vero contra praescriptas formas eligere attentaverint, eligendi ea vice potestate priventur." Cf. Passerini, *De Electione Canonica,* IX, 1; 44.

[44]Can. 11.

[45]Cf. Ferraris, *Bibliotheca,* v. "Electio", I, 23; Laurence of Somercote, *Tractatus de Electione—Lincoln Cathedral Statutes,* II, cxxxvi.

able: a) a solemnity to which an invalidating clause is attached is certainly substantial and essential; b) those solemnities or formalities must be reckoned as essential without which the forms of scrutiny and compromise cease to exist.[46]

A. *Substantial Form of Scrutiny*

Applying the foregoing criteria to the form of scrutiny, the following points must be regarded as essential: a. That there be scrutineers or tellers, for that is of the essence of scrutiny; b. That there be at least two tellers (or, as a bare minimum, one with the president), for, since the votes are cast secretly, the testimony of two witnesses is required to create full proof; c. That the votes be cast by means of some intervention of the tellers; d. That the tellers publish the result in some way.

These four points are simply the unfolding of the bare essentials of scrutiny, *viz.* (a) tellers (b) must intervene in the election. The teller is a witness, therefore at least two are required for full proof. The tellers must intervene, at least by carefully watching the casting of the votes. At the end of the voting the tellers must give their testimony by declaring the final result, at least the bare statement: A has been elected.

By the application of the same criteria the following are not essential for scrutiny: a. That the tellers be selected by secret votes; b. That they take an oath; c. That the votes be cast carefully, singly, and with due observance of the order of precedence; d. That the result of the voting be published in a certain determined way, or that announcement be made as to how many votes each candidate received; e. That the votes be burned.

---

[46]Cf. can. 1680, § 1; see also Maroto, *Institutiones*, I, 788.

B. *Substantial Form of Compromise*

In compromise these three points are essential: a. That the voters consent to the compromise unanimously; b. That at least the greater number of the *compromissarii* have none of the impediments mentioned in canon 167, and that they be priests if the chapter is composed of clerics; c. That the *compromissarii* observe the conditions attached to the compromise.

The unanimous consent required for the bestowal of a compromise is a deduction from canon 101, § 1, n. 1: *Quod omnes uti singulos tangit ab omnibus probari debet*. All are singly surrendering an individual right to vote, therefore all must individually agree to the surrender. Compromise is a form of election, therefore fitness for compromise must be reckoned according to the norms of canon 167. The requirement that the *compromissarii* be priests if the chapter is clerical is required for validity by canon 172, § 2. Canon 173, n. 2 makes it substantial that the *compromissarii* observe the conditions attached to the compromise.

For a valid compromise it is not essential: a. That the compromise be drawn up in writing; b. That all the *compromissarii* be qualified according to canon 167. It is necessary that the deciding vote or votes be given by qualified persons and if an excommunicated person is admitted after sentence to act as a *compromissarius,* the compromise fails.

The neglect of the substantial form of election has two effects: a. The election is invalid and the one chosen acquires no right whatever; b. If the voters have *knowingly* violated the form, they are to be punished by their ordinary; the form of punishment is not determined. Ignorance of the canon law of elections absolves the voters from punishment.[47]

---

[47]Can. 2229, § 2.

ARTICLE V. *Simony*

Canon 2392

Firmo praescripto can. 729, delictum perpetrantes simoniae in quibuslibet officiis, beneficiis aut dignitatibus ecclesiasticis:

1. Incurrunt in excommunicationem latae sententiae Sedi Apostolicae simpliciter reservatam;

2. Ipso facto privati in perpetuum manent iure eligendi, praesentandi, nominandi, si quod habent;

3. Si clerici sint, praeterea suspendantur.

Simony in general[48] is the deliberate design to buy or sell for a temporal price such things as are spiritual, or temporal things so annexed to spiritual things that the temporal objects cannot exist apart from the spiritual.[49]

The essence canonically of the crime of simony lies in the pact between two parties. By nature the crime requires an accomplice. Purely mental simony committed by one party alone is a sin, but canonically regarded it is not a crime.[50]

The simoniacal *pact* may be either: a) *real,* when either the price or the object of the sacrilegious sale has been transferred and the contract has been executed by at least one of the parties; b) *conventional,* when the agreement has not yet been carried out, though it was made either expressly, or tacitly, that is, under circumstances such as to reveal the simoniacal design. Both types of pacts constitute the crime of simony.[51] To prove the censure in the external forum, it must be established that the bribe or price was offered and accepted, or at least an illicit contract was

---

[48]Can. 727.

[49]Cf. Ayrinhac, *Penal Legislation,* p. 360; Ryder, *Simony,* p. 53; Chelodi, *Ius Poenale,* p. 124; Piat, *Praelectiones,* II, 46.

[50]Can. 2195, § 1.

[51]Can. 728; Chelodi, *Ius Poenale,* p. 140; Ryder, *Simony,* p. 128.

made. Where the agreement is only implicit, there is necessary a transfer of the object of the contract by at least one of the parties, otherwise, the simoniacal intention would not be manifested.

The *price* involved may be either: a) *munus a manu,* namely, money or something which can be reckoned in terms of money, for instance, the cancellation of a debt; b) *Munus a lingua,* which comprises oral commendation, public expression of approval, moral support in high places; c) *Munus ab obsequio,* which involves service of any kind either actual or habitual, not due by reason of mutual obligation, but rendered with a view to obtaining a spiritual favor.[52]

The *object of the crime of simony* in elections is a benefice, a dignity, or an office in the strict sense.[53] The proximate object is the *vote.* Simony may creep into all the acts that are necessary for the reception of an ecclesiastical office or benefice, and all who take part in these acts may commit the crime.[54]

The *effect* of simony is, first of all, to render the election invalid. This is the force of the clause in canon 2392, *firmo praescripto* can. 729, for the canon in question declares that the simoniacal provision is devoid of all effect, even though a third party commits the simony without the knowledge of the one elected; in this latter case, however, if the simony was committed fraudulently with the intent to nullify the election of an innocent party, or if the candidate has knowledge of the simony and rejects it, the election is valid.[55]

The *penalties* of simony are as follows: a. an excommunication simply reserved to the Holy See is incurred *ipso facto;* b. the guilty voters are *ipso facto* perpetually de-

---

[52]Ryder, *Simony,* p. 58-61; Passerini, *De Electione Canonica,* VII, 82; Coronata, *Institutiones,* II, 8.

[53]Can. 145, § 2.

[54]Chelodi, *Ius Poenale,*? p. 141; Passerini, *De Electione Canonica,* VII, 24.

[55]Can. 729.

prived of the right to vote; c. if the voters are clerics they are to be suspended. The first two penalties are incurred automatically; the third must be inflicted by the ordinary.[56]

Particular instances of how the crime of simony may be committed in connection with elections:

a. If a price (as explained above) is given in order to obtain a vote for oneself or for another, even when the price is given by a disinterested party who would simply like to see D elected.

b. If, in order to obtain a vote, one promises a prelacy, for instance the office of Guardian.

c. If a price is given in order to divert votes away from another candidate.

d. If one voter agrees to vote for another in this election, provided that other votes for him in a subsequent election.

The foregoing acts of simony would have an effect upon the validity of the election. A further case may be stated which would not affect the validity of the election but would be an instance in which the crime of simony is committed in connection with an election. The case is this: If a price is given in order that someone surrender his right to contest the election, for instance, if one enters this simoniacal pact with someone who has not been summoned to the election.[57]

Having considered simoniacal votes and the effect of a simoniacal election, one may raise a final question as to how many simoniacal votes are required to render an election simoniacal and invalid? Certainly, if the greater part of the voters commit simony, the election is invalid. Likewise, if only a few voters commit simony, but with the connivance of the others, the election is simoniacal. If the one elected has committed simony in purchasing even one vote,

---

[56]Ryder, *Simony*, p. 127-131; Chelodi, *Ius Poenale*, p. 140-141; Cappello, *De Censuris*, p. 310-315; Coronata, *Institutiones*, IV, 642-644.

[57]Cf. Piat, *Praelectiones*, II, 47; Passerini, *De Electione Canonica*, VII, 82-129; Maroto, *Institutiones*, I, 784-785; Coronata, *Institutiones*, I, 273-274.

the election is invalid if the vote was decisive. Since a simoniacal vote is an invalid vote,[58] it can never decide an election.

There are two further possibilities: a) if simony is committed by a third party without the knowledge or against the will of the one elected, the election is valid if the majority of the votes were uninfluenced by simony; b) if the one elected entered simoniacal contracts with a number of the voters, but was elected by a substantial majority of the voters, who were uninfluenced by simony, then the election, according to Passerini, is valid from a processual point of view, but the act should be voided because of the unworthiness of the one chosen.[59] It was noted above, however, that the election of an unworthy person is void from the beginning.[60] Therefore, it must be said that the election is valid from the point of view of canon 729, but void on account of the election of an unworthy person.

ARTICLE VI. *Disregard of Legitimate Authority in Elections.*

Canon 2393

Omnes qui iure eligendi, praesentandi, vel nomiandi legitime fruuntur, si, neglecta auctoritate illius cui confirmatio vel institutio competit, officium, beneficium aut dignitatem ecclesiasticam conferre praesumpserint, suo iure pro ea vice ipso facto privati manent.

Canon 2394

Qui beneficium, officium vel dignitatem ecclesiasticam propria auctoritate occupaverit vel, ad ea

---

[58]Can. 2392, n. 2.

[59]"Electio cassanda . . . non ex defectu electionis, sed ex defectu electi."—Passerint, *De Electione Canonica,* VII, 338. See also *op. cit.,* VII, 335-340.

[60]*Supra* p. 222.

electus, praesentatus, nominatus in eorundem possessionem vel regimen seu administrationem sese ingesserit, antequam necessarias litteras confirmationis vel institutionis acceperit easque illis ostenderit, quibus de iure debet:

1. Sit ipso iure ad eadem inhabilis et praeterea ab Ordinario pro gravitate culpae puniatur;

2. Per suspensionem, privationem beneficii, officii, dignitatis antea obtentae et, si res ferat, per depositionem, cogatur a beneficii, officii, dignitatis occupatione eorumque regimine vel administratione statim, monitione praemissa, recedere;

3. Capitula vero, conventus aliique omnes ad quos spectat, huiusmodi electos, praesentatos vel nominatos ante litterarum exhibitionem admittentes, ipso facto a iure eligendi, nominandi vel praesentandi suspensi maneant ad beneplacitum Sedis Apostolicae.

As was noted in the very first chapter of this study, no office can be validly obtained in the Church unless it is duly granted by competent ecclesiastical authority.[61] Posts of jurisdiction and power in the Church cannot be seized by force nor obtained by usurpation. Even though a group of electors enjoys the right to designate the person who is to receive office, the actual bestowal of the office belongs to the legitimate Church authority. Therefore canon 2393 makes it a punishable offense if a group of voters, who have only the right of designating the person of the office-holder, should neglect the authority of the superior and *presume* to confer the office without waiting for the requisite confirmation. The punishment is deprivation of the right to vote for that single instance incurred *ipso facto*. Since the law uses the word, "presume," anything which tends to diminish

---

[61] Can. 147.

the culpability of the guilty parties will also free them from the punishment.[62]

If one attempts to take office on his own authority or if, having been elected, he spurns the authority of the confirming superior by meddling in the affairs of his office before receiving letters of confirmation, he renders himself ineligible for the office in question and should receive further punishment from the ordinary. These penalties are incurred even in the presence of factors which diminish culpability.

One who takes office on his own authority commits the more serious fault, but one who, in violation of canon 176, § 3, administers his office before confirmation, also disregards the principle that authority in the Church cannot be seized but must be duly conferred. Therefore, canon 2394 punishes both offenders. Chapters, monasteries and all others who abet the usurpers by admitting them without requiring letters of confirmation remain automatically deprived of the right to vote at the pleasure of the Holy See.

In order to force the intruder to relinquish his unlawful administration, canon 2393, n. 2, authorizes the ordinary to inflict, after due admonition, suspension, privation of benefices or offices previously obtained and, if necessary, even deposition.[63]

ARTICLE VII. *Summary of the Causes of Invalid Elections and of Other Electoral Defects.*

As a conclusion to the consideration of invalid elections and of other defects not amounting to invalidity, a brief summary may help towards clarity.

---

[62]Cf. can. 2229, § 2; see also Chelodi, *Ius Poenale*, p. 140; Ayrinhac, *Penal Legislation*, p. 362; Pistocchi, *I Canoni Penali*, p. 334; Salucci, *Il Diritto Penale*, p. 359.

[63]Cf. Pistocchi, *I Canoni Penali*, p. 336-339; Chelodi, *Ius Poenale*, p. 142-3.

A. *Invalid Votes.*

In the first place, one must carefully distinguish invalid elections from invalid votes. The following single votes are invalid, but the election is not invalid, unless these votes determine the result:

a. A vote sent by letter or cast by proxy, unless particular law provides for the valid use of such a method.[64]

b. The excess votes of one who attempts to cast more than one vote in his own name, by reason of several titles to vote.[65]

c. The votes of those enumerated in canon 167, § 1, saving the fact that the wilful admission of a person excommunicated through declaratory or condemnatory sentence nullifies the election.

d. Votes which lack the qualities enumerated in canon 169, § 1, namely, votes that are not free, secret, certain, absolute, and determined.

e. A vote cast for oneself.[66]

B. *Voidable Elections.*

a. An election is valid but voidable if one of the voters who had a right to be summoned was slighted. If the voter can prove his right and can establish the fact that he had recourse to the competent superior within three days of hearing about the election, the superior must nullify the election.[67]

b. Despite force, fraud and illicit procuring of votes, an election will still be valid, if the required majority of votes was cast freely. Nevertheless, it would seem that the competent superior could void such an election at the instance of an injured party, by analogy namely with can. 162, §§ 2, 3. Since the Code strictly safeguards the right of a voter to

[64]Can. 163.
[65]Can. 164.
[66]Can. 170.
[67]Can. 162, § 2.

be physically present at the chapter, it would seem that *a fortiori* his moral presence, namely his ability to vote freely and without constraint, should receive the same protection.

C. *Invalid Elections.*

An election is invalid:

a. If the time-limit for the holding of the election has expired.[68]

b. If less than two thirds of the lawful voters are summoned.[69]

c. If an outsider is admitted to vote.[70]

d. If a secular person votes or otherwise interferes in the elections of clerics or religious.[71]

e. If the decisive individual vote is invalid.[72]

f. If an excommunicated person after declaratory or condemnatory sentence is knowingly admitted to vote.[73]

g. If the substantial form of scrutiny or compromise is not observed.[74]

h. If in any decisive ballot of the assembly more votes are cast than there are voters present.[75]

i. If the election was simoniacal.[76]

D. *Elections Subsequently Invalidated by Law.*

Certain elections may be validly performed, but because of some subsequent defect the law invalidates the election-result. The cases follow:

---

[68]Can. 161.
[69]Can. 162, § 3.
[70]Can. 165.
[71]Can. 166.
[72]Can. 167, § 2.
[73]Can. 167, § 2.
[74]Cf. can. 2391, § 2.
[75]Can. 171, § 3.
[76]Can. 729.

a. If the one elected does not give and notify his consent within eight days of being apprised of his election.[77]

b. If, after giving and notifying his consent, the one elected does not apply for confirmation within eight days.[78]

c. If, before confirmation, the one chosen meddles in the affairs of his office.[79]

ARTICLE VIII. *Devolution of Appointment*

Canon 178

> **Si electio intra praescriptum tempus peracta non fuerit, aut collegium iure eligendi privetur in poenam, libera officii provisio ad eum Superiorem devolvitur, a quo confirmanda esset electio vel cui ius providendi successive competit.**

Ordinarily a chapter which has performed an invalid election can correct the error by proceeding to a new election. In two cases, however, the chapter loses the right to hold a new election and the right of appointment devolves upon the next higher superior.[80] The two cases are mentioned in canon 178: a. If the time-limit set for the completion of a valid election has expired; b. if the chapter has been deprived of the right to vote as a punishment. In all other cases the chapter may rectify its own mistake, by holding a new election.

---

[77]Can. 175.

[78]Can. 177, § 1.

[79]Can. 2394, n. 1.

[80]If the president of the chapter is a voting member and has participated in the invalid election, he will rarely have power to correct the defect. If, however, the presiding officer is truly superior to the chapter (e. g. the local ordinary who presides at an election of nuns) the appointment may devolve upon him in accordance with the norms now to be set forth.

The question of the time-limit within which an election must be held has been fully discussed when considering canon 162. Canon 178 merely repeats the provision already contained in the earlier canon.

The punishment of deprivation of vote is incurred in the following cases:

a. If the voters request or submit to the lay interference forbidden by canon 166. In this instance canon 2390, § 2, says that the "voters" are deprived of the right to proceed to a new election. Therefore, if the majority of the chapter did not consent to the lay interference, the chapter as such is not affected by this punishment.

b. If the individual voters neglect the substantial form of scrutiny or compromise, they are to be punished in accordance with the gravity of their fault.[81] If the chapter as a whole is guilty of this crime, the next higher superior is at liberty to punish them by forbidding them to hold a new election. In this instance the new appointment would devolve upon the higher superior. If certain individuals alone are guilty, then these alone should be punished by the higher superior and the others may proceed to a new election.

c. If the chapter knowingly elects an unworthy person, the entire chapter loses the right to hold a new election. In this instance no distinction is made between the guilty and the innocent; all alike are deprived of the right to hold a new election.[82]

d. If the entire chapter is guilty of simony, then the election will devolve upon the higher superior since the voters are incapable of proceeding to a new election.[83] If some of the voters were innocent, then this innocent minority may proceed to correct the invalid election.

Upon which superiors, in particular, does the appointment devolve? The Code says: upon the superior with whom the right of confirmation rests. Therefore, it is

---

[81]Can. 2391, § 2.

[82]Can. 2391, § 1.

[83]Can. 2392, n. 2.

clear that the local ordinary in whose diocese the election is held has the right to appoint, in accordance with canon 178, the superioress general of a diocesan congregation of women and the officials of lay confraternities.[84] When no confirming superior is designated, it becomes a little more difficult to determine upon which superior the right of appointment devolves. No confirming superior is designated in reference to the election of a vicar capitular, but canon 432, § 2, expressly says that the appointment devolves upon the metropolitan or, if the metropolitan see is in question, upon the senior suffragan of the province, whenever the election of the vicar capitular has not and may not any longer take place in accordance with the law.

It would seem that the local ordinary may appoint the superior general of a diocesan congregation of men, since they are immediately subject to his jurisdiction. It would be anomalous to have recourse in this instance to the Sacred Congregation for Religious. Nuns are said to be subject to the local ordinary or to a regular superior, but the present law does not say that the bishop or regular superior confirms the election as it was stated in the law before the Code.[85]

The law has been changed in this respect. Therefore, unless special law makes other provision, it would seem that the appointment of an abbess or prioress, like the appointment of the Superioress General of a pontifical congregation, devolves upon the Sacred Congregation for Religious, and not upon the local ordinary or the regular superior.

The appointment of the Supreme Moderator in all institutes of pontifical right devolves upon the Sacred Congregation for Religious. Within the institute the appointment of local superiors devolves upon the provincial, and the appointment of provincial superiors devolves upon the highest superiors in accord with the respective constitutions.[86]

---

[84]Can. 506, § 4; 715, § 1.

[85]Cf. Bachofen, *Compendium*, p. 213.

[86]Cf. Larraona, "De Electionibus Religiosorum", *CpR*, VIII (1927), 294.

Provided the legal time-limit has not yet expired and provided no deprivation of vote has been incurred or inflicted, the chapter may rectify an invalid election by simply proceeding to a new election. Therefore, if an election is invalid because, for instance, less than two-thirds of the voters were summoned, this invalidity will ordinarily be corrected by having the chapter proceed to a new election after a valid suummons has been issued to all. The higher superiors, however, may be invested with discretionary powers which will enable them in instances of this sort to prohibit an election even when the common law does not prescribe devolution of appointment.

CONCLUSIONS

The conclusions derived from the foregoing study as listed here are either findings on points not previously considered by canonists since the Code or are the results of a more thorough investigation than that given by the general commentators.

1. Canonical election as described in canons 160-178 is not found before the development of the cathedral chapter in the twelfth century.

2. In the article on elections in the Code, the clause "*nisi aliud iure caveatur*" and other similar phrases refer not only to laws of the Apostolic See but also to laws legitimately promulgated by inferior legislators either before or after the Code.

3. "*Omnes de collegio*" in canon 162, § 1 has not the same meaning as "*omnes qui volunt et debent et possunt commode interesse*" in the pre-Code law.

4. The meaning of the term "*extraneus*" must be interpreted in the light of the former legislation and its classic interpretation.

5. Contrary to the opinion of some recent canonists, "*carentes*" in canon 167, § 1, n. 5, has an exclusively penal meaning.

6. No repetition but a clear distinction is shown to exist between "*secretum*" in canon 169, § 1, n. 2, and "*secreto*" in canon 171, § 2.

7. The local ordinary in the elections of nuns and Sisters may not cast the deciding vote in the event of a tie.

8. The local ordinary (or his delegate) always appoints the tellers in the elections of nuns, even when the regular superior is present.

9. Not only the decision to proceed by way of compromise but also the choice of the several *compromissarii* must be the result of a unanimous decision of the assembled voters.

10. Limited compromise today has lost its juridical significance and has little more than a ceremonial value.

BIBLIOGRAPHY

Sources

Acta Apostolicas Sedis, Commentarium Officiale, Romae, 1909-

Acta Ordinis Minorum, Romae, 1882-

Acta Sanctorum Bollandiana, 54 vols. Antverpiae, 1643-1853.

Bullarium Ordinis Fratrum Minorum Capucinorum, ed. a Michaele a Tugio in Helvetia, 7 vols., Romae, 1740-1752.

Bullarium Romanum, 24 vols. Augustae Taurinorum, 1857-1872.

Canones et Decreta Concilii Tridentini, Taurini: Marietti, 1913.

Codex Iuris Canonici, Pii X Pontificis Maximi iussu digestus, Benedicti Papae XV auctoritate promulgatus, Romae, 1918.

Codicis Iuris Canonici Fontes cura Emi Petri Card. Gasparri editi, 8 vols. Romae [later, Civitate Vaticana]: Typis Polyglottis Vaticanis, 1923-1938. (Vols. VII-VIII ed. *cura et studio Emi. Justiniani Card. Seredi.*)

Constitutiones Fratrum Minorum Capuccinorum, Romae: Typis Polyglottis Vaticanis, 1926.

Constitutiones Generales Fratrum Minorum, Ad Claras Aquas (Quaracchi): Collegium S. Bonaventurae, 1922.

Corpus Iuris Canonici, editio Lipsiensis post Iusti Henningii Boehmeri curas . . . denuo edidit Aemilius Ludovicus Richter, 2 vols., Lipsiae, 1839.

Corpus Iuris Civilis, Vol. III, *Novellae Constitutiones*—R. Schoell; opus Schoell morte interceptum absolvit G. Kroll, Berolini, 1928-1929.

Decreta Authentica Congregationis Sacrorum Rituum, 6 vols., Romae, 1898-1927.

Harduin, Jean, *Acta Conciliorum et Epistolae Decretales ac Constitutiones Summorum Pontificum,* 12 vols., Parisiis, 1715.

Holstenii Codex Regularum Monasticarum et Canonicarum, ed. Marianus Brockie, 6 tomi in 3 vols., Augustae Vindobonorum, 1759.

Mansi, J. D. *Sacrorum Conciliorum Nova et Amplissima Collectio,* 53 vols., Paris, Arnheim, Leipzig, 1901-1927.

Migne, P. J. *Patorologiae Cursus Completus—Series Latina,* 221 vols., Parisiis, 1844-1855; *Series Graeca,* 161 vols., Parisiis, 1857-1866.

Monasticon Anglicanum, William Dugdale, ed. Calley Ellis and Bandinel, 6 vols. in 8, London, 1817-1830.

Monumenta ad Constitutiones Ordinis Fratrum Minorum Capuccinorum, ed. Venantius a Lisle en Rigault, Romae, 1916.

Monumenta Ecclesiae Liturgica, ed. Ferdinand Cabrol and Henri Leclercq, 4 vols., Paris, 1900-1913.

Monumenta Germaniae Historica, Legum Sectio II, Capitularia Regum Francorum, Tom. I, Ed. A. Boretius, Hannoverae, 1883.

Monumenta Germaniae Historica, Legum Sectio III, Concilia Aevi Karolini, Tom. II, pars II, Ed. A. Werminghoff, Hannoverae, 1908.

Monumenta Germaniae Historica, Auctores Antiquissimi, Tom. IV, pars II, *Venantii Honorii Clementiani Fortunati presbyteri Italici opera pedestria*, Ed. Bruno Krusch, Hannoverae, 1886.

Monumenta Germaniae Historica, Scriptores Rerum Merovingicarum, Tom. II, *Fredegarii et aliorum chronica et Vitae Sanctorum*, Ed. Krusch, Hannoverae, 1889; Tom. III, *Passiones Vitaeque Sanctorum Aevi Merovingici et antiquiorum aliquot*, Ed. Krusch, Hannoverae, 1896; Tom. IV, *Passiones Vitaeque Sanctorum Aevi Merovingici*, Ed. Krusch, Hannoverae, 1902.

Monumenta Germaniae Historica, Scriptores, Chronica et Gesta Aevi Salici, Tom. VIII, *Gesta Abbatum Gemblacensium*, Ed. Pertz, Hannoverae, 1848, (reprint, 1925).

Normae secundum quas Sacra Congregatio Episcoporum et Regularium in novis religiosis congregationibus approbandis procedere solet, Romae, 1901.

*Ordinationes Capitulorum Generalium Ordinis Minorum Capuccinor*um, Romae: Curia Generalis O. M. Cap., [1928].

Patres Apostolici, ed. Franz Xaver Funk, 2 vols., Tübingen, 1901.

Rituale Romano-Seraphicum, Romae, 1915.

Sancti Benedicti Regula Monachorum, Editio Critico-Practica, ed. Cuthbertus Butler, Friburgi Brisgoviae: Herder, 1912.

Sancti Thasci Caecilii Cypriani Opera Omnia, ed. Guglielmus Hartel, 3 vols. in Corpus Scriptorum Latinorum Vindobonae, Vindobonae, (1866-), Vol. III, 1868-1871.

Schroeder, H. J., *Disciplinary Decrees of the General Councils: Text, Translation, and Commentary*, London and St. Louis: Herder, 1937.

Authors.

Appeltern, Victor ab, *Compendium Praelectionum Iuris Regularis Adm. R. P. Piati Montani*, Tornaci, 1903.

Ayrinhac, H. A., *General Legislation in the New Code of Canon Law*, New York: Longmans, 1930.

——————*Penal Legislation in the New Code of Canon Law,* New York: Benziger, 1920.

Bachofen, Augustinus, *Compendium Iuris Regularium,* New York: Benziger, 1903.

[Bachofen], Charles Augustine, *A Commentary on Canon Law,* 8 vols., Vol. II, 4 ed., St. Louis: Herder, 1923.

Barbosa, Augustinus, *Collectio Doctorum Tam Veterum Quam Recentiorum in Ius Pontificium Universum,* 6 vols., Lugduni, 1656.

Barraclough, Geoffrey, *Papal Provisions,* Oxford: Blackwell, 1935.

Barret, John D. M., *A Comparative Study of the Councils of Baltimore and the Code of Canon Law,* Catholic University of America Canon Law Studies: No. 83, Washington: Catholic University, 1932.

Bastnagel, Clement V., *The Appointment of Parochial Adjutants and Assistants,* Catholic University of America Canon Law Studies: No. 58, Washington: Catholic University, 1930.

Battifol, Pierre, *Primitive Catholicism,* (transl. Henri L. Brianceau) New York: Longmans, 1911.

Bernardus Papiensis, *Summa Decretalium,* ed. E. A. Th. Laspeyres, Ratisbonae, 1860.

Beveregius, Guglielmus, *Synodicon sive Pandectae Canonum et Conciliorum,* 2 vols., Oxonii, 1672.

Beyer, K. *Die Bishofs-und Abtswahlen in Deutschland unter Heinrich* IV *in den Jahren 1056-1076,* Halle, 1881.

Bonin, *Die Besetzung der deutschen Bistuemer in den letzten 30 Jahren Heinrichs IV, 1076-1106,* Jena, 1889.

Boucharlat, A., *Les Elections Episcopales sous le Merovingiens,* Paris, 1904.

Bouix, D., *De Iure Regularium,* 2 vols., Paris, 1867.

Bradshaw, Henry, and Wordsworth, Christopher, *Lincoln Cathedral Statutes,* Vol. II, Cambridge, 1897.

Butler, Cuthbert, *Benedictine Monachism,* 2 ed., London: Longmans, 1924.

Cappello, Felix M., *Summa Iuris Canonici,* 3 vols., Romae: Apud U. Greg., Vols. I-II, 2 ed., 1932-1934; Vol. III, 1936.

——————*Tractatus Canonico-Moralis de Censuris Iuxta Codicem Iuris Canonici,* 3 ed., Romae: Marietti, 1933.

Carlyle, R. W., and Carlyle, A. J., *A History of Medieval Political Theory in the West,* 6 vols., New York: Longmans, 1903-1936, Vol. IV, 1928.

Castellini, Lucas, *De Electione et Confirmatione Canonica Praelatorum Quorumcumque Praesertim Regularium,* Romae, 1625.

Catholic Encyclopedia, The, 16 vols. and 2 suppls., New York, 1907-1922.

Chapman, John *Saint Benedict and the Sixth Century*, New York: Longmans, 1929.

Chelodi, Ioannes, *Ius de Personis*, 2 ed. a Sac. Ernesto Bertagnoli recognita & aucta; Tridenti: Libr. Edit. Tridentum, 1927.

————, *Ius Poenale et ordo procedendi in iudiciis criminalibus*, 3 ed., Tridenti: Ardesi, 1933.

Cicognani, Hamletus, *Ius Canonicum*, 2 vols., Romae, 1925.

Cicognani, Amleto, *Canon Law*, authorized English version by J. O'Hara and F. Brennan, Philadelphia: Dolphin Press, 1934.

Clarke, Maude Violet, *Medieval Representation and Consent*, New York: Longmans, (1936)

Cocchi, Guidus, *Commentarium in Codicem Iuris Canonici ad usum scholarum*, 8 vols., Vols. III-VII, 3 ed., Vol. II and VIII, 4 ed., Vol. 1, 5 ed., Augustae Taurinorum: Marietti, 1931-1938.

Conte, Matthaeus, a Coronata, *Institutiones Iuris Canonici*, 5 vols., Taurini: Marietti, 1928-1936; *alias*, Vol. I, 1939.

————, *Compendium Iuris Canonici*, 2 vols., Taurini: Marietti, 1937-1938.

De Meester, Alphonsus, *Iuris Canonici et Iuris Canonico-Civilis Compendium*, nova ed., 3 vols. in 4, Brugis: Desclée, 1921-1928.

De Peyrinis, Laurentius, *Subditus, Praelatus, ac Formularium et Privilegia Regularibus praesertim Minimis per Summos Pontifices Sixtum IV usque ad Urbanum VIII Concessa*, Venetiis, 1648-1649.

Dictionaire d'Archéologie Chrétienne, ed. Leclercq, Paris: Libraire Letouzey et Anè, 1921-

Fagnanus, Prosper, *Ius Canonicum seu Commentaria Absolutissima in Decretalium Libros*, 3 vols., Venetiis, 1709.

Fanfani, Ludovicus, *De Iure Religiosorum ad Normam Codicis Iuris Canonici*, Taurini: Marietti, 1925.

Ferraris, J. Lucius, *Prompta Bibliotheca Canonica, Iuridica, Moralis, Theologica, nec non Ascetica, Polemica, Rubricistica, Historica*, ed. Migne, 9 vols., Romae, 1885-1892.

Fontanella, Jacobus, *Canonicarum Quaestionum Resolutiones de Iurepatronatus, De Electione, De Ecclesiae Praelatis, De Collegiata Ecclesia*, Neapoli, 1664.

Funk, Franz Xaver, *Abhandlungen und Untersuchungen*, 3 vols., Paderborn, 1897.

Gerdes, H., *Die Bischofswahlen in Deutschland Unter Otto dem Grossen*, 953-973, Hamburg, 1878.

Geselbracht, Franklin, *Das Verfahren bei den deutschen Bischofswahlen in der zweiten Haelfte de 12. Jahrhunderts*, Weida in Thueringen, 1905.

Gillet, Pierre, *La Personalitè Iuridique en Droit Ecclésiastique*, Malines: Godenne, 1927.

Hefele, Carl, *Conciliengeschichte*, 9 vols. (vols. 8 and 9 continued by Card. Hergenroether), Freiburg in Breisgau, 1855-1890.

Heimbucher, Max, *Die Orden und Congregationen*, 3 ed., 2 vols., Paderborn, 1933-1934.

Hilling, Nikolaus, *Das Personenrecht des Codex Iuris Canonici*, Paderborn, 1924.

Hinschius, Paul, *System des katholischen Kirchenrechts mit besonderer Ruecksicht auf Deutschland*, 4 vols., Berlin, 1869-1888.

Hofmeister, Philipp, *Bischof und Domkapitel nach altem und neuem Recht*, Würtemberg, 1931.

Hostiensis (Henricus de Segusio), *Apparatus super quinque libros Decretalium; Summa Aurea*, Lugduni, 1568.

Imbart de la Tour, P., *Les Elections épiscopales dans l'Eglise de France du IXe au XIe siecle*, Paris, 1890.

Jaeger, Leo, *The Administration of Vacant and Quasi-Vacant Sees in the United States*, Catholic University of America Canon Law Studies: No. 81, Washington: Catholic University, 1932.

Lévy-Bruhl, Henri, *Etudes sur le élections abbatiales en France*, Paris, 1913.

Lijdsman, Bernardus, *Introductio in Ius Canonicum*, 2 vols., Hilversum in Hollandia, 1924-1929.

Maroto, Philippus, *Institutiones Iuris Canonici*, 2 vols., Romae: Apud Commentarium pro Religiosis 1919-1931, Vol. I, 3 ed., 1921.

Michiels, Gommarus, *Principia Generalia de Personis in Ecclesia*, Lublin in Polonia, 1932.

Mocchegiani, Petrus, *Iurisprudentia Ecclesiastica*, 3 vols., Quaracchi, 1904.

Montini, Giovanni Baptista, *Note Scholastiche per la Storia della Diplomazia Pontificia*, Romae: Appollinaris, 1933-1934.

Moersdorf, Klaus, *Die Rechtssprache des Codex Iuris Canonici*, Veroeffentlichungen der Goerresgesellschaft, Sektion fuer Rechts-und Staats-wissenschaft, Heft 74, Paderborn: Schoeningh, 1937.

Mouret, Fernand, *A History of the Catholic Church*, (transl. Newton Thompson), Vol. II, St. Louis: Herder, 1935.

Oesterle, G. *Praelectiones Iuris Canonici*, Vol. I, Romae, 1931.

Oietti, B. *Commentarium in Codicem Iuris Canonici*, 4 vols., Romae: Univ. Greg., 1927-1931.

Orth, Clement R., *The Approbation of Religious Institutes*, Catholic University of America Canon Law Studies: No. 71, Washington: Catholic University, 1931.

Papi, Hector, *The Government of Religious Communities*, New York: Kennedy, 1919.

Passerini, Petrus Maria de Sextula, *Tractatus de Electione Canonica*, Romae, 1693.

Phillips, Georg, and Vering, Friedrich H., *Kirchenrecht*, 8 vols., Vol. VIII, Regensburg, 1889.

Piatus Montensus, *Praelectiones Iuris Regularis*, 3 vols., Tornaci, 1890.

Pirhing, E., *Ius Canonicum in Quinque Libros Decretalium Distributum*, Dillingae, 1647-1678.

Pistocchi, Mario, *I Canoni Penali del Codice Ecclesiastico*, Torino: Marietti, 1925.

Polzin, Johannes Eduard, *Die Abtswahlen in den Reichsabteien* von 1024 bis *1056*, Greifswald, 1908.

Pruemmer, Dominicus, *Manuale Iuris Canonici*, Friburgi Brisgoviae: Herder, 1927.

Raynouard, Francois Juste Marie, *Histoire du Droit Municipal en France*, 2 vols., Paris, 1829.

Reiffenstuel, Anacletus, *Ius Canonicum Universum*, 5 vols., Monachii, 1702.

Reilly, Thomas Francis, *The Visitation of Religious*, Catholic University of America Canon Law Studies: No. 112, Washington: Catholic University 1938.

Rodericus, Emmanuel, *Quaestiones Regulares et Canonicae*, 4 vol., Venetiis, 1611.

Ryder, Raymond A., *Simony*, Catholic University of America Canon Law Studies; No. 65, Washington, Catholic University, 1931.

Saegmueller, Johann Baptist, *Die Bischofswahl bei Gratian*, in Veroeffentlichungen der Goerresgesellschaft, Sektion fuer Rechts-und Sozialwissenschaft, Heft 1, Koeln, 1908.

Saegmueller, Johann Baptist, *Lehrbuch des katholischen Kirchenrechts*, 3 ed., 2 vols., Freiburg im Breisgau: Herder 1914.

Salucci, Raffaele, *Il Diritto Penale Secondo il Codice di Diritto Canonico*, Subiaco, 1926.

Samuellius, Franciscus M., *Disputationum Controversiae de Canonica Electione in regularibus praelatis atque cathedralium ecclesiarum canonicis eligendis*, Venetiis, 1644.

Schaefer, Timotheus, *Compendium de Religiosis ad Normam Codicis Iuris Canonici*, 2 ed., Muenster: Aschendorff, 1931.

Schmalzgrueber, Fr. X., *Ius Ecclesiasticum Universum*, 5 tomes in 10 vols. Romae, 1845.

Schuerer, Emil, *A History of the Jewish People*, Vol. II. (div. 2.), Edinburgh, 1885.

Schur, Johannes, *Koenigthum und Kirche im Ostfraenkischen Reiche vom Tode Ludwigs des Deutschen bis Konrad* I, Paderborn, 1931.

Sipos, Stephanus, *Enchiridion Iuris Canonici*, Pecs, 1926.

Sohm, Rudolf, *Kirchenrecht*, 2 vols., Muenchen und Leipzig: Duncker und Humboldt, 1923.

Smith, S. B., *Notes on the Second Plenary Council of Baltimore*, New York, 1874.

Suarez, F., *Opera Omnia*, 28 vols., Parisiis, 1856-1878.

Toso, Albertus, *Ad Codicem Iuris Canonici Commentaria Minora*, 5 vols., Romae: Marietti, 1920-1934.

Van Espen, Zegerus Bernardus, *Ius Ecclesiasticum Universum*, 5 vols., Lovanii, 1753.

Vermeersch, Arturus, and Creusen, Iosephus, *Epitome Iuris Canonici*, 3 vols., Vols. I and II, 4 ed., Mechliniae, Romae: Dessain, 1929-1930; Vol. III, 3 ed., 1928.

Werminghoff, A., *Verfassung der deutschen Kirche im Mittelalter*, Leipzig, 1913.

Wernz, Franciscus Xaverius, *Ius Decretalium*, 2 ed., Vol. II in 2, Romae, 1906.

Wernz-Vidal, *Ius Canonicum*, 7 tomes in 9 vols., Romae: Apud Aedes Universitatis Gregorianae, 1925-1938; Vol. II, 2 ed., 1928.

Ziegler, A. K., *Church and State in Visigothic Spain*, Washington: Catholic University, 1930.

Periodicals.

Appollinaris, Romae, 1928—

Archiv fuer katholisches Kirchenrecht, Innsbruck, 1857-1861; Mainz, 1862—

Catholic Historical Review, Washington, 1920—

Church Quarterly Review,—London, 1875—

Commentarium pro Religiosis (later, *Commentarium pro Religiosis et Missionariis.)*, Romae, 1920—

Ecclesiastical Review, The (originally *The American Ecclesiastical Review.)*, Philadelphia, 1889—

Homiletic and Pastoral Review, The, New York, 1900—

Periodica de Re Canonica et Morali utili praesertim Religiosis et Missionariis, Bruges, 1905—

Revue de l'histoire des Religions, Paris, 1880—

Theologische Quartalschrift, Tuebingen, 1819—

Theologisch-praktische Quartalschrift, Linz, 1832—

Zeitschrift der Savigny Stiftung—Kanonistische Abteilung, Weimar, 1911—

Zeitschrift fuer Kirchenrecht, Tuebingen und Leipzig, 1890—

Principal Articles

Bannister, A., "The Origin and growth of the cathedral system", *The Church Quarterly Review,* CIV (1927), 86-96.

Barraclough, Geoffrey, "The Making of a Bishop in the Middles Ages", *Catholic Historical Review,* XIX (1933), 275-319.

Boudinhon, A., "Election", *Catholic Encyclopedia,* V, 374-378.

Dulac, A., "Les Elections episcopales dans l'Englise latine au moyen âge", *Revue de l'histoire des religions,* XCIV (1926), 76-113.

Goyeneche, S., "De extensione vocis activae in capitulis generalibus, quae fieri nequit contra statuta", *CpR,* VII (1926), 390-392.

————, "De approbatione electionum religiosorum ab Ordinario", CpR, XI (1930), 31-38.

————, "Interventio Ordinarii in electionibus religiosarum", *CpR,* XI (1930), 399-410.

————, "Schedulae Albae", *CpR,* XV (1934), 24-30.

————, "De electione delegati ad capitulum generale qui aliunde ius habet interessendi eiusque substituti", *CpR,* XV (1934), 115-129.

Haentzsche, C., "Die Entstehung des ausschliesslichen Wahlrechts des Domkapitels zu Hildesheim", *AKKR,* LXXI (1894) 3-14.

Hilling, Nikolaus, "Zur Abtswahl der Benektinerregel", *AKKR,* CII (1908), 55-57.

Larraona, A., "De Electionibus Religiosorum", *CpR,* VIII (1927), 177-184; 284-295; IX (1928) 110-114; 329-340; X (1929) 56-57; 265-271.

Oesterle, G., "Vier Faelle aus dem Ordensleben", *ThPrQS,* LXXXVIII (1935), 354-358.

Pruemmer, D., "An invalid election and its consequences", *Homiletic and Pastoral Review,* XXX (1929), 72-75.

Saegmueller, I. B., "Die Papstwahl durch das Kardinalscollegium als Prototyp der Bischofswahl durch das Domkapitel", *Theol. Quartalschrift,* XCVII (1915), 321.

Sweet, A. H., "The control of English episcopal elections in the XIII century", *Cath. Hist. Rev.,* VI (1927), 573-582.

Vermeersch, A., "De Electione et Postulatione", *Periodica,* XVI (1927), 263*-266*.

————, "De Electione capitulari", *Periodica,* XI (1923), (153).

————, "De utili tempore faciendae electionis", *Periodica,* XIII (1924), (71)-(72).

Wretschko, Alfred von, "Die Electio Communis bei Den Kirchlichen Wahlen im Mittelalter", *Deutsche Zeitschrift fuer Kirchenrecht,* XI (1901) 321-392.

Abbreviations

AAS—Acta Apostolicae Sedis
AKKR—Archiv für katholisches Kirchenrecht
ASs—Acta Sanctorum Bollandiana
Cath. Hist. Rev.—Catholic Historical Review
CpR—Commentarium pro Religiosis
Fontes—Codicis Iuris Canonici Fontes
MGH—Monumenta Germaniae Historica
MPG—Migne, *Patrologia, Series Graeca*
MPL—Migne, *Patrologia, Series Latina*
ThPrQS—Theologisch-praktische Quartalschrift
ZKG—Zeitschrift für Kirchengeschichte
ZSS—Zeitschrift der Savigny Stiftung—kanonistische Abteilung

BIOGRAPHICAL NOTE

Anscar John Parsons was born in Yonkers, New York, April 8, 1911. He attended the Sacred Heart School in Yonkers, New York, and the preparatory seminary of the Capuchin-Franciscan Province of St. Joseph, at Garrison, New York. He entered the Capuchin novitiate, Detroit, Michigan, in 1928 and was professed the following year. His seminary course was made at St. Anthony's Monastery, Marathon, Wisconsin, where he was ordained on June 16, 1935. In September, 1936, he entered the School of Canon Law at the Catholic University of America, from which he received the Baccalaureate in Canon Law in June, 1937, and the licentiate in Canon Law in June, 1938.

ALPHABETICAL INDEX

CANON LAW STUDIES

1. FRERIKS, REV. CELESTINE A., C.PP.S., J.C.D., Religious Congregations in Their External Relations, 121 pp., 1916.
2. GALLIHER, REV. DANIEL M., O.P., J.C.D., Canonical Elections, 117 pp., 1917.
3. BORKOWSKI, REV. AURELIUS L., O.F.M., De Confraternitatibus Ecclesiasticis, 136 pp., 1918.
4. CASTILLO, REV. CAYO, J.C.D., Disertacion Historico-Canonica sobre la Potestad del Cabildo en Sede Vacante o Impedida del Vicario Capitular, 99 pp., 1919 (1918).
5. KUBELBECK, REV. WILLIAM J., S.T.B., J.C.D., The Sacred Penitentiaria and Its Relation to Faculties of Ordinaries and Priests, 129 pp., 1918.
6. PETROVITS, REV. JOSEPH, J.C., S.T.D., J.C.D., The New Church Law on Matrimony, X-461 pp., 1919.
7. HICKEY, REV. JOHN J., S.T.B., J.C.D., Irregularities and Simple Impediments in the New Code of Canon Law, 100 pp., 1920.
8. KLEKOTKA, REV. PETER J., S.T.B., J.C.D., Diocesan Consultors. 179 pp., 1920.
9. WANENMACHER, REV. FRANCIS, J.C.D., The Evidence in Ecclesiastical Procedure Affecting the Marriage Bond, 1920 (Printed 1935).
10. GOLDEN, REV. HENRY FRANCIS, J.C.D., Parochial Benefices in the New Code, IV-119 pp., 1921 (Printed 1925).
11. KOUDELKA, REV. CHARLES J., J.C.D., Pastors, Their Rights and Duties According to the New Code of Canon Law, 211 pp., 1921.
12. MELO, REV. ANTONIUS, O.F.M., J.C.D., De Exemptione Regularium, X-188 pp., 1921.
13. SCHAAF, REV. VALENTINE THEODORE, O.F.M., S.T.B., J.C.D., The Cloister, X-180 pp., 1921.
14. BURKE, REV. THOMAS JOSEPH, S.T.D., J.C.D., Competence in Ecclesiastical Tribunals, IV-117 pp., 1922.
15. LEECH, REV. GEORGE LEO, J.C.D., A Comparative Study of the Constitution "Apostolicae Sedis" and the "Codex Juris Canonici," 179 pp., 1922.
16. MOTRY, REV. HUBERT LOUIS, S.T.D., J.C.D., Diocesan Faculties According to the Code of Canon Law, II-167, pp., 1922.

17. MURPHY, REV. GEORGE LAWRENCE, J.C.D., Delinquencies and Penalties in the Administration and the Reception of the Sacraments, IV-121 pp., 1923.
18. O'REILLY, REV. JOHN ANTHONY, S.T.B., J.C.D., Ecclesiastical Sepulture in the New Code of Canon Law, II-129 pp., 1923.
19. MICHALICKA, REV. WENCESLAS CYRILL, O.S.B., J.C.D., Judicial Procedure in Dismissal of Clerical Exempt Religious, 107 pp., 1923.
20. DARGIN, REV. EDWARD VINCENT, S.T.B., J.C.D., Reserved Cases According to the Code of Canon Law, IV-103 pp., 1924.
21. GODFREY, REV. JOHN A., S.T.B., J.C.D., The Right of Patronage According to the Code of Canon Law, 153 pp., 1924.
22. HAGEDORN, REV. FRANCIS EDWARD, J.C.D., General Legislation on Indulgences, II-154 pp., 1924.
23. KING, REV. JAMES IGNATIUS, J.C.D., The Administration of the Sacraments to Dying Non-Catholics, V-141 pp., 1924.
24. WINSLOW, REV. FRANCIS JOSEPH, A.F.M., J.C.D., Vicars and Prefects Apostolic, IV-149 pp., 1924.
25. CORREA, REV. JOSE SERVELION, S.T.L., J.C.D., La Potestad Legislativa de la Iglesia Catolica, IV-127 pp., 1925.
26. DUGAN, REV. HENRY FRANCIS, A.M., J.C.D., The Judiciary Department of the Diocesan Curia, 87 pp., 1925.
27. KELLER, REV. CHARLES FREDERICK, S.T.B., J.C.D., Mass Stipends, 167 pp., 1925.
28. PASCHANG, REV. JOHN LINUS, J.C.D., The Sacramentals According to the Code of Canon Law, 129 pp., 1925.
29. POINTEK, REV. CYRILLUS, O.F.M., S.T.B., J.C.D., De Intulto Exclaustrationis necnon Saecularizationis, XIII-289 pp., 1925.
30. KEARNY, REV. RICHARD JOSEPH, S.T.B., J.C.D., Sponsors at Baptism According to the Code of Canon Law, IV-127 pp., 1925.
31. BARTLETT, REV. CHESTER JOSEPH, A.M., LL.B., J.C.D., The Tenure of Parochial Property in the United States of America, V-108 pp., 1926.
32. KILKER, REV. ADRIAN JEROME, J.C.D., Extreme Unction, V-425 pp., 1926.
33. MCCORMICK, REV. ROBERT EMMETT, J.C.D., Confessors of Religious, VIII-266 pp., 1926.
34. MILLER, REV. NEWTON THOMAS, J.C.D., Founded Masses According to the Code of Canon Law, VII-93 pp., 1926.
35. ROELKER, REV. EDWARD G., S.T.D., J.C.D., Principles of Privilege According to the Code of Canon Law, XI-166 pp., 1926.
36. BAKALARCZYK, REV. RICHARDUS, M.I.C., J.U.D., De Novitiatu, VIII-208 pp., 1927.
37. PIZZUTI, REV. LAWRENCE, O.F.M., J.U.L., De Parochis Religiosis, 1927. (Not printed.)

38. BLILEY, REV. NICHOLAS MARTIN, O.S.B., J.C.D., Altars According to the Code of Canon Law, XIX-132 pp., 1927.
39. BROWN, MR. BRENDAN FRANCIS, A.B., LL.M., J.U.D., The Canonical Juristic Personality with Special Reference to Its Status in the United States of America, V-212 pp., 1927.
40. CAVANAUGH, REV. WILLIAM THOMAS, C.P., J.U.D., The Reservation of the Blessed Sacrament, VIII-101 pp., 1927.
41. DOHENY, REV. WILLIAM J., C.S.C., A.B., J.U.D., Church Property: Modes of Acquisition, X-118 pp., 1927.
42. FELDHAUS, REV. ALOYSIUS H., C.PP.S., J.C.D., Oratories, IX-141 pp., 1927.
43. KELLY, REV. JAMES PATRICK, A.B., J.C.D., The Jurisdiction of the Simple Confessor, X-208 pp., 1927.
44. NEUBERGER, REV. NICHOLAS J., J.C.D., Canon 6 or the Relation of the Codex Juris Canonici to the Preceding Legislation, V-95 pp., 1927.
45. O'Keefe, REV. GERALD MICHAEL, J.C.D., Matrimonial Dispensations, Powers of Bishops, Priests and Confessors, VIII-232 pp., 1927.
46. QUIGLEY, REV. JOSEPH, A.M., A.B., J.C.D., Condemned Societies, 139 pp., 1927.
47. ZAPLOTNIK, REV. JOHANNES LEO, J.C.D., De Vicariis Foraneis, X-142 pp., 1927.
48. DUSKIE, REV. JOHN ALOYSIUS, A.B., J.C.D., The Canonical Status of the Orientals in the United States, VIII-196 pp., 1928.
49. HYLAND, REV. FRANCIS EDWARD, J.C.D., Excommunication, Its Nature, Historical Development and Effects, VIII-181 pp., 1928.
50. REINMANN, REV. GERALD, JOSEPH, O.M.C., J.C.D., The Third Order Secular of Saint Francis, 201 pp., 1928.
51. SCHENK, REV. FRANCIS J., J.C.D., The Matrimonial Impediments of Mixed Religions and Disparity of Cult, XVI-318 pp., 1929.
52. Coady, Rev. John Joseph, S.T.D., J.U.D., A.M., The Appointment of Pastors, VIII-150 pp., 1929.
53. KAY, REV. THOMAS HENRY, J.C.D., Competence in Matrimonial Procedure, VIII-164 pp., 1929.
54. TURNER, REV. SIDNEY JOSEPH, C.P., L.U.D., The Vow of Poverty, XLIX 217 pp., 1929.
55. KEARNEY, REV. RAYMOND A., A.B., S.T.D., J.C.D., The Principles of Delegation, VII-149 pp., 1929.
56. CONRAN, REV. EDWARD JAMES, A.B., J.C.D., The Interdict, V-163 pp., 1930.
57. O'NEILL, REV. WILLIAM H., J.C.D., Papal Rescripts of Favor, VII-218 pp., 1930.

58. Bastnagel, Rev. Clement Vincent, J.U.D., The Appointment of Parochial Adjutants and Assistants, XV-257 pp., 1930.
59. Ferry, Rev. William A., A.B., J.C.D., Stole Fees, V-135 pp., 1930.
60. Costello, Rev. John Michael, A.B., J.C.D., Domicile and Quasi-domicile, VII-201 pp., 1930.
61. Kremer, Rev. Michael Nicholas, A.B., S.T.B., J.C.D., Church Support in the United States, VI-136 pp., 1930.
62. Angulo, Rev. Luis, C.M., J.C.D., Legislation de la Iglesia sobre la intencion en la application de la Santa Misa, VII-104 pp., 1931.
63. Frey, Rev. Wolfgang Norbert, O.S.B., A.B., J.C.D., The Act of Religious Profession, VIII-174 pp., 1931.
64. Roberts, Rev. James Brendan, A.B., J.C.D., The Banns of Marriage, XIV-140 pp., 1931.
65. Ryder, Rev. Raymond Aloysius, A.B., J.C.D., Simony, IX-151 pp., 1931.
66. Campagna, Rev. Angelo, Ph.D., J.U.D., Il Vicario del Vescovo, VII-205 pp., 1931.
67. Cox, Rev. Joseph Godfrey, A.B., J.C.D., The Administration of Seminaries, VI-124 pp., 1931.
68. Gregory, Rev. Donald J., J.U.D., The Pauline Privilege, XV-165 pp., 1931.
69. Donohue, Rev. John F., J.C.D., The Impediment of Crime, VII-110 pp., 1931.
70. Dooley, Rev. Eugene A., O.M.I., J.C.D., Church Law on Sacred Relics IX-143 pp., 1931.
71. Orth, Rev. Clement Raymond, O.M.C., J.C.D., The Approbation of Religious Institutes, 171 pp., 1931.
72. Pernicone, Rev. Joseph M., A.B., J.C.D., The Ecclesiastical Prohibition of Books, XII-267 pp., 1932.
73. Clinton, Rev. Connell, A.B., J.C.D., The Paschal Precept, IX-108 pp., 1932.
74. Donnelly, Rev. Francis B., A.M., S.T.L., J.C.D., The Diocesan Synod, VIII-125 pp., 1932.
75. Torrente, Rev. Camilo, C.M.F., J.C.D., Las Processiones Sagradas, V-145 pp., 1932.
76. Murphy, Rev. Edwin, J., C.PP.S., J.C.D., Suspension Ex Informata Conscientia, XI-122 pp., 1932.
77. MacKenzie, Rev. Eric F., A.M., S.T.L., J.C.D., The Delict of Heresy in Its Commission, Penalization, Absolution, VII-124 pp., 1932.
78. Lyons, Rev. Avitus E., S.T.B., J.C.D., The Collegiate Tribunal of First Instance, XI-147 pp., 1932.
79. Connolly, Rev. Thomas A., J.C.D., Appeals, XI-195 pp., 1932.

80. SANGMEISTER, REV. JOSEPH V., A.B., J.C.D., Force and Fear as Precluding Matrimonial Consent, V-211 pp., 1932.
81. JAEGER, REV. LEO A., A.B., J.C.D., The Administration of Vacant and Quasi-Vacant Episcopal Sees in the United States, IX-229 pp., 1932.
82. RIMLINGER, REV. HERBERT T., J.C.D., Error Invalidating Matrimonial Consent, VII-79 pp., 1932.
83. BARRETT, REV. JOHN D. M., S.S., J.C.D., A Comparative Study of the Third Plenary Council of Baltimore and the Code, IX-221 pp., 1932.
84. CARBERRY, REV. JOHN J., PH.D., S.T.D., J.C.D., The Juridical Form of Marriage, X-177 pp., 1934.
85. DOLAN, REV. JOHN L., A.B., J.C.D., The Defensor Vinculi, XII-157 pp., 1934.
86. HANNAN, REV. JEROME D., A.M., S.T.D., LL.B., J.C.D., The Canon Law of Wills, IX-517 pp., 1934.
87. LEMIEUX, REV. DELISLE A., A.M., J.C.D., The Sentence in Ecclesiastical Procedure, IX-131 pp., 1934.
88. O'ROURKE, REV. JAMES J., A.B., J.C.D., Parish Registers, VII-109 pp., 1934.
89. TIMLIN, REV. BARTHOLOMEW, O.F.M., A.M., J.C.D., Conditional Matrimonial Consent, X-381 pp., 1934.
90. WAHL, REV. FRANCIS X., A.B., J.C.D., The Matrimonial Impediments of Consanguinity and Affinity, VI-125 pp., 1934.
91. WHITE, REV. ROBERT J., A.B., LL.B., S.T.B., J.C.D., Canonical Ante-Nuptial Promises and the Civil Law, VI-152 pp., 1934.
92. HERRERA, REV. ANTONIO PARRA, O.C.D., J.C.D., Legislation Ecclesiastica sobra el Ayuno y la Abstinencia, XI-191 pp., 1935.
93. KENNEDY, REV. EDWIN J., J.C.D., The Sprecial Matrimonial Process in Cases of Evident Nullity, X-165 pp., 1935.
94. MANNING, REV. JOHN J., A.B., J.C.D., Presumption of Law in Matrimonial Procedure, XI-111 pp., 1935.
95. MOEDER, REV. JOHN M., J.C.D., The Proper Bishop For Ordination and Dimissorial Letters, VII-135 pp., 1935.
96. O'MARA, REV. WILLIAM A., A.B., J.C.D., Canonical Causes For Matrimonial Dispensations, IX-155 pp., 1935.
97. REILLY, REV. PETER, J.C.D., Residence of Pastors, IX-81 pp., 1935.
98. SMITH, REV. MARINER T., O.P., S.T.Lr., J.C.D., The Penal Law For Religious, VII-169 pp., 1935.
99. WHALEN, REV. DONALD W., A.M., J.C.D., The Value of Testimonial Evidence in Matrimonial Procedure, XIII-297 pp., 1935.
100. CLEARY, REV. JOSEPH F., J.C.D., Canonical Limitations on the Alienation of Church Property, VIII-141 pp., 1936.

101. GLYNN, REV. JOHN C., J.C.D., The Promoter of Justice, XX-337 pp., 1936.
102. BRENNAN, REV. JAMES H., S.S., A.M., S.T.B., J.C.D., The Simple Convalidation of Marriage, VI-135 pp., 1937.
103. BRUNINI, REV. JOSEPH BERNARD, J.C.D., The Clerical Obligations of Canons 139 and 142, X-121 pp., 1937.
104. CONNOR, REV. MAURICE, A.B., J.C.D., The Administrative Removal of Pastors, VIII-159 pp., 1937.
105. GUILFOYLE, REV. MERLIN JOSEPH, J.C.D., Custom, XI-144 pp., 1937.
106. HUGHES, REV. JAMES AUSTIN, A.B., A.M., J.C.D., Witnesses in Criminal Trials of Clerics, IX-140 pp., 1937.
107. JANSEN, REV. RAYMOND J., A.B., S.T.L., J.C.D., Canonical Provisions for Catechetical Instruction, VII-153 pp., 1937.
108. KEALY, REV. JOHN JAMES, A.B., J.C.D., The Introductory Libellus in Church Court Procedure, XI-121 pp., 1937.
109. MCMANUS, REV. JAMES EDWARD, C.SS.R., J.C.D., The Administration of Temporal Goods in Religious Institutes, XVI-196 pp., 1937.
110. MORIARTY, REV. EUGENE JAMES, J.C.D., Oaths in Ecclesiastical Courts, X-115 pp., 1937.
111. RAINER, REV. ELIGIUS GEORGE, C.SS.R., J.C.D., Suspension of Clerics XVII-249 pp., 1937.
112. REILLY, REV. THOMAS F., C.SS.R., J.C.D., Visitation of Religious, VI-195 pp., 1938.
113. MORIARTY, REV. FRANCIS E., C.SS.R., J.C.D., The Extraordinary Absolution from Censures, XV-334 pp., 1938.
114. CONNOLLY, REV. NICHOLAS P., J.C.D., The Canonical Erection of Parishes, X-132 pp., 1938.
115. DONOVAN, REV. JAMES JOSEPH, J.C.D., The Pastor's Obligation in Pre-nuptial Investigation, XII-322 pp., 1938.
116. HARRIGAN, REV. ROBERT J., M.A., S.T.B., J.C.D., The Radical Sanation of Invalid Marriages, VIII-208 pp., 1938.
117. BOFFA, REV. CONRAD HUMBERT, J.C.D., Canonical Provisions for Catholic Schools.
118. PARSONS, REV. ANSCAR JOHN, O.M. Cap., J.C.L., Canonical Elections.
119. REILLY, REV. EDWARD MICHAEL, A.B., J.C.L., The General Norms of Dispensation.
120. RYAN, REV. GERALD ALOYSIUS, A.B., J.C.L., Principles of Episcopal Jurisdiction.

www.ingramcontent.com/pod-product-compliance
Lightning Source LLC
LaVergne TN
LVHW050250080826
844660LV00012B/617

* 9 7 8 0 8 1 3 2 2 3 0 7 0 *